DOUG CASEY

MATT SMITH & MAXIM SMITH

I0453112

THE PREPARATION

HOW TO BECOME COMPETENT CONFIDENT AND DANGEROUS

Copyright © 2025 Doug Casey, Matt Smith, and Maxim Smith

All rights reserved. No part of this publication may be reproduced, distributed, or transmitted in any form or by any means, including photocopying, recording, or other electronic or mechanical methods, without the prior written permission of the publisher, except in the case of brief quotations embodied in critical reviews and certain other noncommercial uses permitted by copyright law.

For permission requests, visit: nowforthefuture.org, thepreparation.com

ISBN 979-8-9938603-1-2

Cover and interior design by Ljiljana Pavkov / bookwormsdesign.com

First Edition 2025

TABLE OF CONTENTS

Preface 8

Introduction 14

Chapter 1   How to Use This Book 26

Chapter 2   The Wrong Question 32

Chapter 3   The Core Problem: Wanting What Others Want 34

Chapter 4   How To Actually Get Ahead In Life 48

Chapter 5   New Rules–Your Personal Code 56

Chapter 6   Why You Need A Personal Code 68

Chapter 7   Forget Mentors, Find a Patron 80

Chapter 8   Wealth & Economics 94

Chapter 9   How to Finance The Preparation 116

Chapter 10 Becoming Future Proof 122

Chapter 11 What's Included In The Cycles 134

Chapter 12 Anchor Courses: Hands-On Learning at the Core of Each Cycle ... 144

Chapter 13 Academic Program 160

Chapter 14 Activities–DO FUN SHIT 176

Chapter 15 Unlocking New Possibilities By Holding Yourself Accountable ... 198

Chapter 16 Managing Your Mind 202

Chapter 17 Cycles of The Preparation 214

Chapter 18 How to Build Your Own Cycle 246

Chapter 19 Resources Academics, Books, Classical Music Guide, Movies Worth Watching 256

THE
PREPARATION

Doug Casey is part Indiana Jones, part Socrates, part James Bond—and he's lived different chapters of his life like each of them.

He's traveled to over 175 countries in search of fun and profit, searched for sunken treasure, befriended generals, negotiated with presidents, and traded stories with mercenaries. Along the way, he built real wealth and carved out a life entirely on his own terms.

My friends and I sometimes joke that Doug might actually be "the most interesting man in the world"—but it's only a joke because it's probably true.

Through his adventures, investments, and writing, Doug has helped shape how millions of people think about wealth, risk, and personal sovereignty.

Doug likes to say, "When I come to a fork in the road, I take it."

This book is your fork in the road. Take a chance. Take the fork. You won't regret it.

Matt Smith

PREFACE

BY MAXIM SMITH

This book is as much a gift to you as it is to me, your future kids, and mine.

I'm Maxim Smith, the beta tester for the book. I've been taking the ideas from this book and putting them into practice.

You'll hear The Preparation referred to as a program, but really, it's a way of life — a new way of doing things. The magnitude of change it has brought to my own life is impossible to explain in any way that would do it justice.

Let me give you a glimpse into it all...

Over the course of 2 years I've scuba dived in murky Texas lakes and cold Punta del Este water, learned the basics of wrangling horses from a man in Wyoming, learned to fly a plane in Colorado, worked long nightshifts on wildfires in Oregon as an EMT, been apprenticed to an Uruguayan gaucho who taught me how to drive tractors, fix fences, shoe horses, and treat and raise cattle.

I've written 10s of thousands of words documenting my journey and thoughts which helped me become a better writer. I've become a competent chess player, a Spanish speaker. I've spent several days in the Colorado mountains learning horse/mule packing from one of the most impressive men I have ever met...

I've climbed to the top of several 14,000ft mountains, sailed around the Falkland Islands and through the Strait of Magellan, hiked through the hot Nevada desert while working on a geophysics crew, became an EMT, and did additional wilderness first responder training in the high desert of Colorado...I've spent 5 days at a rope rescue course in South Dakota; studied economics, flying, copywriting, regenerative agriculture, and several different eras of history. Along with that, I've read more books than I can recall.

I've made money from writing, working at Office Depot, delivering pizzas, treating patients as an EMT on wildfires, and apprenticing on a geophysics crew. My passport is filling up with stamps from places I never thought I'd go. And, I've done all of this before the age of 20.

But, more importantly...

I've moved closer to becoming the man I want to be.

Yet, it wasn't too long ago that I was completely lost.

You see, for years I knew that I didn't want to go to college. It wasn't an option in my mind. I pay tens or hundreds of thousands of dollars and for what? A piece of paper? I never loved sitting in a classroom. The idea of spending another four years in a lecture hall sounded terrible to me. Plus, I had no idea what I wanted to do as a career. College seemed like a mistake.

As you may know, a college education is among the largest investments most Americans will make. The total cost of attending a public college is about $36,000 a year, and the average length of time to a degree is nearly five years. Tack on debt service for student loans and the opportunity cost of not working while in school, and the real cost of college can easily pass $300,000—more than the median net worth of most families.

SCAN ME   — **THE WALL STREET JOURNAL — WHY AMERICANS HAVE LOST FAITH IN THE VALUE OF COLLEGE**

More than the money, the biggest problem was that I had no clue what I wanted to do. My father, Matt Smith, is an entrepreneur. He's built businesses since he was my age starting with painting houses to a job board for recent college grads, a digital advertising agency, several niche publishing businesses to the first marketplace for music royalties, and for the last few years, a regenerative cattle ranch in Uruguay.

I figured that I'd likely go down that route. Even then, that path was vague. In fact, my entire future after the age of 18 was shrouded in a vague mist. I didn't know what I was going to do or how I was going to do it, but I still thought that everything would somehow work out.

I didn't begin to think seriously about the future until I turned 17. I wanted to do something to get ahead of the rest. The ambition and drive were there, but what was I to do?

This question stood at the forefront of my mind for the entirety of my 17th year. Yet, as the year passed I made no significant progress in any way. Time marched on and anxiety began to creep in. I was in a rut that I didn't know how to get out of. I hadn't found a "why" and, in consequence, I didn't have a "how". It caused a lot of pain in the way that my inaction would lead to anxiety, leading to further inaction...creating a terrible cycle.

To put it bluntly: I was lazy, unskilled, closed off to the world, fearful, and disappointed with myself at the realization of how far I was from being the man I could be.

All of the anger and frustration that I held with myself was projected onto the world. I blamed the world and the people around me for my condition. The world, as it seemed to me, was not a place of opportunity, creation, and beauty, but more of a prison cell.

This is a dark view, but it's one I held during that time. I suspect many young men today can empathize with this.

I needed something to grab onto – something meaningful to me, something that was beyond the typical "life checklist":

- ▶ Get through K-12
- ▶ Go to college
- ▶ Get a job
- ▶ Get married
- ▶ Have kids
- ▶ Retire

While some of these things are good, there's no beauty in living life in a linear, formulaic process.

What I wanted (and I didn't realize this until later) was to *become* someone. To hold the ultimate version of myself in my mind and to do the things necessary to become that man.

Well, in late July of 2023, a spark was lit that would lead me to that realization and, later, to finding my own path.

I was speaking with my dad about a book (this book) that he and Doug Casey were planning on writing. They had both seen that young men are having a rough time today. The usual routes of the military, college, or a dead-end job are kind of bleak and uncertain. Even worse, the premier path — college — simply doesn't work anymore. I didn't want to follow any path that might lead to a life of sorrow and servitude. Not only that, but society shames masculinity, one of the key components which drives men to do great things. I refused to participate in any institution that supported these ideas.

This topic requires a deeper dive, but to make a long story short: Young men have no clear meaningful path to follow, no understanding of success, society doesn't value them, and they have few people to emulate or admire.

My father and Doug began to think, "Can these problems be solved? If so, what would uplift young men to take action and direct their own lives? What would a young man need to do to become competent, educated, valuable, fulfilled, dangerous..."

From these questions Doug came up with a short list of games, activities, and occupations which he believed would make a man much more capable than most.

Now, Doug is the sort of man you want to listen to intently. He has lived a long, impressive life. For those who don't know him, Doug Casey is a legendary speculator, investor, the original International Man, best-selling author, economist, philosopher, and my father's mentor.

Doug is both well-read and widely-read. He has written 9 books. One of them, Crisis Investing, was a huge #1 best seller. He published a newsletter for decades. He has traveled to over 175 countries

Figure 1 **Doug Casey, Matt Smith and Maxim Smith during a fuel stop in Lima, Peru.**

and lived in 10. He was a polo player, skydiver, martial artist, scuba diver, auto racer, and competitive shooter.

His list of games, activities, and occupations was the spark I needed. All of the sudden my idea of life, my perspective, changed. That list (and the goal of it) made me realize that what's important is being and doing, not just having (something we will get into later on).

My mind was now oriented to doing the things that the man I want to be would do. And, my primary focus was now to become the man I wish to be. So, because of Doug's list, I decided to read more, learn how to play chess, improve my Spanish, take a 4-month class to become an EMT, and take on a menial job to earn some money to help fund my pursuits.

I found the beginning of my path. I want you to find yours. That's what this book is all about.

Doug's list is the origin of a program we've developed for young men. We like to call this program, "The Preparation". As an alternative to college, this program is self-directed and designed for driven individuals who seek to go their own path in life.

The goal of college is to receive a degree to get a job which will hopefully turn into a career. Financial independence is the outcome they hope for and it's a worthy goal, but one that few actually achieve.

That goal can be achieved through The Preparation, but as you'll see, financial independence is a byproduct of being a man of substance and doing things that create value. This book will show you how.

The ideas in this book are bolstered by the contributions of three generations of men. Doug Casey graduated from Georgetown University. My father dropped out of the University of Illinois after three semesters. And I am doing what Doug and my father would have done if they could start over today.

To avoid confusion, we'll label each author at the start of each chapter. Also, throughout the book all three of us contribute "Pro Tips" within the body of each chapter.

With this book, we're laying out everything crucial to a young man's education that is otherwise unavailable today. And we'll do it in a way filled with adventure those stuck in college lecture halls daydream about.

Money making is a key component of this program, but with the tools you'll acquire from this book, it may be the easiest thing you'll do. We will show you how to develop your character and live a virtuous life. We will give you a detailed set of high-value skills you can learn, and, on top of that, you'll get the exact locations where you can go to learn them. We'll Provide you a blueprint to follow and show you how to personalize it if you choose.

We want you to become a virtuous, competent, and educated man. If you're up for the task, this book will show you the way.

Trust me, you have no idea how much you can accomplish within 4 years. While your peers are letting time slip away at an institution, you'll be doing extraordinary things in interesting places and becoming more and more valuable each day. When your peers finally graduate, you'll be so far ahead, you'll leave them in the dust.

In less time than it takes most to graduate college, you could become a competent fighter, healer, horseman, and pilot. But that's not all...you'd still have time left over to learn how to sell and start your own business. You could learn how to design and build your own home. You could obtain the skills to survive in the wild, and you could learn to comfortably speak a second or third language. Along the way, you could build an international network of good, valuable people.

All of this (and more) is possible, but there's one thing we need you to bring to the table.

Ambition. Great achievements can come to anyone, anywhere, in any situation – if they have ambition. One young man will read this book, see the tools before him, and he will let them sit there. Another will pick up the blueprint, get to work, and create his success. It's up to you to decide who you want to be.

When I started The Preparation, I had some resources at my disposal. My father had set aside an amount of money for me equivalent to a year's worth of tuition at a prestigious university. However, I still took on a job at Office Depot and I worked as a pizza delivery driver to pay for the different classes and courses I took. The point is, whether you're starting off with a little bit of cash, an unlimited budget, or nothing at all – you can make your way through The Preparation, build a stack of accomplishments, and become a man among men.

So, without further ado...let's get into The Preparation.

INTRODUCTION

BY DOUG CASEY

This book will change the course of your life.

I earned, or at least received, a B.A degree from Georgetown in 1968 in an era when relatively few went to college and a degree was arguably worth something. Although I enjoyed my time on campus, college didn't prepare me to deal with life and face the world. If I'd had good counsel—or had a book like this—I would have used those four years more productively.

I consider college to have been a misallocation of time and money. in the context of today's world, I'd say it's far worse than a misallocation. It's worse than a waste. It's a negative, a detriment, worth less than zero.

If you go to a school with a serious intent to qualify for a STEM (Science, Technology, Engineering, Math) degree, that's one thing. Those are serious subjects, requiring rigorous study, testing, and often lab work. If you're interested in STEM it might make sense to go out into the world and then go back to a specialized university, once you're sure that's the direction you want to go.

However, non-STEM courses often fill minds with harmful ideologies requiring years to unlearn. Formal college courses like gender studies, sociology, government, and psychology usually amount to indoctrination, with approximately zero value in the real world. Your main take-aways will be a degree—which, after your first job, nobody will care about or ask to see—and an albatross of debt around your neck that can't be discharged and will continue growing larger as it accumulates interest.

You can learn the liberal arts and all the material in non-STEM courses without going to college, without accruing debt, and without poisoning yourself with academia's toxic indoctrination.

But, you may ask, what about the network, the connections you'll make with other students at college? Fair question. First, the fact is that you'll meet people and make friends wherever you go. Remember that. And then consider that the kids you'd meet in college will be as lost and perhaps even more ill-informed than you are. There once was a time when having the will and ability to get into a college would set you apart; colleges were generally small, serious, and selective. That's no longer the case.

If college still meant that you'd meet other bright, upwardly mobile people who could act as a cohort aiding each other through life, that would be—and once was—a reason to go. But today that's only likely if you go to an expensive and prestigious college that attracts smart rich connected kids. If you attend a local college, you'll get none of that. Most of the 4,000 odd colleges in the US are worth little or nothing from that viewpoint because, well, they're not magnets for smart, connected kids from rich families. The pool is increasingly diluted by affirmative action students who are there because they've been suckered into thinking it will help them. Truly, it only helps the university administration show how much they value "diversity," at the expense of those affirmative action students who delay by 4–6 years their ability to start accumulating wealth. Such connections won't move you forward.

If you do go to a college surrounded by the smart, connected, and rich—and get to know them— great. Some might become friends for life. But you don't need to go to college to meet those kinds of people. And as a matter of fact, if they're sitting there in college, they're probably just drones, albeit smart drones from well-to-do, well-connected families. In other words, the second biggest reason for going to college—making connections—is as much of a chimera and delusion as the main reason: getting an education.

Nonetheless, like about 40% of young men, you are probably headed to a college or university. The chances are that you're going primarily because many or even most of your high school classmates are going. You've been told or led to believe that it's what you're supposed to do, that it's the natural progression for a young man such as you.

It's not.

There was a time, which ended a couple of generations ago, when a college degree was your entrée to a prestigious job and a high income. There was some truth to that when getting into college was a big deal that would set you apart. It no longer is.

There was a time when most students could work their way through college. Now the sticker price for attending a name brand institution can run close to $100,000 for a nine— month year. (The cost of going to college has gone up by 3x in the last 30 years while the median earnings of college graduates have gone up only 2x.)

You may qualify for grants or scholarships to reduce the financial burden, but when and if you graduate in four years (only 41% do), you'll enter the real world with little useful knowledge and a mountain of student loans that will keep you indentured for decades.

After graduation, you will face the daunting task of finding a job—ideally one that justifies your financial investment and offers some relief from the crushing weight of your loans. But what practical skills will you really have? College graduates typically leave with a paper credential but lack the hands-on experience and marketable skills to thrive.

Worse, you'll find that some of the best years of your life were frittered away. As Rick Blaine said in the movie **Casablanca**, "You'll regret it. Maybe not today, maybe not tomorrow, but soon, and for the rest of your life."

In college you'll gain only a limited amount of knowledge and very few skills with direct application in the real world. It's great to meet the other kids, but they won't have very much life experience either. It can be fun hanging out with them (and hanging out is typically 80% of the college experience) but we promise that you'll have much more fun hanging out with the people you'll meet in the Preparation. Plus you will learn much more, have many more great experiences, build yourself into the type of man you want to be, and come out hundreds of thousands of dollars ahead.

THE KIND OF EDUCATION YOU REALLY WANT

Robert Persig's book "Zen and The Art of Motorcycle Maintenance" discusses the interrelation of all areas of knowledge and the value of curiosity. In one vignette, we find a poor, uneducated, greasy-haired (but curious) motorcycle mechanic who realizes that if he's going to torque a bolt properly, he should learn a bit about metallurgy and how aluminum relates to steel. That leads him to chemistry. An interest in that leads him to physics. Which will lead him to astronomy and astrophysics. Which leads him to philosophy. Which takes him to ethics. Which leads to ancient history. Then modern history and English literature. Over time he may still fix motorcycles to put bread on the table, but he's opened the entire expanse of human existence, just by pursuing one thread.

Those thoughts in the book led me to a long discussion with Sonny Barger (president of the Hells Angels) when he came to a meeting of the Eris Society, a gathering I sponsored in Aspen for many years. We became friends. Sonny was—surprising to many—quite well read. I have no doubt that the fact that he was among the most knowledgeable of the club's 5000 members helped keep him on top of the heap. You never know where pursuing a thread of knowledge will take you.

The journey of Pirsig's motorcycle mechanic can and should apply to everyone and anyone. The only requirements are curiosity and diligence. The mechanic transformed himself into a modern-day Renaissance Man, someone with a broad range of interests, knowledge, and skills. Starting with almost nothing.

A.E. Van Vogt put his finger on the end phenomenon of this in "The Voyage of the Space Beagle." In an interstellar redux of Darwin's voyage, the Space Beagle is chock full of scientists. But there's a non-specialist on board that Van Vogt calls a Nexialist, a generalist who (paradoxically) specializes in seeing the connections between things. His wide breadth of knowledge, abilities, and experience allowed him to interpret situations in ways that a specialist might be unable to see. The Nexialist, who saves the Space Beagle from numerous dangers, is a type of Renaissance Man.

As is Edmond Dantes, The Count of Monte Cristo, hero of the novel by Alexandre Dumas. We make reference to the Count, as a model, in this book. I'd also draw your attention to another fictional character, Paladin, who we'll discuss later.

Which brings me to the point of this book and why it could very well be the most important thing you'll ever read. That's because it's a practical guide for young men who are trying (probably haphazardly) to figure out what to do with their lives. The typical drill is to log eight years in grade school, get through high school, go to college, get a job, climb the corporate ladder, and retire.

I know that may sound like a cynical oversimplification, but it's the path most men take. But you don't have to live your life that way—not even remotely. That rat race starts with school.

School is the central experience of the first 22 years of your life. For some people the first 24 or 26 years—a third of your life. Sure, you gain some basic knowledge, at least via osmosis, through logging many hours sitting behind a desk. But it's a painfully suboptimal way to prepare for life. The fact of the matter is that once you're competent at reading, writing, and arithmetic, the whole world of knowledge is open to you. Most of the time in school thereafter is wasted. And the higher the grade, the more true that is. Think back to the years you spent in classrooms, waiting for time to pass, for the clock on the wall to grant you freedom. How much knowledge did you gain? But, looking at the bright side, at least there were few out— of-pocket costs—until you get to college.

BECOMING A RENAISSANCE MAN

The term "**Renaissance Man**" suggests a person of many accomplishments. Not an expert or a specialist, not someone who knows everything about just a few things, but someone who knows more than a little about everything.

That paraphrases Charles van Doren, ex-editor of the Encyclopedia Britannica. He's right, but incomplete. That definition just covers intellectual knowledge, the ability to grasp facts and reason. That's more the definition of a *polymath*. A Renaissance Man, as we define it in this book, is broader. He doesn't just know things, but he can also do things, has a wide range of experiences, and a moral basis for his life.

The object of the Preparation is to get you on the way to being what Renaissance Italians called an *uomo universale*, a Universal Man. Or what we today call a Renaissance Man.

Aristotle said *"Every systematic science, the humblest and the noblest alike, seems to admit of two distinct kinds of proficiency; one of which may be properly called 'scientific knowledge' of the subject, while the other is a kind of 'educational acquaintance' with it. For an educated man should be able to form a fair off-hand judgment as to the goodness or badness of the method used by a professor in his exposition.* **To be educated is in fact to be able to do this;** *and even the man of universal education we deem to be such in virtue of his having this ability."*

Regrettably, for someone who was an extremely clear thinker, Aristotle often comes off as unclear and obscure. Probably because everything we have from him is in the form of notes from his students. In any event, what we're hoping to do in The Preparation is to make sure you get what Aristotle called an educational acquaintance, not scientific knowledge. Life—not to mention just four years—is too short for the latter.

"Scientific knowledge" here is for a specialist. "Educational acquaintance" means you have a sound enough grip of the basics to allow you to tell the difference between sense and nonsense.

Following the path laid out in this book should give you a much, much, better education than logging four years in any college. That's true for several reasons. One, you'll be learning from some of the very best teachers in the world.

Two, you won't suffer the distractions of being surrounded by teenagers. Most of them have little knowledge, experience, or wisdom, but lots of bad habits.

Three, you'll be doing things in the real world, not just sitting behind a desk. You'll gain competence in a broad range of activities. The typical college grad has no real competence in anything.

The Preparation will direct you in maximizing your mind (your intellect and thought processes), your body (your vehicle for dealing with the material world), and your character (the most important of the three). Without a sound foundation to differentiate what's right from what's wrong, the knowledge of good vs. evil, and the ability to make wise choices, you'll find the knowledge, experience and power you'll gain during your life are hollow or worse.

A Renaissance Man is someone with a broad range of knowledge, experience, and skills. He hasn't just memorized the answers to some questions, but uses critical thinking skills to dig into the why and how. He questions everything, including, or even especially, authority. A broad base of knowledge and experience lets him come up with answers.

A Renaissance Man knows a lot about many things. But while you want as much knowledge as you can get, it's still only a possession, like a car, a house, or money—albeit knowledge is the most personal of possessions. Knowing a lot about a lot of things is a foundation for being a Renaissance man; but it's really only a stepping stone to success and happiness.

If you make the effort to understand the courses we recommend, the academic part of The Preparation should give you a broader and deeper knowledge of the world than four years in any university in the world. In part, it's because you're in charge of the process, so you will care to learn, and you will learn your way. 16 quarters of The Preparation will immerse you into the real world. The academic knowledge base you'll learn will prepare you to do many practical hands-on things. That knowledge, combined with the skills you'll acquire, the places you'll go, and the people you'll meet will let you stand head-and— shoulders above your contemporaries.

As did Leon Battista Alberdi (1404–1472), who is often singled out as the first Renaissance Man, a generation before Leonardo da Vinci. He was a polymath, but best known as an artist, architect, writer, linguist, poet, cryptographer, and philosopher. Not just an intellectual, he was notably tall, strong, and in his autobiography he claims to "excel in all bodily exercises; could, with feet tied, leap over a standing man; could in the great cathedral, throw a coin far up to ring against the vault; amused himself by taming wild horses and climbing mountains." He summed up his life when he said: "A man can do all things, if he will."

Be–Do–Have

Like Alberti, you should want to be a polymath. But a Renaissance Man can also put the theory into practice. It's here we get down to the three most important verbs in any language: Be, Do, and Have.

"Do" is the practical, the operative, partner in this verbal triumvirate. We live in a world of cause and effect. You want to be the cause, not the effect. If you Do things, you cause effects. The result should be an increase in what you Have. The more you Have, the more you're in a position to Do more.

It's great to have lots of things, as long as you don't let them capture you. Things are described by nouns. There are many thousands of them—including knowledge, health, ability, and money. In addition to making life more pleasant, having things—especially the most fungible of things, money—helps you to Do more.

Verbs (there are thousands of them) include thinking, working, creating, traveling, and enjoying. Verbs are more important than nouns in life. A virtuous circle. Having and Doing should put you on the road to Being. Or perhaps we should say Beingness, a state of reality, and transforming yourself into your own ideal.

The result, the end phenomenon, should be serenity, confidence, strength of character, self-actu-alization, and a sense of inner power. These things are what mystics, ascetics, gurus, and monks spend a lifetime trying to achieve. They attempt to gain Beingness by swearing off the material world, with practices like meditation, prayer, fasting, and yoga. These practices can be useful, of course. But The Preparation is intended to set you on a course to master reality by confronting it, not avoiding it. We can't promise that all the Have and Do elements of the Preparation will get you to Be. But the four years involved with the Preparation will get you a lot further than four years at a college. People overemphasize Havingness. Having things is important as a means, but it should never be an end. Doing can change your essence, enabling you to Be what you wish. At the same time, by virtue of Doing things, you get to Have things. Knowledge, money, possessions, power, and skills. People respect the wealthy. Calvinists believe success is a proof of righteousness. For Catholics success is an outward sign of inward grace. They're both right, assuming that the success is achieved ethically.

You don't want to be overly concerned with Have (things you possess). "I must have prestige." "I must have power." "I want to have a strong, athletic body." "I need to have money." "I want to have a beautiful mate." This is a huge and stupid trap. Having things is only a consequence of Doing. There's nothing wrong with wanting to have any and all these things; the more the better. But, remember, Have is only a consequence.

"Do" is what is in your control right now. Doing things results in having things. And having things makes it easier to do more things: a positive feedback loop.

But the essence of life is Beingness. Who, in fact, are you? That's a question that's rarely asked. Few people want to pursue their essence, to see what's there. Beingness isn't a chalice or object of some kind, it's the real Holy Grail. It's why we find monks devoting their lives to work and prayer, living simply and following orders. Even more extreme, some become ascetics, scourge their bodies and live as hermits, denying themselves food and every kind of comfort. They're looking for the meaning of life. I think, however, they're going at it in the wrong way. Fighting against the concept of Have is to fight reality.

Perhaps that's because they're afraid of finding and having to confront failures, lies, betrayals, cheats, stupidities, shameful aggressions, or thefts. These things result in shame or guilt and are burdens that you always carry with you. They erode your very Being. How do you avoid that? By adopting a personal code of ethics. By always doing the right thing. By being a stand-up guy. In this book, we'll help you develop your own personal code. A personal code grounded in moral-ity and virtue should keep you from Doing harm and wanting to Have destructive things. It will make it easier to Be. Doing moral things allows you to Be something that you want to be; to mold yourself into the man you want to be.

Don't be afraid of virtue (which makes many people flinch today). The meaning, the essence, of the word has been degraded. It's associated with religious concepts, more suited to clergy than men living in the world. We don't mean to disparage anyone's religious beliefs, but the origin of *virtue* is the Latin word *vir*, which means "man." Real virtue is to be manly, like the Homeric heroes Achilles, Hector, or Odysseus. There are long lists of virtues (and vices) depending on who's talking. There's often confusion between the Classical and the Theological virtues. The Classical virtues date from ancient times and include courage, justice, honesty, temperance, and hospitality. Theological virtues are concepts more along the lines of faith, hope, charity, humility, and chastity seem more appropriate for cloistered nuns than young virile men.

Building a strong virtuous character is the most important part of a proper education. But it's the least likely thing you will gain from four years in college. In fact, swimming in a tepid pool of Wokeness for four years is going to do the opposite.

Figuring out what's right and wrong (today's world doesn't much use the words Good and Evil) is actually the most important thing you can learn in the process of becoming a Renaissance man. While people appreciate the company of others who Have things, they much more value the company of people who are capable and can Do things. But most valuable of all are those who Are: those whose essence is admirable and virtuous. Men who can be counted on, who are wise, brave, and trustworthy.

The ideal of molding yourself stands in opposition to the idea of college, where you're theoretically supposed to be remade by the institution. Academia generally despises autodidacts—those who dispense with their services, and instead educate themselves. To go to Harvard is to be molded into a *Harvard Man*. But is becoming *a Harvard* Man a desirable goal? In the past it had desirable elements. But no longer. Higher education is no longer about gaining the knowledge you need to think critically and rationally to arrive at independent conclusions. It's much more about political indoctrination. Autodidacts and independent researchers are discouraged. Students get higher grades if they regurgitate their professors' opinions.

The very model of being molded by a school is wrong. You're not a piece of clay.

"Be" is the most important verb in life. It connotes character and ethics. These aren't *Have* things. They're part of your essence. Unlike possessions, they can't be taken from you. You could master all other aspects of being a Renaissance man, but if you lack good character and ethics you've failed.

A large part of this book is to spell out what it means to do the right thing, to be a stand— up guy. It doesn't matter how much Do and Have you've got. If you lack virtue, you'll be untrustworthy, disloyal, dishonest, imprudent, and unworthy.

This book is not for everybody. What it recommends is not only unconventional, but scary to most people.

Why do people go to college today? Why do people go to high school for that matter? Was it a mistake even going to high school? What could and should you do in those four years while surrounded by young yahoos? That's a question you should ask yourself.

We believe parents should—ideally—homeschool their children. Does it make sense to shunt them off to an institution manned by employees for eight hours a day? I would give the example offered by the movie *Twins* with Arnold Schwarzenegger and Danny DeVito. DeVito's character grows up conventionally in the city; he's a mental, physical, and moral disaster. His knowledge and skills consist solely of scamming and manipulating. Arnold's character, on the other hand, grew up on a desert island, away from distractions and the deleterious influences of young yahoos. He occupied his time reading great books and making himself into a physical specimen. As the title suggests, they were twins separated at birth. The homeschooled Arnold became a brilliant Adonis and Danny became a surly troll.

I went to a four-year military academy for high school. I went to college because I didn't know any better. Everyone in my class went to college, even those at the bottom of the academic barrel. If not college, what? Get an entrance level job doing something I had no interest in? It would have been considered malpractice if any teacher had counseled that there was not only another possibility, but a much better one. What should you do?

In both high school and college I took the required courses: Literature, History, Science, Philosophy, Math, Political Science, Foreign Language. People think college means an education. But the fact of the matter is, when you're sitting at a desk 30 hours a week, you'll often fall asleep in class because you've stayed up late the night before, partying. Perhaps you'll cut the class because the professor is predictably boring and incompetent or the subject is irrelevant or made impenetrable. Your mind will wander during the class, and if the professor says something of value, you could easily miss it. Most of the time, the professor is just droning on, saying the same things he's said for many years, with no particular competence about either what he's saying or how he says it. If you're at a prestigious university you'll occasionally get a great professor. Is it worth four years of time and a quarter million dollars? I think not. Especially when there are much better alternatives. You want the knowledge, and you should, you can get a college education by listening to courses online. I'm a big fan of the Teaching Company. They've sought out some of the world's best instructors, who are paid to, and generally succeed at, giving a commanding performance. Best of all, you can listen to these truly excellent courses as many times as you'd like. At a college, a lot of the time, you won't be listening to a professor anyway. You'll likely be listening to a teaching assistant who is regurgitating what the professor taught him, flavored with his own activist bias and spin.

Going to college today has nothing to do with walking around with Plato at his Academy, or Aristotle at his Lyceum. The chances of finding a modern Socrates at a university are Slim to none, and Slim's out of town. Socrates didn't teach because he needed a job; he taught to uncover wisdom, and what was right or wrong. At college you'll rarely discuss things with somebody like Socrates, pursuing a subject to understanding. An overwhelming percentage of professors today are Woke, socialists, or some variety of doctrinaire leftist. So, if you go to class, you'll sit through 50 minutes of a professor presenting material that is bent, confused, befuddled, murky and outright harmful. Today's college experience is totally dysfunctional. Socrates would not approve.

Going to college today delays getting into the real world. It prolongs childhood. And for that, you're paying hundreds of thousands of dollars, which will turn you into an indentured servant for years to come. It's actually quite insane. Repeat this for emphasis: Outside of STEM fields, by going to college, you're wasting, or at best seriously misallocating, time and money which could have been used more profitably and more enjoyably. But it's even worse. College today is just a neutral halfway house for gaining some maturity. It's a negative value, because almost all of the professors, certainly in the so-called liberal arts, are doctrinaire leftists who will act to corrupt you. Because they're in positions of authority and you're paying them a lot of money, you naturally feel you ought to absorb what they're telling you. And because you're just out of high school, you simply don't have the experience to know that you're being actively corrupted. Going to college is almost always a mistake for almost everybody.

The idea of paying an institution for an education is foolish. Education is something that you do for yourself.

PART 1

Chapter 1

HOW TO USE THIS BOOK

MATT SMITH

There are things every man should know—things you could eventually learn on your own but that nobody will ever tell you. Even if they did, you probably wouldn't listen. This book is about those things. It is designed to Prepare you for your future and in doing so, answer the question, "What exactly should I do to become the man I want to be?"

The summer before Maxim's 18th birthday I knew that he was facing this problem. This book is for him. At its core, this is a father's best effort to prepare his son for an important and uncertain time.

Of course, this book doesn't cover everything Maxim (or YOU) will ever need to know. That book would be impossibly long, with most parts irrelevant to the challenges he faces today.

We formulated a structure for young men like my son to become competent, confident, and dangerous. The philosophical ideas along with exactly how to make it happen. Hopefully this gives you a way to visualize a plan to maximize your time, energy, and money to become the man you want to be.

Maxim has been following The Preparation for two years, and the results speak for themselves. He's not the same person he was even a year ago. He started the preparation as a boy. Today, already, he is a man.

To most people, the benefits of being competent and confident are probably self-evident. But the idea of becoming "dangerous" might take some readers aback. It shouldn't.

A dangerous man isn't merely able to defend himself (important as that is), but to think for himself: to critically assess and question any information he receives and even his own built-in beliefs. He is resourceful and independent. A dangerous man can chart his own course and doesn't rely on the herd for protection.

WHAT DOES IT MEAN TO BE COMPETENT, CONFIDENT, AND DANGEROUS?

To be competent is to possess the knowledge and skills necessary to excel in a variety of domains. Competence is the foundation of effectiveness and the ability to solve problems under pressure.

Competence sets a man apart from the masses of drones meandering through life. A competent man can make things happen and shape the world around him.

To be confident is to carry yourself with self-assurance born of real accomplishments. Young men feign confidence all the time, but that's not what we're talking about here. True confidence is not arrogance but a quiet belief in your capacity to succeed, even in unfamiliar or challenging situations. True confidence will inspire and comfort those around you.

To be dangerous is to possess the capability to assert yourself, protect others, and achieve your goals with precision and decisiveness. It is not about recklessness or harm but about having the skills and mindset to face any challenge head-on. A dangerous man is disciplined, focused, and relentless in pursuing what is meaningful, able to defend his principles and those he cares about. As outlined later in the book, this quality embodies controlled strength and strategic thinking—essential traits for navigating life with purpose and integrity.

The goal of The Preparation is to instill these qualities in every participant, ensuring they emerge ready to lead, adapt, and excel in life.

THE TWO PARTS OF THIS BOOK

This book is divided into two essential parts:

PART 1: FOUNDATIONAL IDEAS: The first section equips you with the philosophical and intellectual groundwork necessary for growth. Not the abstract musings of existentialists like Kierkegaard, though I've read my share, but the kind of philosophy that helps you answer, Who am I? How does the world work? How can I successfully engage with it? It includes lessons on building character, developing a personal code, and understanding the economic and social forces shaping our world. These ideas form the bedrock of becoming a competent, confident, and dangerous man.

PART 2: ACTIONABLE STRATEGIES: The second section focuses on tangible, actionable steps. The curriculum here, you'll find detailed guidance on how to execute The Preparation's cycles, master new skills, and undertake challenges that will transform you into a well-rounded, resourceful individual. This is where theory meets practice.

WHAT ARE CYCLES?

At the heart of The Preparation's curriculum are 16 "cycles"—three-month thematic programs, such as Cowboy, Pilot, or Fighter. Each cycle combines:

- ▶ **AN ANCHOR COURSE:** The centerpiece of the cycle, providing immersive, hands-on experiences.
- ▶ **ACADEMIC COURSES:** Online or self-guided studies to deepen knowledge.
- ▶ **READING ASSIGNMENTS:** Books tied to the cycle's theme, offering historical, philosophical, or technical insights.

- ▶ **SKILL-BUILDING ENJOYABLE ACTIVITIES:** Do Fun Shit, purposeful challenges like learning chess, mastering a musical instrument, or skydiving.
- ▶ **REFLECTION AND ACCOUNTABILITY:** Weekly writing exercises to track progress and reinforce learning.
- ▶ **OPTIONAL WORK OPPORTUNITIES:** For those who wish to earn while learning, any job—even temporary—can add valuable insights and financial support.

This structure ensures a balanced mix of physical, intellectual, and reflective growth. Each cycle is designed to maximize your time, with 40 productive hours per week culminating in a minimum of 480 hours per cycle.

We've gone through the effort of laying out the cycles for you. We tell you where to go and what to do. If you follow the cycles we've laid out, we have no doubt that you'll become a modern day Renaissance Man. Whether it's gaining medical skills as an EMT, navigating the skies as a private pilot, or mastering Muay Thai in Thailand, these experiences are designed to push your boundaries and expand your horizons.

WHY CHOOSE THE PREPARATION?

The Preparation's 16 cycles can be completed in four years—the same time it takes to earn a college degree—but at every step, you'll build practical skills, gain meaningful knowledge, and cultivate a powerful network that amplifies your earning potential.

According to recent estimates, the cost of a four-year college degree in the U.S. averages at least $140,000, and many graduates leave school with tens of thousands or even hundreds of thousands of dollars in student loan debt.

The Preparation offers a radically different path. All 16 cycles can be completed over four years, **all for the cost of a single year at a prestigious university.**

PREPPERS—as we call those who follow The Preparation—gain real-world skills of economic value. Unlike college, The Preparation is designed so that, if you need to, you can pay your way through it. Each cycle allows participants to take on work opportunities that not only offset costs but also add to their skill sets and networks. By the end of the program, Preppers emerge debt-free, and armed with a portfolio of competencies that dramatically increase their future opportunities and earning power.

Imagine the contrast: after four years of college, most graduates have theoretical knowledge and debt. After four years of The Preparation, Preppers are skilled EMTs, pilots, welders, ranchers, and much more. They've learned to navigate real-world challenges, adapt to diverse environments and develop practical skills. The Preparation is a crucible. Preppers pass through it, starting as a young man with few advantages and emerge anew—A man with character, abilities, confidence, clarity, and surprising opportunities.

Hands-on-skills are a priority, but are only a component of becoming a well-rounded man. Preppers don't skimp on academics including economics, foreign language, history, and science. Today, you can attend classes of America's greatest professors for virtually free–online.

Doug and I are both considered "rich guys". We are subject matter experts in economics, wealth creation, and entrepreneurship. These skills have never been more relevant than they are today, and we've incorporated them into The Preparation.

Preppers learn critical financial principles such as understanding sound money, analyzing market trends, and recognizing opportunities for wealth preservation and growth. Unlike traditional education, which often neglects these real-world essentials, The Preparation ensures every participant leaves with a firm grasp of how to manage and grow their financial resources.

The Preparation encourages entrepreneurship. We show participants how to lay the groundwork for building their own businesses and creating value. Whether it's launching a service, crafting a product, or investing in opportunities, we provide the tools and mindset to think creatively and take calculated risks—empowering young men to carve their own paths.

Furthermore, Preppers learn what few others can: the art of finding and developing relationships with mentors. Drawing from the "Forget Mentors, Find a Patron" chapter, readers discover how to identify influential individuals who can guide and open doors for them. This ancient but under-appreciated practice, rooted in the Roman patron-client relationship, equips Preppers to build connections that lead to transformative opportunities.

The Preparation isn't just about gaining skills; it's about building a foundation for a life of purpose, independence, and impact. While college students spend their 20s trying to climb out of debt and establish themselves, Preppers are already living meaningful lives, contributing to their communities, and pursuing opportunities that align with their passions and goals.

THE POWER OF CYCLE-STACKING

Cycle-stacking— completing multiple cycles consecutively— has a compounding effect. Skills learned in one cycle often complement the next, building momentum and confidence. For example, the resilience developed in a Fighter cycle may enhance your adaptability during a Survivalist cycle. Over time, as you will see, this deliberate practice transforms you into the resourceful, capable, and independent man.

WHY THE PREPARATION WORKS

Traditional education measures effort in credit hours, but The Preparation redefines productivity. While a college student might log 840 hours annually (15 credit hours and 13 study hours per week over 30 weeks), a single year of The Preparation amounts to 1,920 hours of intentional effort. These hours are not just more numerous but also more impactful, combining real-world application with personal growth.

Unlike college, which often allows for passive participation, The Preparation demands active engagement. Imagine learning to pack mules and lead them through the wilds of Idaho, learning to sail near Cape Horn, or becoming a private pilot in Alaska. These aren't hypothetical scenarios; they are real opportunities available through this program. Each experience builds skills, expands networks, and offers stories worth telling. And all for a fraction of the cost of a university "education".

GETTING STARTED

Part 2 of this book is all about the curriculum. Keep in mind, you don't need to commit to all 16 cycles right away. The key is to begin. Choose a cycle that excites you—one that aligns with your interests or sparks curiosity. Completing your first cycle will provide the momentum and confidence to pursue others. With each cycle, you'll discover that you, with expanded capabilities, have changed and, at the same time, new and unexpected opportunities will emerge.

As the philosopher, Epictetus said, "The world turns aside for the man who knows where he is going." The Preparation is your launchpad to a life of purpose and achievement. It won't be easy, but nothing worthwhile is easy. Dive into your first cycle, embrace the challenges, and get momentum working in your favor. Let The Preparation show you the way.

Chapter 2

THE WRONG QUESTION

BY MATT SMITH

Recently, I was at a gathering and overheard an older fellow talking with two young guys—19 and 22. Neither was going to college, which I happen to think is often a smart choice these days. Inevitably, though, the older guy asked the typical question: "So, what are you going to do?" By this, of course, he meant the grown-up version of what adults always ask little kids: "What do you want to be when you grow up?"

Kids typically respond with something exciting—like fireman, policeman, or astronaut. When you're around college age, the expected answers revolve around schools, majors, and careers—the usual dreary treadmill leading to what people call a "good job." The unspoken assumption is that a job alone is something to aspire to—as if climbing a corporate ladder is the highest purpose in life.

Both young men struggled to articulate an answer. So, naturally, I stepped in. I said, "Forget jobs for a moment. A job is just a way to make money. The real question is: What kind of man do you want to become?"

Their eyes lit up, and their posture improved immediately. Instead of vague answers, they began to talk about virtues, character, and ambition.

Young men instinctively want something meaningful and noble—something worthy of their potential. A mere job won't inspire anyone, let alone young men with ambition.

Next time someone asks you, "What do you want to be when you grow up?" answer them plainly: "I'll earn a living, sure, maybe through a job. But right now, I'm focused on becoming the kind of man I want to be."

That picture in your mind—the image of the confident, competent, and dangerous individual you're meant to be—will become clearer as you keep reading. By the end of this book, you'll know exactly what it means to be that kind of man

Chapter 3

THE CORE PROBLEM: WANTING WHAT OTHERS WANT

MATT SMITH

"I can teach anybody how to get
what they want out of life.
The problem is that I can't find anybody
who can tell me what they want."

—MARK TWAIN

Have you ever set your sights on something—a good grade, a car, an award, or a university acceptance letter—only to later question why you wanted it in the first place? Maybe you worked hard for it, achieved it, and still felt unfulfilled. This puzzling experience is rooted in a concept called mimetic desire, a term introduced by the French thinker René Girard.

Girard's groundbreaking idea reveals a surprising truth about human behavior: much of what we want isn't chosen independently. Instead, we imitate the desires of others. As Girard famously said,

"Man is the creature who
does not know what to desire,
and he turns to others in order
to make up his mind.
We desire what others desire
because we imitate their desires."

The first dozen years of my adult life were lived in "monkey see, monkey do" fashion. I pursued the same things people around me pursued. And even in success, I was dissatisfied and unhappy. How could it be otherwise?

When you play a game for a prize you care nothing about, winning cannot bring satisfaction. The solution is simple: to play your own game and only for prizes you truly desire. The question, however, is complicated: How do I make sure my aim is true?

WHAT IS MIMETIC DESIRE?

René Girard, a literary critic and philosopher, observed that human beings often don't know what they want. Instead of forming desires on their own, people look to others— whether friends, family, celebrities, or even strangers—to figure out what to value. This creates a dynamic where we imitate not just behavior but also the desires of those around us.

Imagine scrolling through social media and seeing a friend's vacation in Bali. You weren't thinking about traveling, but now you find yourself yearning to book a similar trip. That's mimetic desire at work—your friend's desires influenced your own. Recognizing these moments helps you separate what you truly want from what society tells you to want.

Girard described desire as a triangle:

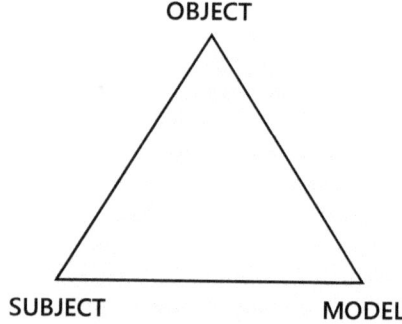

THE SUBJECT: You, the person wanting something.

THE OBJECT: The thing you desire (e.g., a job, a degree, or a car).

THE MODEL: The person (or people) whose desire influences your own. As a young person this is typically your peers and parents.

Mimetic desire isn't just a theoretical concept; it's something I lived, often without realizing it. Like many, I followed paths shaped by others—whether it was societal expectations or the desires of people around me.

FOLLOWING THE CROWD

Early on in school they placed me in the "gifted" program. I never felt gifted and, in fact, school always felt like a prison to me. What I really wanted to do was make an escape, and yet, I still pursued good grades like everyone else in my peer group.

When my release date from lockup (aka graduation) was finally on the horizon I somehow decided, I should go to college. Why? Because the mimetic contagion of wanting to go to college was all around me. Everyone I knew was going to college. Even the college I chose to attend wasn't chosen by me. All the smartest students without rich parents wanted to go to the best state school, the University of Illinois.

Not only was this a stupid idea, but it also never even occurred to me that I could have gone to Harvard or West Point. Or, better yet, I could have gone to Oxford or the Sorbonne. My scope of vision was way too limited and local. The University of Illinois in Urbana, IL was the only college I even applied to. Monkey see, monkey do.

When you follow mimetic desire, eventually you'll find yourself in a place you never wanted to be. A reckoning ensues.

My college reckoning came late one Friday night, when I was out for a jog around campus. A few miles into my run I turned onto Green Street just when the bars were closing. As the crowd of partygoers emerged, I slowed to a walk. And with the clarity of a runner's high, I saw my fellow students. Good-natured but loud and obnoxious, some staggered, and one vomited in the street. In the clarity of a runner's high, the scene struck me as grotesque. It was like I was driving down the interstate and just realized I'd missed my exit a ways back. I was in the wrong place. How did I get here?

Don't get me wrong, I've been that guy who went out for fun and drank too much. I don't recommend it, but neither am I trying to condemn it. The problem wasn't my fellow students. The problem was me. And it was visible to me that night in stark relief. Going with the flow, following the crowd, I'd ended up in a place where I didn't belong. I'd been drawn to the idea of college. A place to improve ourselves, but we had enough free time during the weeknights to go barhopping till daybreak.

Mimetic desires are borrowed desires and can drive you far from your true path.

The moment of clarity caused a reckoning with the fact I'd outsourced my own wants to the crowd, and it landed me in a place where I didn't belong. After that night I couldn't imagine dedicating the next 2.5 years to a degree because I realized it was never what I genuinely wanted. I didn't even have a declared major. I thought a degree would give me the skills and credentials to get me a job, that's what conventional wisdom suggests.

I never attended another University class, that night I couldn't shake the feeling that there had to be another way to get the success and working opportunities I wanted.

HOW MIMETIC DESIRE LEADS US ASTRAY

Mimetic desire isn't all bad. When a society holds high ambitions, the upward trajectory of desire will motivate us to improve our lot in life. Likewise, when a society's desires degenerate, it can lead us like lemmings off a cliff. In either case, whenever we get sucked into adopting the desires of the crowd in place of our own, it can lead to serious problems.

Chief among these problems is unfulfillment. Look around at the world today, at the 40–60-year-olds you know. How many of them are stuck in jobs they hate or tolerate? How many are living the life you aspire to? Have time to do what they really want to do? How many are truly happy, healthy, and (at least) reasonably prosperous?

How many of them have become the man they hoped to be? Unfulfillment isn't the only problem.

Mimetic desire can lead to rivalry and conflict. In Girard's framework we tend to see others not only as models but also as rivals because when multiple people want the same thing, competition arises.

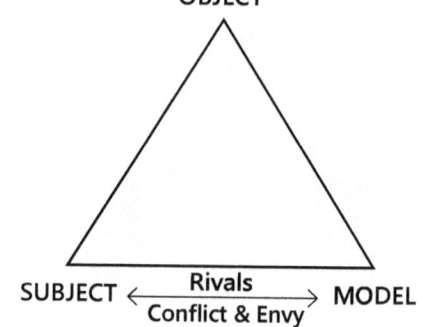

Competition is great in sports, it's wonderful for building comradery amongst teammates, it is a critical mechanism in free markets, and it can serve as a priceless feedback tool for us, personally. But, as a byproduct of everyone desiring the same thing, it is toxic and leads to jealousy, envy, and strained relationships.

Mimetic desire can trap us in cycles of conflict and dissatisfaction unless we take steps to break free.

Like a black hole's inescapable pull, mimetic desire exerts such powerful gravity that most people never realize they're caught in its orbit, endlessly pursuing borrowed desires. They chase ghost after ghost, convinced that the next achievement will finally make their world feel right.

There are two paths to escape this gravitational well.

The first is through conscious effort–developing such a deep understanding of our own authentic motivations that they burn bright enough to overcome the pull of the crowd's predictable wants. Like a star generating enough energy to resist collapse, we must kindle our own inner fire.

The second path, as was true in my case, requires a tragedy powerful enough to tear through the fabric of our assumptions. Like a violent cosmic event that can distort even a black hole's pull, sometimes only a major personal crisis can break us free from the orbit of mimetic desire.

BREAKING FREE OF BORROWED DESIRES

When I arrived on the scene, my mom and step-dad were there along with some of my younger brother's friends. Three cops and the petite medical examiner were standing in his driveway talking. She was wearing a white lab coat which I thought, at the time, to be odd.

My younger brother, Aaron, had spent the last couple of years remodeling the house himself. Our elder brother, Josh, skipped college altogether and I'd dropped out, so it was left to Aaron to be the first in the family to graduate. He got a double major in Mathematics and Philosophy. Smarter than me and certainly better educated, he was also good with his hands. He was something of a renaissance man. He played drums in a rock band, could fix anything mechanical, and rebuilt old cars for fun. When one of his old cars was on its last leg, he signed up for a local demolition derby so he could send the car to its demise in the most spectacular way possible.

Aaron's girlfriend discovered his body at home after she learned he didn't show up for work and wasn't answering calls. She stumbled into what must have been a grisly site. He'd fired a .357 round through the roof of his mouth and out the back of his head. He was 13 days from his 27th birthday. It was late 2005.

I wanted to see him. I insisted on it. Only my mom went into the house with me. The smell is what I remember most. When blood is exposed to air, it oxidizes and produces an iron— like smell. And there was a lot of blood.

I didn't see the worst of it, thankfully. The medical examiner had already moved him from the spot where he did the deed and placed him on a stretcher. The catastrophic exit wound was mostly concealed by a sheet.

There were more than 300 people at his funeral. I was amazed. I knew if it were me that had died, there **might** be 50 or 100 people there. The guy was even more popular than I knew. He was smart. He was capable. He mattered to so many people.

I have no idea why he did it. I expected some revelation to emerge to explain things. I went through all his belongings looking for answers. Nothing turned up. It remains a mystery.

I saw it was a tragedy within a tragedy. That he was gone was bad enough, but what was worse was the fact that, for him to do this, I knew he must have been suffering. Shouldn't I, as his brother, have seen it coming? How could I be so oblivious? That's the part that really got me then. It still does almost 20 years later.

Aaron's death shattered the illusion I'd been living. Everything I thought I wanted, suddenly didn't matter. In his absence I was forced to confront the truth. After leaving University years before, much of my life, even my success, had still been dictated by desires I'd absorbed from others. His tragedy was a wake-up call, pushing me to ask what really mattered and what I truly wanted, independent of societal expectations.

MIMETIC RECKONING

Aaron's suicide hit me like a brick. I was 30. I'd worked virtually every day since my first paper route at nine. My first big win began in 2002 when I started an internet advertising agency. That first year, I was hoping to earn at least $60,000. But sometimes success sneaks up on you. By the end of that first year the business generated almost $750,000 in profit. More money is a thing everyone wants, so I wanted it too. I never asked myself why I wanted the money, or why I was working this hard. When Aaron died, I was the richest person I'd ever met. It's not as impressive as it sounds, I didn't know anyone.

Just to illustrate how pervasive mimetic desires were in my life—Even the house I owned, I bought BECAUSE it was the most desired house in town. Here I was, living in Iowa in what everyone referred to as the "castle house". It was nice, but I didn't even want to live in the Midwest. The house was filled with things I didn't care about or want. It felt fake. It was fake. Delivered by seeking borrowed desires.

The one stark exception to the rule was my new son. I really wanted to be a dad and just two months before Aaron's death, Maxim was born. Life and death, joy and tragedy at the same time. The range of emotions was wild. I'd see-saw from a sense of wholesomeness with Maxim to unrelenting sadness about Aaron.

I called it a sabbatical. I needed time to think. I took a step back from my work. I moved my young family to the mountains outside Asheville, North Carolina. Where I could read and spend time with my new son. Any mimetic desire I'd once had was eviscerated. And in the void that remained, I began the hard work of figuring out what I truly wanted. I needed to know what makes a life worth living.

WHY A MAN NEEDS A PHILOSOPHICAL CORE

Without a philosophical core, a man drifts through life like a ship without a rudder. He gets moved around by whatever winds happen to be blowing—chasing what others chase, wanting what others want, never knowing his own mind. I see it all around me: men who seem successful on the outside but still feel something is missing.

Every man must discover these truths for himself. You can be told what matters in life, but until you truly understand it—until you find that philosophical core—you're just borrowing someone else's compass. The ancient Greeks and Romans understood this. Look at Athens in its golden age: philosophers like Socrates, Plato, and Aristotle weren't just writing theories—they were teaching men how to live with excellence. They developed concrete ideas about courage, justice, wisdom, and self-control. These virtues shaped both the individual and society. When a young Alexander the Great needed a teacher, his father Philip II chose Aristotle—because he knew that wisdom must precede power.

The Romans built on this foundation. Cicero showed how virtue and duty could guide both personal conduct and public service. Seneca taught that true freedom comes from mastering yourself, not your circumstances. Marcus Aurelius proved that even an Emperor needs philosophy to live well. These weren't just ideas—they were the bedrock of a civilization that produced men of extraordinary capability and character.

When Rome fell, trade routes collapsed and technologies were forgotten—the famous Roman concrete, the engineering of aqueducts, the art of building roads that would last millennia. And we lost something even more vital: we lost the philosophical foundation that had created so many great men. The ideas that drove both personal and civilizational excellence were buried and forgotten. Europe entered the Dark Ages.

This darkness lifted when scholars like Petrarch discovered Cicero's letters in an old monastery. Later, Manuel Chrysoloras brought the lost works of Plato and Aristotle back to Florence. This rediscovery sparked what the era of change we call the Renaissance–a rebirth of ancient wisdom. As these ideas spread across Europe, they awakened something that had been sleeping for centuries.

The Dark Ages ended because men rediscovered how to think about what matters.

Today, we're facing another dark age. Most men don't think about virtue anymore. We chase status, comfort, and whatever everyone else is chasing. But these ancient ideas about excellence and purpose are still there, waiting to be rediscovered. Just as every civilization must find its way back to wisdom, every man must find his philosophical core. The path to excellence hasn't changed–we just need to discover it for ourselves.

The first step of The Preparation is to help you undergo a renaissance of your own–to re-discover ancient wisdom and take the actions necessary to shape yourself into the man you want to be–Competent, Confident, and Dangerous.

REDISCOVERY

Living with a philosophical core begins with observing the events that happen to us. It provides a toolkit to reinterpret these experiences in the most constructive way. Many people struggle here because a part of us clings to the idea of being victims of circumstances beyond our control. But if you can overcome that instinct, you'll find a small but profound space within yourself—a beachhead, your own sovereign domain.

From this foundation, you can build something extraordinary: an empire of the individual, where you hold the power to chart your own course and shape the person you aspire to become.

I found my own way back to these ancient truths through Epictetus, a stoic philosopher born a slave in ancient Rome. During my sabbatical, I did little else but read his words and think about how this ancient wisdom could light my own path forward. Like the Renaissance scholars who rediscovered Cicero's letters, I found something powerful in these old ideas.

Most people think being 'stoic' means being emotionless, like some kind of robot. But that misses the point entirely. Stoics feel everything–grief, joy, anger, love–they just refuse to be ruled by these emotions. Instead, they learn to master themselves. Epictetus taught that self-mastery was the key to freedom and a meaningful life. He saw philosophy as a practical tool for living, not an academic exercise.

Among the men known to have studied stoic philosophy we find people like: Marcus Aurelius, the Roman Emperor who studied Epictetus's teachings religiously. George Washington shaped his character–his famous self-control and integrity–through stoic principles. When Teddy Roosevelt ventured into the uncharted Amazon during his "River of Doubt" expedition, he carried the works of Epictetus with him. Roosevelt later captured a core stoic theme in his famous line, "Do what you can, with what you've got, where you are."

Philosophy should provide a useful intellectual framework for understanding reality. The appeal of stoicism to men like Roosevelt and Washington is that it's practical. It provides a model for how the world works and guidance to succeed within it. Unlike religion, philosophy does not require faith, nor does it contradict it. It simply provides an effective perspective for interpreting our life experience, understanding our highest motivations, and directing our actions toward a fulfilling end.

PREDESTINATION VS. PERSONAL AGENCY

The stoics believe in two ideas that seem in opposition—predestination and personal agency. Predestination is the basis for Amor Fati or Love of Fate. It's a view that whatever happened to us, outside our control, was destined to happen—It literally had to happen, and, despite its unpleasantness, it happened for our own good. The stoics viewed fate not as a random or indifferent force, but as a wise teacher, providing individuals with exactly what they need to grow in virtue and wisdom.

Epictetus doesn't believe in good fortune or bad luck. By his reading, the death of my brother could not be bad because the situation was out of my control. I could imagine him saying, "He's dead, now what will you do?" On the other side of the coin, he'd look at the wealth I'd managed to accumulate and be unimpressed. It was neither good nor bad. For him, what people often call "good luck" or "bad luck" are simply external events, neutral in themselves, that we interpret based on our judgments and reactions.

What we do when fate comes is completely up to us. We don't have control over the world, but we always have total personal agency. And whatever fate might bring; we have the opportunity to be virtuous in our thoughts and actions. Our reactions are totally up to us. Our fate, as harsh as it may appear at times, is always an opportunity for personal agency and growth.

AMOR FATI

Love of Fate is a simple idea with profound implications. It doesn't matter what other people do or say. Every circumstance I find myself embroiled in, every difficulty I face from birth to death, is something I should embrace.

Shouldn't difficulty be avoided? Sure, if it's in your control – by all means. So long as you don't compromise yourself by abandoning virtue.

But let's stick with what we can't control for now—all the circumstances that make life feel unfair and often come to negatively dominate our view of the world and our role in it. Maybe, for instance, you're like me and grew up in a bad family situation?

My dad and mom split up before my fourth birthday leaving my mother with four young kids in dire straits. Mom was forced to take a job to try to keep a roof over our heads. She succeeded although the power was frequently disconnected by the utility company due to late payment and the cupboards were always bare.

Except for the rare times mom was around, my brothers and I grew up living like characters from "The Lord of the Flies". It was easy to blame dad for those years of trouble. My dad died in 2018. But to this day, my siblings only ever referred to him by his first name, Fred. The hurt and resentment run deep.

Trauma is as old as time. There's no escaping it. Much of my own was rooted in the day my mom & dad split up and cascaded from there. When things happen to us we are forced to respond.

Growing up, food was a big problem for my family. There was never enough to eat. Mom was too proud to accept public aid. Although, I'll never forget the time I watched her unload a cardboard box of canned food and pasta onto the table. Looking at the spread "Wow, where did you get this?", I asked. "The church pantry", she said. "Sometimes they give stuff like this to needy families." I suspect the little food we did have came from the generosity of strangers.

Poor me, right? That's how I once saw it. But Amor Fati is a powerful idea. With Epictetus' help I started to see my past in a different light.

As a kid, I always felt like I was starving. It drove me to work as soon as I could and in any way I could. Shoveling driveways, mowing lawns, and my regular paper route gig at nine. Nobody had to suggest these things to me. I wanted to eat. To eat, I needed money. To get money I had to work. It became a compulsion totally unnoticed by me until one day I looked up and was a millionaire.

As the actress Mae West famously said, "I've been rich and I've been poor. Rich is definitely better." But would I have become rich if it weren't for the dire straits I experienced as a child?

Epictetus makes clear that difficulty is an opportunity, "Difficulty shows what men are. Therefore, when a difficulty falls upon you, remember that God, like a trainer of wrestlers, has matched you with a rough young man. Why? So that you may become an Olympic conqueror."

Not long ago, I was catching up with my older brother, Josh. At one point he brought up the current beef he was having with mom. He still holds bitterness toward mom and long dead, "Fred".

I asked my brother if he thought I was a good father. He said, "Yeah, obviously". I told him, "I owe it all to dad. The most vivid memory I have of dad growing up was standing at the front door waiting to be picked up for a weekend visit. It was winter. Pickup time was 8am. I had my coat and shoes and backpack on so he wouldn't need to wait. By the time 9:00 rolled around mom came down the stairs and told me she didn't think he was coming. She was right. I remember dad as a no-show. It's because of him that I show up for my kids. Dad showed me what I didn't want to be and that was a gift. I have a great relationship with my kids because I showed up. I get all the rewards of being a father because he inadvertently showed me the way. I'm actually grateful for dad."

My brother and I experienced the same things. He feels resentment. I feel gratitude. The only difference is I embraced Epictetus' idea that: "It is not things themselves that disturb people, but their judgments about these things."

You will suffer and remain rattled from past events and the actions of others until you learn to recognize the value of these external events toward your development as a man. Amor Fati.

ON THE ACTIONS OF OTHERS

What other people do can drive us crazy, especially when we're children and totally dependent on them. We see their behavior or hear their words and want them to be different. We expect better. As reality fails to meet our expectations, we can become bitter and even vengeful.

Few of us are lucky enough to grow up with parents wise enough to avoid causing harm. The stoics believe knowledge and virtue are deeply intertwined. Epictetus says ignorance is the cause of most human error and vice. So, we shouldn't be surprised when an ignorant person doesn't behave virtuously. When people lack the wisdom to distinguish between true and false goods, they act on faulty assumptions. Out of ignorance they behave in foolish or even vicious ways.

Epictetus tells us, "No one does wrong willingly." Wrongdoing stems not from malicious intent but from ignorance or a mistaken understanding of what is truly good or right. According to Epictetus, if people knew better, they would act better.

Knowing the difference between good and bad might seem like a trivial thing. But, even the evillest person you can think of believed they were doing the right thing and for good reasons. From common thieves to uncommon criminals like Hitler and Stalin—all believed they were doing the right thing.

If you lack the wisdom to discern right from wrong, you'll make mistakes. Most mistakes aren't 'make it or break it'–just stupid or short-sighted. But some are actively self— destructive or evil. Ignorance leads to error. And only a fool believes "ignorance is bliss".

No matter who or where you are, you'll notice people around you doing stupid and vicious things. What can we do? First, recognize that the source of this behavior is ignorance. Second, recognize that we also do stupid things when we act out of ignorance. And while malice is hard to forgive, ignorance in ourselves or others is easy. Finally, we can make it a priority to reduce our own ignorance and, perhaps, that of others.

In this light, I came to see that my dad's actions didn't stem from malice. I could see that while his ignorance did cause me harm, he really harmed himself. By his actions, he denied himself the many rewarding benefits of being a father. I don't feel sorry for myself, I feel sorry for him.

A strange and unseen burden was lifted from me once I took on this perspective. It was easy to forgive and transcend any harm. It freed me. Jesus had it right when he said, "Forgive them father for they know not what they do."

Much of stoic philosophy comes down to how we interpret reality. It's not useful to ever think of yourself as a victim of circumstances or another person. A "poor me" perspective makes you weak and disempowered. Your energy is squandered, lamenting the things you can't control rather than fully leveraging all that you can.

It's a fool's errand to try to control others, but you can control yourself. You can always choose how to respond to the actions of others–Amor Fati. And you can work to extinguish your own ignorance so that you are not the source of foolish and vicious behavior. By improving our understanding, we can act in ways that are genuinely good, not only for ourselves but for others as well.

Only you can control your thoughts, attitudes, and actions. In this domain you are king. Everything else–circumstances, outcomes, and the opinions of others, are not up to us. It's fine to win the race or land a dream job. But these achievements are not entirely up to us and should not be of great concern. Our task: do the best we can with what we have, then–let go of the rest. Remember–Amor Fati.

WISDOM

What's the difference between a wise man and a fool? Watch how they make decisions.

A fool rushes in, driven by impulse and short-term desires. He takes the easy money, betrays a friend's trust, or compromises his principles "just this once."

A wise man sees further. He understands three things the fool doesn't: himself, how the world actually works, and how to use his power effectively within it. This understanding leads to something rare and precious–moral clarity. When you can see clearly, the right path becomes obvious, and you find the courage to take it.

This is righteousness—not some abstract religious concept, but practical wisdom in action. And nothing shows this better than George Washington's defining moment.

After defeating the British, Washington was the most powerful man in America. He commanded a loyal army and had widespread public support. Many expected him to seize power–it's what military leaders had done throughout history. Even King George III was watching to see what he'd do.

When told that Washington planned to simply return to his farm, the King was stunned. "If he does that," he declared, "he will be the greatest man in the world."

Think about this: Washington's righteousness was so clear that even his defeated enemy recognized it. Why? Because a wise man knows that true power isn't in controlling others—it's in controlling himself. While fools grab for quick power, the wise man's choices echo through history.

Wisdom's reward: the ability to see the right path and the strength to take it, regardless of the temptations before you. A fool stumbles through life, collecting regrets. A wise man builds a legacy that even his enemies must respect. As ignorance is reduced, wisdom emerges. And wisdom leads to a trait universally admired, but difficult to define–righteousness.

THE ART OF LIVING: MEN WITH A PHILOSOPHICAL CORE

A philosophical core is central to The Preparation and your path to becoming competent, confident, and dangerous. Without it, all your efforts lack direction and staying power. Vague ideas like "being a good person" or "working hard" aren't enough; you need a tested framework, like stoicism, to guide your actions and decisions. If you know who you are, you'll know what to do.

Consider the stark difference a philosophical core makes by comparing two Roman emperors: Marcus Aurelius and his son Commodus.

Marcus Aurelius, ruling Rome at its height, lived by strict philosophical principles. He began each morning examining his thoughts and actions, writing, "Waste no more time arguing what a good man should be. Be one." During a plague, he stayed to comfort the sick. When generals rebelled, he chose justice over vengeance. Marcus lived by a code greater than himself, and under his leadership, Rome endured.

Commodus, inheriting his father's empire, lacked any guiding principles. Driven by impulse and emotion, he skipped governance for gladiatorial games and pleasure. Criticism led to paranoia and cruelty, as he executed nobles and emptied the treasury for elaborate spectacles. Styling himself as a god, his erratic rule brought Rome to the brink of collapse. Ultimately, Commodus's own inner circle assassinated him, ending his reign in disgrace.

Marcus Aurelius is remembered as a great philosopher-king. Commodus, by contrast, marked the beginning of Rome's decline—a megalomaniac and homicidal narcissist to boot. He declared himself a living god and styled himself as Hercules reborn. Commodus had the same advantages, same opportunities—the difference? One built on philosophical bedrock; the other on shifting sand.

Now consider two American Revolution figures: John Paul Jones and Benedict Arnold. Both rose from modest beginnings. Both displayed courage and brilliance. But their philosophical cores shaped their legacies.

Arnold was ambitious, confident and possessed virtues like courage. But he was unprincipled, and let resentment consume him after political setbacks. His bitterness led to treason, plotting to surrender West Point for money. When the plot failed, he fled to England, dying in obscurity and remembered only as a traitor.

Jones, guided by steadfast principles, faced adversity with resolve. When asked to surrender during a naval battle, his ship in tatters, he famously replied, "I have not yet begun to fight!" He turned the tide, capturing the enemy ship. Today, Jones is honored as the "Father of the American Navy," his legacy a testament to unwavering principles.

Same challenges, same opportunities. The difference? One acted on enduring principles; the other, fleeting emotions and short-sighted gain. A philosophical core doesn't just guide you—it defines the legacy you leave behind.

PUTTING IT ALL TOGETHER

Focus only on what you can control—your attitude, your thoughts, and your actions. Everything outside your control, no matter how unfair it may seem, is not your concern. Life's challenges and setbacks are opportunities to grow into the man you are meant to be. Embrace Amor Fati—love your fate—and welcome all that life brings as a chance to build strength and character. Let virtue and righteousness guide your every decision.

Living with a philosophical core doesn't mean giving up on material success or leading an austere, uneventful life. Quite the opposite. Once I embraced stoic principles, my aimlessness disappeared. I gained clarity and a renewed curiosity that led me in directions I could never have imagined. I was able to reorient my work to what mattered to me, rather than just to make money. I purposefully made time to challenge my views of the world. I traveled the world—from Bhutan to Palau, Chile to Slovakia, Japan to Panama— expanding my horizons and deepening my understanding of life. I even moved my family to Argentina, forging new relationships with fascinating, capable people. I became known in circles not just for "working hard" but for my integrity and values. Along the way, I experienced wild adventures, acquired invaluable skills, and built several successful businesses, earning more than I ever thought possible.

This isn't about sacrifice;
it's about personal mastery.
When you align your life
with principles, success
becomes a byproduct
of clarity and purpose.
It's not called the Art of Living
for nothing.

HOW TO ACTUALLY GET AHEAD IN LIFE

BY MATT SMITH

Now we need to talk about what you can do to change the world around you; the specific actions you can take to construct a reality you desire and the steps you can take to become the man you want to be.

Conventional wisdom suggests that to succeed it's best to focus on a single path of specialization. They tell you to become an expert with a PHD, MD, or MBA. That is terrible advice. As the great sci fi writer Robert Heinlein said, "specialization is for insects."

Embedded in the belief that traditional career paths lead to success is the idea of "climbing the ladder." It starts with school, normalizing the idea that you make progress by following the instructions of an authority figure. It includes getting good grades, jumping through hoops to qualify for scholarships, and eventually acceptance into supposedly prestigious universities all to join another crowd climbing a new ladder.

After graduation, guess what? A new ladder awaits with the corporate or career hierarchy, promising advancement and fulfillment at the top. Be good, work hard, and be patient. Your time is coming, they tell you. But all you've become is a "professional" at doing what you're told to do and not asking questions. But you should ask questions.

What is this ladder? Who built it, and for whose benefit? Was it constructed to help you succeed, or does it serve someone else's agenda? Is there a better way to get there? Most importantly, why is everyone climbing it without asking these questions?

The idea of climbing the ladder assumes there's something meaningful at the top.

As a good rule of thumb, don't ever climb someone else's ladder. If you're going to climb, build your own ladder, one that leads to where you know you want to go.

Better yet, think of your path to success like building a spider's web. A spider begins its web by releasing a single silk thread into the wind, letting it drift and attach to a solid surface. This becomes the anchor point. That first thread into the wind is your first novel action—taking a chance, trying something new, a step into the unknown. You don't know exactly where it will land, but you trust that it will find an anchor point. Once it does, you can build from there.

Each action you take, each connection you make, strengthens your web. From that single starting point, you expand outward, creating a structure that supports your goals, adapts to challenges, and catches the many opportunities that will come your way.

Imagine your skills and network as a spider's web, each thread representing a competency or connection. The more threads you weave, the stronger your web becomes. Even if one thread breaks, others support you. By contrast, a ladder offers no backup; one slip and you fall.

- ▶ A ladder is a nasty competitive field. You try to pull the person down who is ahead of you and grease the steps for the people below you.
- ▶ A ladder makes you reliant on a single path. If it breaks, you're stuck.
- ▶ It forces you to follow someone else's rules to move forward.
- ▶ It's a slow, step-by-step progress that might not even lead where you want to go.
- ▶ You're vulnerable to gatekeepers who decide your worth.
- ▶ When the ladder tips, there's nothing to catch you on the way down.

By contrast, a web is like a net. Each thread represents a skill, a connection, or an opportunity you've created. If one thread breaks, others hold strong, and the web continues to function.

Your web grows stronger and more expansive the more you weave into it, capturing opportunities effortlessly. Unlike a ladder, where progress stops if you slip, a web provides resilience—and the freedom to explore in every direction.

Because The Preparation is envisioned as an alternative to college, we outline a four-year plan comprising quarters we call "cycles". Each cycle has a theme. You can do them in any order you please. Each cycle is wildly different from any other. They provide hands-on skill development. Each skill has practical value and could turn into a profession. After completing some cycles, you'll see a clear path to a job if not a profession. You'll be tempted to take it. We recommend continuing with the next cycle. Cycle-stacking is the idea.

The idea isn't entirely new. Robert Heinlein, the author of the excellent Sci-fi novel, "The Moon is a Harsh Mistress", described it this way, "A human being should be able to change a diaper, plan an invasion, butcher a hog, conn a ship, design a building, write a sonnet, balance accounts, build a wall, set a bone, comfort the dying, take orders, give orders, cooperate, act alone, solve equations, analyze a new problem, pitch manure, program a computer, cook a tasty meal, fight efficiently, die gallantly. Specialization is for insects."

Man is not designed for specialization. And the full capability of man is unlocked by combining a variety of skills.

Scott Adams, the creator of the Dilbert comic series and author of many interesting and successful books explains the concept compellingly. He calls it skill-stacking. During this process, an individual learns a variety of skills rather than focusing on one, making himself vastly more valuable and unique. Skill stacking is a cheat code for life. It creates 2 + 2 = 5 types of results for individuals who do it.

Cycle-stacking is Skill-Stacking on steroids.

With 16 cycles laid out for you in this book there's plenty to do. But in 16 cycles, we couldn't conceivably cover all the possibilities. So, we'll show you how to build your own cycle as well.

It is our contention, proved true by Maxim's experience over the last 2 years, that if you complete even a few cycles, you will be a new man. As you become competent, confident, and dangerous, exciting possibilities will unfold for you that are completely off your radar today.

Expanding your capabilities requires focus and courage. The cycles are meant to facilitate the focus, but you'll need to supply the courage. As Epictetus says, "If you want to improve, be content to be thought foolish and stupid."

MAKE SEEMINGLY RANDOM CONNECTIONS

As you **do** novel things, you'll meet all kinds of people seemingly at random. I met Jean— Luc Moreau, a retired officer of the French Foreign Legion, on an airplane to Panama. I met my good friend, Craig Ballantyne, at an otherwise unproductive business meeting. I bumped into the man who would become my mentor, Doug Casey, as I walked out of my hotel lobby onto the streets of Buenos Aires.

Building rich and rewarding social relationships is important and should not be left to the accidental coincidence of school or employment associates. You can and should have a much bigger and more powerful social network which spans the globe. Having a deep Rolodex of competent and interesting people who encourage and enable you is a force multiplier to your life. In a later chapter, the Preparation will show you how to achieve it.

The point is this: by doing new and unconventional things, you naturally attract fascinating people—friends, mentors, teachers, collaborators, even individuals you might have admired from afar. If you're genuinely open and interested, you'll find yourself building valuable relationships with ease. These seemingly random connections can dramatically elevate your life in unexpected ways. They form the threads that weave your expanding web of opportunity.

PRO TIP

It bears repeating because most people don't believe it: if you show up consistently as someone dependable, curious, and authentic, people will genuinely want to help you. They'll enjoy spending time looking for opportunities to connect you with others who could transform your life in ways you can't yet imagine.

DIFFERENTIATE YOURSELF

As you start taking bold actions and forming meaningful connections, you'll quickly grasp a crucial truth: success in life isn't about fitting in—it's about standing apart. You must differentiate yourself, and the simplest way to do that is to become genuinely interesting.

There are two effective strategies to become interesting. The first is simple: be genuinely interested. Be curious about everything—ask insightful questions, listen carefully, and sincerely try to understand other people's experiences and perspectives. Curious people naturally draw others to them.

The second way to stand out is to do things most people either can't or won't do. Step out of the ordinary. Challenge yourself with experiences that push your limits and break you out of the mundane routines everyone else follows.

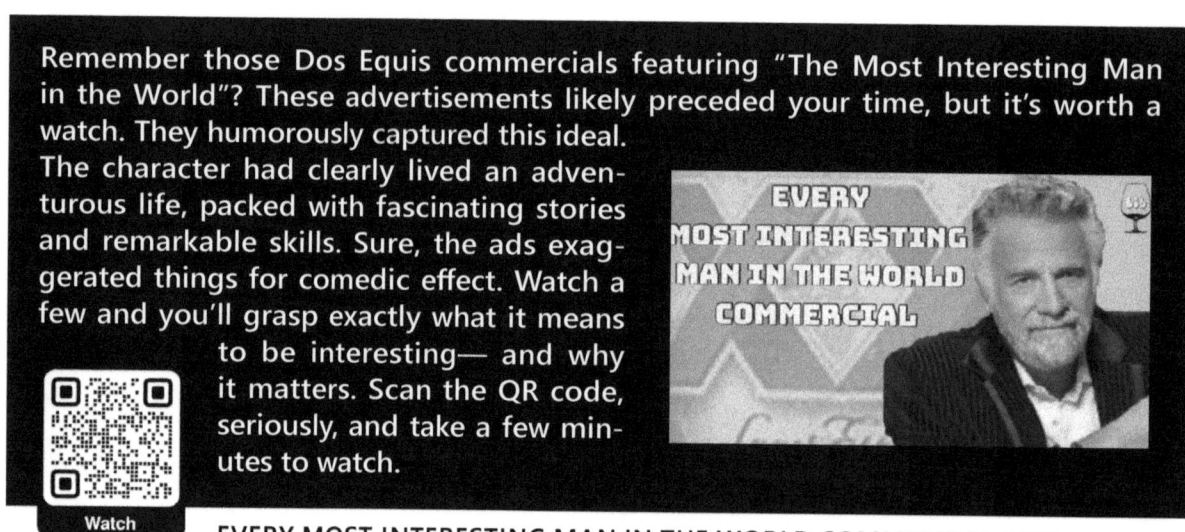

Remember those Dos Equis commercials featuring "The Most Interesting Man in the World"? These advertisements likely preceded your time, but it's worth a watch. They humorously captured this ideal. The character had clearly lived an adventurous life, packed with fascinating stories and remarkable skills. Sure, the ads exaggerated things for comedic effect. Watch a few and you'll grasp exactly what it means to be interesting— and why it matters. Scan the QR code, seriously, and take a few minutes to watch.

EVERY MOST INTERESTING MAN IN THE WORLD COMMERCIAL EVER

The Dos Equis campaign worked so brilliantly because it zeroed in on a profound truth we all recognize: interesting people hold unique power. They're admired and respected because they've earned it through doing things others haven't dared to try.

Dos Equis' hero is an older man enjoying the reputation earned over decades of living an interesting life. He didn't start off "finding the Fountain of Youth but not drinking because he wasn't thirsty." He had to start from where he was and you'll need to do the same.

The possibilities are endless. Here are some random examples that could be part of your preparation:

- ▶ Travel to an exotic locale like Mongolia or Namibia and immerse yourself completely—learn the language, explore local customs, and make friends who can open doors.
- ▶ Master a demanding physical discipline, like mixed martial arts or competitive sailing, to forge mental toughness and genuine self-confidence.
- ▶ Start a profitable side hustle—something that sharpens your business instincts while earning money.

- ▶ Study practical survival skills—become proficient at wilderness navigation, first aid, and self-reliance techniques that most people only read about.
- ▶ Learn precision shooting and marksmanship—not just to develop discipline and patience but to understand responsibility and self-control.
- ▶ Start now by building a meaningful **body of work**—paintings, insightful articles, provocative books, or a photographic series documenting your adventures. A body of work is tangible proof of your passion and effort. It shows you're not a mere spectator; you're someone who contributes something original and valuable to the world.

When you leverage your greatest asset, your ability to take novel action, in pursuit of unique interests, you don't just gain new skills and stories—you also develop confidence, resilience, and a perspective that sets you apart. The result—you'll be a more interesting and capable man.

Being interesting isn't about being better than anyone else. You aren't in a competition to climb a ladder. It's about being yourself in a way that's undeniable. It's about letting the world see the full scope of your potential and passions.

NOVEL ACTION IS THE CATALYST FOR EVERYTHING (DO)

Massive Novel action is the key to the DO portion of BE. DO. HAVE. If you've got good character, aspire to virtue, and build capabilities along the way, everything compounds and connects in ways you can't currently envision.

At this point in your life, forget about money, experience, or connections—you likely don't have much, and nobody really cares anyway. Your grades, your AP classes, your varsity sports—none of it matters. Trust me on this.

You stand here as a young man, perhaps with only a modest set of accomplishments behind you. But make no mistake: history shows your age is no excuse for hesitation or mediocrity. Today's culture infantilizes young men, expecting little and allowing adolescence to drag on indefinitely. Yet this modern attitude is absurd when judged against history.

Throughout history, young men your age commanded armies, forged empires, wrote profound works, and decisively shaped civilization. Consider Alexander the Great. By eighteen, he was already a seasoned warrior, educated personally by Aristotle, and rigorously trained in military strategy by his father, King Philip II, from age eight. At sixteen, Alexander was entrusted to rule Macedon as regent during his father's absence, a moment his father's enemies mistakenly believed was their chance. Expecting an easy victory against an inexperienced youth, they revolted. But Alexander swiftly crushed the rebellion, proving his skill beyond doubt, and founded the city of Alexandropolis to commemorate his triumph.

Age, then, is clearly no barrier to greatness—only a modern excuse for delaying it.

At 18, an age when modern society hands you a High School diploma and pats you gently on the head, Alexander faced a coalition of Greek city-states, including Athens and Thebes, at the Battle of Chaeronea. Leading 2,000–3,000 troops on the crucial Macedonian left flank, he went up against twice as many seasoned Greek warriors, including the legendary Sacred Band of

Thebes—previously undefeated and famed for routing the Spartans. For Alexander, this was a decisive moment—sink or swim. He didn't just swim; he utterly annihilated the Greeks and permanently shattered the Sacred Band.

Of course, Alexander enjoyed wealth and privilege. But what truly sets him apart is something you already possess: the capacity to act decisively.

John Paul Jones possessed the very same asset. Born in Scotland, he went to sea as a mere apprentice at age 13. By 21, he was already commanding a merchant ship on transatlantic trade routes. His life took a dramatic turn in 1770 when, after killing a mutinous sailor in self-defense, he fled Britain for America. Lucky for the colonies. Jones joined the Continental Navy in 1775 and quickly distinguished himself through boldness and skill.

Jones is remembered today as the "Father of the American Navy". He refused to surrender despite severe damage to his ship and captured the powerful British warship HMS Serapis in a remarkable upset.

These historical examples are numerous. Pascal published groundbreaking work on geometry at 16. At 19, Augustus Caesar was assembling armies, forging alliances, and launching his campaign to become the first Roman Emperor. Beethoven supported his entire family at 18 as a court musician. George Washington was surveying the rugged Virginia frontier at 17. John Stuart Mill published his first major essay at 17, already fluent in Greek, Latin, and French. By age 20, Genghis Khan had united scattered tribes and was already a feared conqueror.

Don't let anyone convince you to think of yourself as a child. Even at 13, you're fully capable of thinking, acting, and shouldering responsibility as an adult.

These exceptional young men came from diverse backgrounds and eras. Sure, some had innate talents or advantages, but most did not. Their true common denominator—and your greatest asset—is the ability to take decisive, bold action.

YOUR GREATEST ASSET

Your greatest asset, one you probably haven't given enough thought to, is your ability to act—specifically, your willingness to take "novel" action. Novel action means stepping into new and unfamiliar territory, meeting different people, and encountering fresh ideas. Any one of these new experiences can dramatically alter the course of your life. Massive, sustained novel action will stack opportunities in ways you can't currently imagine.

At this age you have endless energy to do something radical. Most teenagers today want to do cool things but the best they can come up with is video games, sport, or organized play. These are distractions. We are presenting a totally different choice.

So start showing up in new places (see Part 2 of this book). Show up sincerely, no matter how small or trivial the task appears. Use your personal code, have a give a shit factor. Be dependable, resourceful, and respectful. When others hesitate, you move forward. When others doubt, you press on. When others wait for permission, you create your own opportunities.

Children wait for authority to present them with choices. Responsible adults know they possess the power to create their own opportunities. Action generates momentum, and momentum attracts even more people and possibilities. Each action you take in The Preparation expands your web, building an ever-expanding universe. Most individuals wait like a fool for someone else to act first, which is why they spend their lives climbing someone else's ladder. Be the man who moves first, have courage to go your own way. You'll soon discover the immense power inherent in simply doing novel things.

THE COMPOUNDING EFFECT OF REPUTATION

With every action you take and every relationship you nurture, you're building something invaluable: your reputation. Your reputation isn't just what people say about you—it's the energy you bring into the world.

People will start to associate you with certain qualities:

▶ "He's the one who's always dependable."
▶ "He's the one who's curious about everything."
▶ "He's the one who's constantly doing cool shit"

This reputation has a compounding effect. It opens doors you didn't even know existed.

People start to think of you when opportunities arise. They recommend you, introduce you, or offer you a seat at the table.

And as your reputation grows, so does your influence—not in a superficial "influencer" way, but in a way that allows you to shape your own path; to choose your own adventure.

A Renaissance Man becomes known by the things he's done and the type of man he is. Reputation isn't just based only on what you've done but who you are.

Ultimately, you must decide not what you're going to do–if you enlist in The Preparation, you will have many options. The critical decision for you is: **what kind of man do you want to Be?**

It is important to start with defining this for yourself, so you don't become defined by someone else. Or be defined by something you did because you didn't think about how it would affect the shaping of your character.

Our reputation is an outward sign of inner virtue and so is entirely within our control if you adopt a personal code. In this next chapter we are going to teach you how to build one.

A man is made up of a few discernible building blocks, those blocks are Character, Virtues, and Capabilities. This is where we should focus all our energy.

NEW RULES— YOUR PERSONAL CODE

MATT SMITH

Your generation is the most hassled, monitored, scheduled, surveilled, and unfree generation in history. You were raised in a sea of rules and laws that regulate virtually anything you might want to do. Some of these rules may have merit, but the combined mass is smothering and disempowering.

The exceptions are those restrictions we impose on ourselves. The difference between a man and any other animal is that we have a rational mind and the ability to choose our thoughts and actions. A Prepper can create rules for himself that bring his conduct into alignment with his ideals.

This takes self-discipline. This **is** self-discipline. And self-discipline is a muscle that grows stronger through exercise. Where should we direct our self-discipline? Our rational mind points us in the right direction. Nobody is more aware of our personal failings than we are. And it is left to us to correct them.

> "Whatever rules you have adopted,
> abide by them as laws, and as if you
> would be a sinner to transgress them;
> and do not regard what anyone says of you,
> for this, after all, is no concern of yours."
> EPICTETUS IN ENCHIRIDION, 50.

When you do something you shouldn't, you don't need an authority figure to tell you. You know it. Certain actions degrade us. We feel it. The same thing happens when we avoid doing something we know we should do. Each degrading action is akin to living small. But through self-awareness and self-discipline we can consciously choose to live big.

Character is formed by our choice to not act in ways that degrade ourselves. Character emerges as we draw a line in the sand and say to ourselves, "no more!" With each action toward living big, we expand our sense of self-respect. True self-respect is the foundation of any great man.

WHAT DOES IT MEAN TO LIVE BIG?

Living big, means to live in a way that dignifies yourself. When a man exercises self— discipline by choosing actions that dignify rather than degrade himself, honest self— esteem is the result.

Setting rules for yourself is the way. Your rules will be unique to you and designed to combat the private behavior that makes you feel degraded. This will require introspection on your part. I can't pretend to know what happens in your mind. But to make the point, let me share some examples with my corresponding rules. Let's start with what we may call Public Conduct.

MY RULES FOR PUBLIC CONDUCT

Through introspection and observation, I realize that every time I hide or, understood differently, each time I don't show up properly, I degrade myself.

In class, the teacher asks questions about a book that students are supposed to have been read- ing. She ignores raised hands and calls on lowered heads instead. You hope she doesn't pick you, and force you to reveal you haven't read the book. You try to look invisible. Naturally, she calls on you. To make matters worse, you bullshit your way through an answer. She knows you didn't read it. You know you didn't read it. You wonder how obvious it is to everyone else. But your answer buys you a sort of 'plausible deniability'. You feel some relief to have made it through. But you still feel degraded.

How different it would have been if you'd read the book. Even better, what if you'd had an inter- esting opinion to offer? Failing that, the next best thing would've been to speak the truth. "I didn't read the book. I regret not having done it. But that doesn't change the fact I haven't read the book and I can't honestly answer the question." That kind of frankness is rare and bold and doesn't come without risks. You could get a bad grade, subject yourself to discipline, or just end up on the teacher's shit list. Still–saying it will make you feel big rather than small. Every time you lie to cover up for a personal failing your dignity pays the price.

> ***My Rule:*** **Confront and accept the Consequences. Don't Hide or Avoid. Instead, be prepared. Do what you've agreed to do. If you fall short, be frank. No Excuses.**

If you pay attention, you'll notice everyone is hiding everywhere they go. Avoiding eye contact is the key. Like an ostrich with our head in the ground, we think, "If I can't see them, they can't see me." Your mobile phone provides a ready hole to hide in in public.

Try the opposite. When you go to a place, BE in that place. See the people there and be willing to be seen. Be open. Learn to engage people in simple and polite conversation and practice it until you're a pro.

The truth is everyone feels a little degraded when they hide and they're hiding because their prior choices make them feel degraded, just as you do. It's another doom loop society is trapped in at the moment. But humans love dignity, and to be seen by others for the dignity they possess. See others, and risk being seen yourself.

> **My Rule:** **When in public, take time to see others and be friendly. Be open and present so you can be seen as well.**

Not long ago I was at the checkout lane in a Walmart. The checkout lady avoided eye contact but responded to my "good morning" with a halfhearted reply. I could see her irritation with something as she scanned my purchases. The way she'd snatch things up and put them down in the bagging area wasn't exactly wrong. But it was clearly filled with negative emotional energy. Rude is how I first took it. "What's her problem?", I wondered, now growing a little irritated myself.

Here I had a choice. Fortunately, I had a rule, one I'd created to resolve a problem I saw in myself. When I hide, I degrade myself. When I choose not to see others, I degrade myself and everyone I encounter.

I set aside my mild irritation. I looked at her name badge, "Pam". Then I asked the question as sincerely as I could muster. "Pam, (pause) I'm sorry. Did I do something to irritate you?"

It turns out it was Pam's last day at work. She was 72. She'd been working at Walmart for 16 years. Last year she tried to intercede when thieves were walking out with stolen goods. She got a disciplinary write-up for her actions. At her recent annual review, they only gave her a $.15/hour raise. She told me this was punishment for trying to stop the thieves.

But Pam didn't learn her lesson. Earlier this week it happened again. Once more, she tried to intervene. "I just couldn't watch it happen", she told me. And today word came from management that this would be her last shift.

Pam told me all this because I chose to see her and asked a few sincere questions. Pam is a hero in my eyes. I told her that as our brief, but deep, conversation came to a close. I raised my hand to shake hers and if the counter hadn't been between us I would have offered a hug.

Pam was having a bad day. I could have taken it personally. I could have ignored it. I chose to take a moment to see her instead, to offer a little dignity to a "rude" old lady. But why? Who cares? For me, giving dignity to another human being has a huge payoff—it bolsters my own dignity.

> **My Rule:** **Dignity & Respect. Dignify yourself by dignifying others. When you're in a place, be in that place. When you're with someone, be with them.**

I have other public conduct rules as well, but they're more banal. Things like never drinking alcohol to the point where I begin to lose control. And general things like, don't do anything that might make me later feel ashamed of myself. And, as a happily married man who values my marriage as something sacred, never meet or speak with another woman alone.

The important thing to keep in mind is that these rules are by me and for me. They resonate with me. But I have no expectation that anyone else should follow them. It's up to you to create your own rules for public conduct. Your rules should be based on your own observations and introspection. Ultimately, you must determine where you'll draw the line regarding your own public conduct.

RULES FOR PRIVATE CONDUCT

Private Conduct is a whole other matter. Frankly, it's a greater challenge, since private conduct is where we spend most of our time. And, being private, it's easier to lie to ourselves when we fall short.

Only we know if we're putting 10% of our energy into a task, truly giving it all we've got, or choosing to ignore the task completely and instead waste irretrievable moments on Twitter, Tiktok, or Instagram.

It's the things we do, or don't do, in private that most undermine our dignity and make character formation impossible. It's up to us to draw the line. We must set standards we expect from ourselves. And only we will know whether we achieve them.

The focus here is on the things you do which you already know aren't good. The things you choose to overlook rather than confront. There is no greater action you can take to become the man you want to be than to assert authority over the actions you know are destructive.

I asked ChatGPT for the worst habits of young American men. Clearly, the list is a summary of complaints about "kids today!" from parents, employers, and teachers. What young man would list "Disrespect for Authority" as one of his bad habits?

The list is a joke but because of the contrast with the next it is useful. But you shouldn't concern yourself with what authority figures think. Instead, focus on the habits that you yourself know are bad for you and ignore the noise.

Question to ChatGPT:
What are the worst personal conduct habits of young men in America ages 18–25?

BAD HABIT	DESCRIPTION
Lack of personal responsibility	Blaming others for failures and avoiding obligations like work or family duties.
Excessive screen time	Overuse of social media, video games, and streaming at the expense of productivity.
Unhealthy lifestyles	Neglecting physical health through poor diet, lack of exercise, or substance abuse.
Financial irresponsibility	Impulsive spending and lack of understanding of financial basics or saving habits.
Entitlement mentality	Expecting success without hard work and avoiding tasks deemed beneath them.
Disrespect for authority	Disregard for parents, teachers, or mentors and resistance to constructive feedback.
Inconsistent work ethic	Quitting jobs or projects prematurely and failing to follow through on commitments.
Relationship challenges	Immaturity in dating or friendships, prioritizing fleeting interactions over depth.
Overdependence on technology	Difficulty navigating life without digital aids, leading to reduced problem-solving skills.
Lack of purpose or direction	Drifting through life without setting goals or pursuing meaningful activities.
Poor emotional regulation	Struggling to handle stress or failure, leading to anger or emotional withdrawal.

A more useful list is one that contains the opinions of your peers about themselves. I asked ChatGPT: "What do the young men themselves say? Exclude what parents, teachers, and employers might say. What habits have young men identified for themselves as bad habits that they know they should stop?"

Question to ChatGPT:

What do the young men themselves say? Exclude what parents, teachers, and employers might say. What habits have young men identified for themselves as bad habits that they know they should stop?

BAD HABIT	DESCRIPTION
Procrastination	Delaying tasks until the last minute, causing stress and inefficiency.
Overusing social media	Spending too much time scrolling and comparing themselves to others.
Lack of sleep	Staying up late unnecessarily and feeling tired during the day.
Poor time management	Wasting time on unimportant activities instead of prioritizing goals.
Skipping workouts	Failing to maintain consistency with physical fitness routines.
Overeating or unhealthy eating	Consuming too much fast food or snacks, leading to health issues.
Vaping or smoking	Continuing harmful habits despite knowing their negative effects.
Excessive gaming	Playing video games excessively while neglecting responsibilities.
Lack of self-discipline	Struggling to stay consistent with personal goals and commitments.
Avoiding difficult conversations	Fearing confrontation or vulnerability in important conversations.
Neglecting relationships	Not putting effort into maintaining friendships or family ties.
Overthinking	Dwelling on problems excessively instead of taking actionable steps.

Epictetus delivers a bitter pill when he says, "No man is free who is not master of himself." Who can deny the truth of his statement?

Some things in the list above may apply to you. Some will not. Take a hard look at all the actions you take which deny your dignity and hold you back. Then, take a stand. Draw a line in the sand by creating rules for your private conduct and hold yourself accountable to them.

As my great friend, Craig Ballantyne first said (before Jocko Willink) Discipline = Freedom. With your rules in place, you have the power to change everything. In one moment, you are a slave, in the next you can be master. The choice is up to you. And, when you decide, you can become the master... Right. Now.

THE POWER OF "NO"

The failures of men today (and society for that matter) are all rooted in the lack of character. It's the inability to discern things as good or bad, or an unwillingness to draw a line in the sand.

Somehow, we've forgotten that the greatest manifestation of masculine power isn't violence. It's the ability to say "no".

A Man ought to be able and willing to draw a line in the sand, a point beyond which he will not go, a limit to what he will do or accept. Both the horrors of the world, and our quiet internal horrors like depression, anxiety, frustration, and disappointment would end immediately if men would just say no.

It all starts inside each man who can say "no" to himself and hold the line on his Personal and Public Conduct. It isn't easy, but a man knows it must be done because holding the line provides the fuel for one of man's greatest assets: **upholding his self-respect.**

With self-respect, a man can see to the horizon. He can begin to understand what he is both capable and worthy of. It is from this vantage that the pursuit of virtue and capabilities serve him well.

> **PRO TIP**
>
> The fastest path to becoming a man of character is adopting a Personal Code
>
> **CHARACTER = RULES + VIRTUES + CAPABILITIES**

A Personal code helps you determine the man you are or want to Be. Character is developed by an understanding of what is right and good. We don't love rules— except those we create for ourselves as part of our Personal code.

YOUR personal rules define the things you will and will not allow yourself to do. It's where you draw the line in the sand for others, and more importantly, for yourself. A man knows how to hold the line.

Virtues are the values and standards of conduct modeled by ancient heroes which we strive to emulate. We will at times fall short of our own high standards – we're not demigods. But, in failure, we can choose to redouble our efforts toward virtue. The amazing thing about the pursuit of virtue is that it's gratifying regardless of outcome. Knowing you've acted rightly to the best of your ability nourishes the soul in the way no trophy or cash reward might – it's not even close.

Capabilities are the product of your actions. Novel action gives you experience. Focused action leads to skill development. The combination of experience and skill produces a competent man, while the pursuit of virtue gives a man something worthy to strive toward.

ANCIENT VIRTUES

Ancient Greek and Roman virtues laid the bedrock for the rise of Western civilization. These civilizations emphasized character, reason, and the pursuit of excellence.

The Greeks, embodied in Socrates and Aristotle, introduced the concept of virtue as the key to human flourishing. Socrates taught the importance of examining one's life and living in accordance with justice, courage, and temperance. Aristotle expanded on this, defining virtue as the golden mean between extremes, and emphasizing practical wisdom as essential for navigating life's complexities. These ideas provided a blueprint for individual and communal success.

The Romans adopted and adapted Greek virtues, embedding them into their legal and political systems. Cicero championed justice, prudence, and magnanimity as vital for sustaining a republic. The Stoics, like Epictetus and Marcus Aurelius, added resilience and inner discipline, teaching that virtue aligned with nature leads to true freedom. Roman leaders governed with these principles in mind, creating institutions that promoted order, responsibility, and civic duty.

This foundation of virtue ethics including the very notion that men could shape and improve themselves in the pursuit of virtues, influenced every aspect of Western development. It inspired the democratic ideals of the Enlightenment, the principles of modern law, and the values of individual responsibility and community. The emphasis on character and reason as cornerstones of society allowed Western civilization to grow, innovate, and adapt over centuries.

Without the virtues of the Greeks and Romans, the Western world never would've obtained the moral and intellectual grounding that brought it to its peak. Unfortunately, recent generations awash in material success have lost connection with the foundational elements that made us who we are. In its place we feel a void. It is up to us as individuals to re-establish the link with the noble pursuit–the pursuit of virtue.

Below you'll find a table of Ancient Virtues both Greek and Roman. There is some overlap between them. Read through the list. Some are more relevant to life in Athens or Rome in particular and won't strike you as something worthy of pursuit. **What you're looking for is five to seven virtues that really speak to you. If you've got a pen, circle them.**

▶ **Auctoritas** (Roman) / No direct Greek equivalent:
  The sense of social standing, respect, and influence gained through experience, wisdom, and integrity.
  Historical Example: Augustus Caesar–He embodied auctoritas through his leadership, reforms, and influence that stabilized Rome after civil war.

► **Comitas** (Roman) / No direct Greek equivalent:
An approachable, kind, and polite demeanor that fosters goodwill and sociability.
Historical Example: Cicero–Known for his wit and diplomatic style, Cicero modeled comitas in Roman public life.

► **Clementia** (Roman) / No direct Greek equivalent:
The virtue of mercy, leniency, and showing compassion, particularly in leadership and towards those in need.
Historical Example: Julius Caesar–Famously showed clementia by pardoning his enemies after the civil war.

► **Dignitas** (Roman) / **Philotimia** (Greek):
A sense of self-worth and personal honor derived from living a virtuous and responsible life.
Historical Example: Cato the Younger–His unwavering moral stance and eventual suicide were seen as expressions of his dignitas.

► **Disciplina** (Roman) / **Paideia** (Greek):
The pursuit of education, training, and discipline to achieve self-control and excellence.
Historical Example: Marcus Aurelius–His philosophical writings and disciplined reign reflect a life guided by rigorous self-control.

► **Firmitas** (Roman) / **Andreia** (Greek):
Steadfastness and mental strength in adversity.
Historical Example: Scipio Africanus–Demonstrated resolve in defeating Hannibal.

► **Frugalitas** (Roman) / **Metriotes** (Greek):
Simplicity, thrift, and moderation.
Historical Example: Cincinnatus–Returned to his farm after serving as dictator.

► **Gravitas** (Roman) / **Sophrosyne** (Greek):
Seriousness, dignity, and moral weight.
Historical Example: Seneca–Known for stoic composure even in political upheaval.

► **Honestas** (Roman) / **Kalon** (Greek):
Moral uprightness and integrity.
Historical Example: Fabricius Luscinus–Famously rejected bribes and stayed virtuous.

► **Humanitas** (Roman) / **Philia** (Greek):
Kindness, education, and cultural refinement.
Historical Example: Pliny the Younger–Advocated for justice and humane values.

► **Industria** (Roman) / **Arete** (Greek):
Hard work and excellence through effort.
Historical Example: Trajan–Tireless administrator and leader.

- ▶ **Iustitia** (Roman) / **Dikaiosyne** (Greek):
  Justice and fairness in law and conduct.
  Historical Example: Antoninus Pius–Ruled with equity and legal reform.

- ▶ **Pietas** (Roman) / **Eusebia** (Greek):
  Devotion to family, country, and the divine.
  Historical Example: Aeneas–Mythical hero known for his dutiful piety.

- ▶ **Prudentia** (Roman) / **Phronesis** (Greek):
  Practical wisdom and sound judgment.
  Historical Example: Solon–Crafted balanced reforms for Athens.

- ▶ **Severitas** (Roman) / **Sophrosyne** (Greek):
  Strictness and disciplined conduct.
  Historical Example: Lucius Junius Brutus–Executed his sons for justice's sake.

- ▶ **Veritas** (Roman) / No direct Greek equivalent:
  Truthfulness and honesty.
  Historical Example: Socrates–Died rather than compromise truth.

- ▶ **Virtus** (Roman) / **Arete / Andreia** (Greek):
  Valor, excellence, and manly strength.
  Historical Example: Horatius Cocles–Defended the bridge against invaders.

Greek Virtues Without Roman Counterparts

- ▶ **Xenia** (Greek):
  Hospitality and respect for guests.
  Historical Example: Odysseus–Both gave and received it in Homeric tales.

- ▶ **Nomos** (Greek):
  Respect for law and social order.
  Historical Example: Lycurgus–Spartan lawgiver who established strict codes.

- ▶ **Kleos** (Greek):
  Glory earned through heroic action.
  Historical Example: Achilles–Lived and died for eternal fame in the Iliad.

- ▶ **Orphrosyne** (Greek):
  Balanced moderation and joy.
  Historical Example: Pericles–Governed Athens with poise and prudence.

- ▶ **Sophia** (Greek):
  Higher wisdom and philosophical insight.
  Historical Example: Plato–Pursued truth and understanding through philosophy.

Make sure you've identified half a dozen or so virtues that really speak to you. Pick virtues that both impress you and feel authentic to your sense of self because with this program you'll learn to follow them and they will, indeed, shape the man you'll become. Later we'll incorporate them into your personal code. But, first let's see how Ben Franklin used virtues as a life-long constant improvement exercise.

Benjamin Franklin, one of America's founding fathers, was not only a statesman and inventor but also a man deeply committed to self-improvement. Inspired by his belief that moral perfection was attainable through deliberate effort, Franklin devised a system to cultivate his character through 13 virtues.

At the age of 20 (You're never too young to start crushing it), Franklin set out to master these virtues, creating a small book to track his progress. Each page was dedicated to one virtue, marked with seven columns representing the days of the week and rows for recording any lapses. His goal was to focus on one virtue per week, cycling through all 13 four times a year.

Although Franklin admitted he never achieved perfection, his disciplined practice of these virtues profoundly shaped his character. The system allowed him to grow as a person, balancing Franklin's virtues were not merely a list but a lifelong framework for living with purpose, discipline, and integrity.

Chapter 6

WHY YOU NEED A PERSONAL CODE

BY MAXIM SMITH

"Do what manhood bids thee do,
from none but self expect applause.
He noblest lives and noblest dies who
makes and keeps his self-made laws."

—SIR RICHARD FRANCIS BURTON

You must set your sights on the man you'd like to be. Ask yourself, who is he? What is he capable of? How does he live his life? Your answers to these questions will show you how to formulate your personal code. If you ponder long enough you'll have a very clear idea of how the man you want to be would act, and from that, which virtues he possesses.

Courage, humility, compassion, honesty, magnanimity, honor, temperance...whichever virtues you picked from the list earlier and reasons you have for picking them will be a direct reflection of your (current, and desired) character. They show who you are and who you want to be at your core.

Virtue completes a man. As Aristotle said, "Without virtue, man is most unholy and savage..."

All of us believe that becoming a capable man is admirable and impressive. Yet, if that man is not virtuous, he is incomplete, and much less worthy of admiration.

Socrates was admirable because of the great synergy between his capabilities and the virtue he—without any doubt—embodied. Not only was Socrates a philosopher and excellent orator, but he was a soldier, and a good one at that. During the Peloponnesian war his fellow Athenian soldiers would watch as he would spend hours thinking while sitting out in the cold, probably thinking over philosophical ideas. A student of his, Alcibiades, was saved by Socrates on the battlefield during the Battle of Potidaea (432 BC).

At the loss of the Battle of Delium (424 BC), Laches, a general, said Socrates walked calmly and deliberately during the retreat, deterring enemies from attacking him due to his confident presence.

He was a great teacher, philosopher, Hoplite infantryman, wrestler, orator...He was a man who was known to withstand cold, fatigue, hunger, hardship, and the draw of base pleasure. Everything from integrity, courage, humility, wisdom, justice, discipline, and absolute self-control was a part of who he was.

Within him, capability and virtue were intertwined. This should be your goal.

There's a reason why Ben Franklin wished to, "Imitate Jesus and Socrates."

All great men–men worthy of admiration–follow their own code. This code outlines how you will act, in public and private, to walk the morally straight and narrow path to become the man you want to be.

Let me tell you how to structure your own personal code...

STRUCTURING YOUR PERSONAL CODE

My personal code starts with a preamble acknowledging my mission and responsibility–to focus on what is in my control as I work to assemble the building blocks of manhood–Character, Virtue, and Capability. You could copy my preamble, but it's best if you really think it through for yourself.

The preamble makes clear that Character matters and it is formed by our choices and actions. It is our responsibility to make good choices, to never act in a way that degrades us and encourages us to abandon fear and live big. The line in the sand; the place where men do or do not form character is in their ability to say "no". For instance, 'No, I will not allow myself to do things that compromise my sense of virtue.' "No, I will not participate in a fraud, lie, or deceptive act including lying to myself." By saying no, we take the reins of our life and hold ourselves to a standard worthy of a man.

YOUR RULES

After the preamble, the personal code lists **your** rules, for **your** conduct and attitude. Forget about the rules your parents or other authority figures think you ought to follow. These rules are your rules – for you exclusively. Nobody knows better than we do when we fall short. It's our job to draw the line in the sand for ourselves by writing our own set of rules and, as an act of honor, abiding by them. Explain what each virtue means for both your Public and Private conduct.

VIRTUES

After rules, we have virtues. These are the ideals that inspire us. I look to men real and imagined, people like Edmond Dantes, Socrates, Louis L'Amour, and Teddy Roosevelt for examples. The virtues of my heroes inspire me. By actively pursuing them, I will eventually embed them into my identity and truly become virtuous like some of my fictional heroes and the great men who came before me. List all the virtues that you choose to aspire toward. List the virtue and explain what living with that virtue will look like in your life.

COMPETENCY

Your personal code is a work in progress. You may add or remove rules as needed. And you might find that over time, certain virtues speak to you more than others. That's fine, feel free to make changes. But this is your compass. When you're lost and unsure what to do, your rules and the virtues you aspire to will have an answer for you.

Over time, you may alter your formal rules or make changes to the virtues that motivate you within your personal code. But, for the most part, the lists stay fairly static.

What won't be static is the list of competencies. The truth is you'll learn so much and so fast within the program that you'll likely learn new skills you forget you know – lost amongst all that you can recall off the top of your head. For that reason, we added competencies to the personal code. **This is an ongoing list. When you get a good grasp of a new skill, write it down. Write them all down. You'll keep this book as a log book of your progress. As you learn new skills be sure to add them to your list of competencies.**

I learned to tie a bunch of knots, it's not a big deal except most people can't do it. Compared to some of the other things I've learned this seemed like nothing. But, it's not. It's a skill I acquired as a prepper and it should be included. What's amazing is this living list grows overtime and, trust me, you'll look back and see where you were and how far you've come and it'll help you understand that anything is possible.

Revealing my own personal code feels a bit uncomfortable for someone as private as me. But I'm taking one for the team. Hopefully, my example makes it easier to complete your own.

In a moment, you'll create your own Personal Code. But before you get started here's mine to give you a sense of what you're trying to create.

MAXIM SMITH'S PERSONAL CODE

A man is made up of a few discernible building blocks entirely within our control. Those blocks are Character, Virtues, and Capabilities. This is where we should focus all our energy.

CHARACTER

Character is formed by our choice to not act in a way that degrades ourselves, but to live big. Character emerges as we draw a line in the sand and say to ourselves "no more!" With each action toward living big, we expand our sense of self-respect. True self-respect is the foundation of any great man.

PART 1: I Govern myself. These are My Rules

PUBLIC CONDUCT	PRIVATE CONDUCT
I will be aware of my surroundings at all times.	I will work consistently to make myself a better man and produce products which are a net positive to myself, family, friends, and those I seek to aid.
I will act openly, with the knowledge that I must live in harmony with my fellow man.	I will not engage in any act that degrades my soul. Any negative attribute will see swift and aggressive action against it.
I will be present in each moment. Anyone who comes in contact with me will have my full attention.	I will uplift myself and refocus my aim whenever I go off course.
I will not allow evil to continue within my presence, and will combat it as necessary.	I will not complain about any endurable condition.
I will uplift the mood.	I will be industrious, working hard in any venture I undertake.
I will speak clearly and confidently but, in the presence of those who	I will watch myself to look for any undesirable conduct or thoughts
I seek to learn from, I will either ask questions or remain silent to listen to them if I believe that to be the best course of action.	that need to be put to an end and replace it with positive action and forward-thinking.
I will treat others with respect.	I will focus on what is in my control.

THE VIRTUES TO WHICH I ASPIRE	WHY? WHAT WILL IT LOOK LIKE AS IT MANIFESTS?
Discipline	Discipline is necessary for a life worth living. Without it I would fall to the whims of short-term desire. With discipline I can make progress at a steady pace and maintain my personal dignity. As it manifests it shows itself in the ever-increasing list of skills and accomplishments. Along with that, it displays itself in my character as I am able to hold myself with an air of focus, persistence, and will.
Courage	I have encountered fear in everything I do. There's always a voice in the back of my head telling me to take the easy route. It's diminishing and degrading. Courage is necessary in order to overcome it. As courage manifests itself it allows me to go leaps and bounds further in life, experience unique things, meet new people, and do the things I personally believe I must do.
Wisdom	Wisdom adds to the substance of life. It comes directly from experience. It is battle tested and gives rise to good decision making. It will manifest itself as I continue to gain real life experience. The width and depth of my understanding of life will continue to increase. The essential truths of life will come to light as I gain more experience.
Strength	Strength, both mental and physical, should never be understated. A strong body reflects the use of discipline as well as the ability to assert yourself and protect yourself and those you love. Mental strength allows a man to maintain a steady course—always able to set himself back on track or focus his aim. As strength manifests itself I will not only become more physically dangerous, but mentally dangerous as well. Meaning that I can control my mental state and think critically about ideas.
Compassion	Compassion is a difficult virtue to maintain. It requires you to step outside of yourself and see the world through the eyes of another. It isn't just about having sympathy for the suffering other people endure—it's about seeing clearly that the negative actions of someone else come from a place of ignorance, not malice. As compassion manifests itself, I will free myself from my own negative thoughts of other people. Without anger towards others I can act justly to them.

THE VIRTUES TO WHICH I ASPIRE	WHY? WHAT WILL IT LOOK LIKE AS IT MANIFESTS?
Honesty	A man who cannot tell the truth manipulates himself and other people... in fact, he manipulates the world. Lies, deception, and manipulation lead down a path of Hell. When I am honest I allow things to be as they should be–clear and true. I admit to my own failings, speak the truth against unjust forces, and encourage others to do the same.
Humility	A person with humility strips himself of a false persona. He is as he is–no more and no less. Humility aligns with truth and gives a man the opportunity to develop a strong character. As I hold the virtue of humility I can act in a way which moves me closer to the man I wish to become. With it, I can see myself with clarity–all the faults and all the good. From there, I can take clear and conscious action to become a better man.
Magnanimity	A magnanimous man is generous and forgiving. Like the virtue of compassion, magnanimity lets you step outside of yourself and seek to create a good outcome for everyone–some may call it "Taking the high road." As I act with magnanimity I cause others to endear me because I forgive them and am generous in my efforts to seek a good outcome for all. Gaining friends becomes immensely easier. Good, long— lasting friendships can blossom and remain strong.
Temperance	Temperance, in a word, is about self-control. It's essentially a combination for several different virtues including strength and discipline. Without the ability to control himself, what is a man? Nothing but a beast. With the virtue of temperance I, like a blacksmith forging a sword, can craft myself into who I wish to be–rejecting everything opposed to my ultimate aim. My character will grow stronger and, because of that, my life will be much more pleasant to live.

PART 3: Capabilities (As of July 13, 2025 – Skills Acquired)

- ▶ Knot Tying
- ▶ Inspecting/treating cattle knowledge of regenerative agriculture
- ▶ Expanded knowledge of history
- ▶ Sales
- ▶ Marketing
- ▶ Copywriting
- ▶ Social Skills (for a natural introvert)
- ▶ BJJ
- ▶ Kickboxing
- ▶ Wildland firefighting skills
- ▶ Spanish as a second language
- ▶ Persuasive writing
- ▶ Rock Climbing
- ▶ Land Navigation (orienteering)
- ▶ EMT Skills
- ▶ Rappelling/rope skills

- ▶ Motorcycle riding
- ▶ Scuba diving
- ▶ Public speaking
- ▶ Horsemanship/Wrangling
- ▶ Mule packing
- ▶ Chess
- ▶ Wilderness first aid Operating tractors Basics of guitar
- ▶ 27 hours flying a plane Fixing fences
- ▶ Animal butchering
- ▶ Sailing skills (chart work, rope work, helming)
- ▶ Learned to cook a few great meals
- ▶ Experience working on a geophysics crew
- ▶ Expanded knowledge of geology and mining (from field work)

SCAN ME

NOW IT'S TIME TO CRAFT YOUR PERSONAL CODE.

Consider it a living document that will require updates as you progress. Use the next pages to fill out your own personal code. Or you can the QR code for a separate form.

_____ 'S

PERSONAL CODE

A man is made up of a few discernible building blocks entirely within our control. Those blocks are Character, Virtues, and Capabilities. This is where we should focus all our energy.

CHARACTER

Character is formed by our choice to not act in a way that degrades ourselves, but to live big. Character emerges as we draw a line in the sand and say to ourselves "no more!" With each action toward living big, we expand our sense of self-respect. True self-respect is the foundation of any great man.

PART 1: **New Rules, My Rules**

PUBLIC CONDUCT	PRIVATE CONDUCT

PART 2: **Virtues**

THE VIRTUES TO WHICH I ASPIRE	WHY? WHAT WILL IT LOOK LIKE AS IT MANIFESTS?

THE VIRTUES TO WHICH I ASPIRE	WHY? WHAT WILL IT LOOK LIKE AS IT MANIFESTS?

Part 3: **Capabilities**

List of The Capabilities/Skills I've Acquired In The Preparation

▶ _____   ▶ _____

▶ _____   ▶ _____

▶ _____   ▶ _____

▶ _____   ▶ _____

▶ _____   ▶ _____

▶ _____   ▶ _____

▶ _____   ▶ _____

▶ _____   ▶ _____

▶ _____   ▶ _____

▶ _____   ▶ _____

▶ _____   ▶ _____

FORGET MENTORS FIND A PATRON

BY MATT SMITH

If there's one truth about achieving everything you want in life, it's this: you can't do it entirely alone. The most successful people in history didn't just rely on their intelligence, talent, or work ethic—they had mentors to guide them, challenge them, and open doors they couldn't open themselves. Building trusted relationships with the right people is the fastest and most effective way to accelerate your success.

What we're going to discuss here is akin to a secret formula I developed over years building my own rags to riches story. But, riches are just part of it. There are certain rooms you want to be in that are totally off limits to anyone without an invitation.

These informal networks are where all the magic happens from access to incredible deals to adventures that'll take you places... and in ways that you can't imagine.

My mother would be upset to hear me say it, to any rational outsider looking at my childhood – I was poor white trash. Sounds harsh, but I don't even mind the label. We grew up rough, but that's all long in the past. My point is, this formula works for people starting way, way down the totem pole. It can work for you too.

The Formula I'll tell you about in this chapter will allow you, assuming you're a man of honor, to become a welcomed member in the most exclusive groups in the world. It's incredible.

And, if you're lucky and smart enough to seize the opportunity dressed up falsely as self— sacrifice, you'll find yourself a true mentor, a man worthy of your respect and service. And in return he'll open a whole new world to you.

MENTORSHIP IS A FAILED MODEL

The trouble is, the modern idea of mentorship is broken. Young men are told to "find a mentor," as if some wise elder can be found who will take them under his wing out of sheer generosity. If you ask someone to be your mentor, you are adding to his workload, asking for his time and energy, as well as his secrets to success just because you showed up. It's a one-way street where the mentee passively absorbs advice and provides nothing in return— it is doomed to fail.

The ancient Romans had a better system—one that actually worked. It was called the patron-client relationship, and it's still alive today, hidden in plain sight.

A patron was a man with power, influence, and resources. He had the ability to mentor, but why should he? Patrons were much like mentors today, the real difference comes down to the client. Unlike a mentee, a client wasn't a passive recipient of wisdom; he was an ambitious operator who earned his way into the patron's circle by proving his usefulness. In exchange, the patron provided access, protection, and opportunity. Unlike modern mentorship, which often dies after a few coffee meetings, this was an ongoing relationship that evolved as the client grew, succeeded, and ultimately became powerful in his own right.

THE ROMAN WAY

The patron-client relationship thrived in Ancient Rome and played a crucial role in the fabric of Roman society. This symbiotic bond between the wealthy and influential patrons and their less fortunate or experienced clients was a cornerstone of Roman life, providing a means of social mobility, political advancement, and economic stability.

The patrons, often members of the elite class, wielded significant power and resources. They were the ones who could open doors, grant favors, and provide protection to those in need. In return, the clients, typically upstarts or from the lower echelons of society, offered their loyalty, support, and services to their patrons.

To catch the eye of a potential patron, clients had to demonstrate their worth and value. They would go to great lengths to showcase their skills, their knowledge, and their connections.

Roman society that valued oratory and rhetoric; the ability to speak well and engage in intelligent discourse was highly prized. Would-be clients would spend hours honing their verbal skills and sharpening their minds with the latest philosophical and political ideas.

Being interesting, intelligent, and energetic helped one stand out in the ancient world. The same is true today although the methods may be different.

Ancient relationships followed well— known societal norms. Once an aspirant was accepted as a client he went to great lengths to prove his worth, demonstrate his loyalty, and offer his skills and knowledge in service to his patron. They would publicly praise their patron's achievements, defend their reputation, and rally support for their political ambitions.

Then as now—Clients work to serve the interests of their patron, but don't be mistaken—the client is not a subordinate. For the patron, clients are assets worthy of further investment. Being a client doesn't diminish your potential, it dramatically expands it.

Imagine for a moment the benefit of having a wise and powerful man whose loyalty and esteem you've earned. Imagine the advantage that'd give you over your peers in whatever career you pursue. Imagine the doors that might be open to you. In ancient Rome, being a client was an opportunity to move well beyond your station and limited only by your competency and courage. The same is true today.

HOW CLIENTS BECOME LEADERS

Take Julius Caesar and Gaius Marius. Marius, a towering figure in Roman politics, was more than just an uncle to Caesar—he was his patron, providing him with connections, status, and protection. But this was not a one-way relationship. As a client, Caesar didn't just sit back and absorb wisdom—he made himself valuable.

He aligned himself with Marius's political faction, strengthened family ties through strategic marriages, and ingratiated himself with Rome's ruling class. By doing so, he reinforced Marius's influence while securing his own future.

Over time, Caesar surpassed his patron's legacy. He built his own network of clients, and became a patron himself, backing ambitious men who, in turn, propelled him forward. Eventually, he seized power and took control of Rome itself. The lesson? A great client doesn't stay a client forever—he becomes the patron.

PATRON CLIENT RELATIONSHIPS TODAY

These mutually beneficial relationships didn't die with the Roman Empire. They are widely practiced in America today, but they're never discussed. Unlike Rome, today patron/client relationships form on an informal basis and evolve naturally.

What hasn't changed is smart would-be clients know they could benefit tremendously if they had a Patron. Likewise, Patrons who 'have it all' still have unfulfilled ambitions. A reliable, energetic, and intelligent young man can be a great asset to a patron looking to expand his capabilities.

Just look at Peter Thiel and America's Vice President–J.D. Vance.

In 2011, J.D. Vance was a Yale Law student attending a guest lecture series by Peter Thiel, the billionaire co-founder of PayPal. Vance was handpicked along with fewer than 20 other students to participate.

The lectures were part of Thiel's effort to share his unconventional views on entrepreneurship, technology, and society with a small group of handpicked students. Thiel's lectures focused on a range of topics, including how the future of innovation could unfold and the importance of pursuing bold ideas, challenging the status quo, and thinking differently.

Thiel had an alternate motive. As we'll see, he was looking for clients. Three of those ten "handpicked" students stand out.

Vivek Ramaswamy who later made a name for himself on Wall Street, founded a biotech company (Roivant Sciences), and entered the 2024 presidential race. According to public records, Thiel had no part in Vivek's later success.

Blake Masters took detailed notes during Thiel's Stanford class, and those notes eventually became the foundation for the bestselling book Zero to One, which he co-wrote with Peter Thiel in 2014. I've read the book. It's good. It's a worthwhile read, particularly if you're interested in entrepreneurship.

After the class, Masters worked closely with Thiel—serving in leadership roles at Thiel Capital and the Thiel Foundation—and became known as one of Thiel's protégé. Over time, Masters transitioned into the political arena, running for the U.S. Senate in Arizona in 2022 and later for the U.S. House in 2024. Masters remains a client of Thiel.

The third standout student was, of course, JD Vance. Thiel didn't just give Vance career advice—he opened doors. He brought him into Mithril Capital, one of his venture firms, where Vance gained insider knowledge of Silicon Valley, high finance, and power dynamics at the highest levels.

While working for Thiel in 2016, Vance wrote "Hillbilly Elegy", a memoir about his Appalachian upbringing. The book became a bestseller, resonating with millions and attracting Hollywood's attention. It was eventually adapted into a film directed by Ron Howard. While there's no public record of Thiel directly securing the book deal, it's naive to think Thiel's network and influence played no part. Two clients, two best— selling books.

But the real turning point in the Thiel/Vance relationship came in 2021 when Vance decided to run for U.S. Senate. Political campaigns require serious money, and most newcomers struggle to raise enough to be competitive. Vance didn't have that problem. Thiel poured $10 million into a super PAC backing his campaign, instantly making Vance a viable contender in the race. It wasn't just money—it was a signal to other power players that Vance was worth betting on. And it worked. Vance won his seat and, in 2024, became Vice President of the United States.

Thiel put two dark horse candidates in the 2022 senate race. The bet on JD Vance paid off. Masters, not so much, even though Thiel donated $15 million to Masters' campaign for the Senate the same year as Vance.

If Vance or Masters had approached Thiel asking for mentorship, they'd all probably still be another forgotten law graduate. Instead, they proved themselves valuable and, in exchange, earned a patron.

PATRON CLIENT RELATIONSHIPS ARE A TWO WAY STREET.

With the quick rise from obscurity to fame, power, and fortune–It is clear how JD Vance benefited from the relationship. But how might Vance have made himself valuable to Peter Thiel, a man who already has everything?

At the 2011 guest lectures most students likely saw Thiel as a billionaire celebrity, but Vance saw a potential patron—and more importantly, he understood Thiel's worldview.

Thiel has always positioned himself as an intellectual outsider, a critic of the establishment who believes that elites are stifling innovation and that America's best days lie ahead— but only if the right people take power. Vance recognized this and aligned himself with it. He wasn't just another Ivy League lawyer climbing the corporate ladder; he was an outsider himself, a kid from Appalachian Ohio who had served in the Marine Corps and rejected the prevailing ideology of his elite academic environment. This made Vance useful to Thiel in several ways:

He reinforced Thiel's narrative about American decline.

- ▶ Thiel has long believed that America is in decline due to stagnation, bureaucracy, and failing leadership.
- ▶ Hillbilly Elegy, Vance's memoir, fit perfectly into this framework, painting a picture of a broken America in need of bold leadership and new ideas.
- ▶ It's not an accident that his book validated many of Thiel's core beliefs, cementing him an intellectual ally with real-world credibility.

He gave Thiel a bridge into conservative populism.

- ▶ Thiel is awkward – Vance is smooth and likeable.
- ▶ Thiel had always been a tech outsider and libertarian thinker, but Vance gave him a direct link to the emerging populist right.
- ▶ As an Ivy League-educated Appalachian conservative, Vance could speak to both the elite and working-class voters, making him a perfect frontman for a new political movement.
- ▶ If Thiel wanted political influence beyond Silicon Valley, Vance was a useful vehicle for that ambition.

He became a political asset at the right moment.

- ▶ By the time Vance entered politics, Thiel was looking for candidates who weren't just typical Republicans but outsiders who could reshape the system.
- ▶ Thiel didn't just throw money at Vance ($10 million into a PAC backing his Senate campaign)-he invested in him because he saw a man who could win and advance their shared vision.
- ▶ Vance proved Thiel right by winning his Senate race and later securing the Vice Presidency—a move that, in turn, increased Thiel's own influence over the political landscape.

Vance's rise wasn't just luck. He understood what Thiel valued, aligned himself with those interests, and proved himself useful before ever asking for anything in return. And Thiel, in turn, understood that a powerful client makes the patron even more powerful. Thiel opened doors in ways Vance could barely imagine.

This is how real patron-client relationships work. A smart client doesn't beg for guidance—he brings value. A smart patron doesn't just hoard power—he builds powerful allies. And together, they can reshape the world.

THE SYSTEM WORKS—IF YOU WORK IT

This is not about sucking up to powerful men for scraps. Patron-client relationships are built on mutual respect and value creation, not charity. A patron isn't doing you a favor— he's making an investment. And a client isn't a subordinate—he's an asset.

The best patrons don't just give their clients opportunities; they expect results. The best clients don't just take from their patrons; they prove their value every step of the way. This is why the system works—everyone involved flourishes.

If you want to get ahead, stop looking for a mentor to give you career advice or throw you a bone. Instead:

▶ Become useful – Bring skills, energy, and value to the table. Power respects competence. Adopt their vision and help them make it real.
▶ Align with the right people – Find those building something bigger than themselves and help them win.
▶ Be loyal – Clients who jump ship at the first opportunity never last. Those who build long-term alliances thrive.
▶ Play the long game – The best patron-client relationships evolve. If you succeed, you won't just have access—you'll become a power player yourself.

HOW PATRON-CLIENT RELATIONSHIPS BEGIN

If you're ambitious the question to ask yourself is "How do I make myself an asset to a powerful man?"

Patron-client relationships don't start with a handshake agreement or some formal mentorship program. They begin when a young, ambitious client aligns his interests with someone who has already built something significant. This isn't about blind loyalty—it's about recognizing where real power and opportunity lie.

When a client first enters a patron's world, he often abandons his own preferences to serve the patron's interests. Not because he's weak or without ambition, but because he understands some-thing most people don't: his best path to power is by making himself indispensable to someone who already has it.

This is how Julius Caesar started under Marius. He didn't walk in demanding favors—he served. He used his family name and charm to strengthen Marius's political faction, aligning himself completely with his patron's ambitions. It wasn't about losing himself—it was about positioning himself for the future.

The best clients recognize that serving a great patron is not a sacrifice, but an investment. They play the long game, proving themselves in small ways until they become so valuable that their patron wouldn't dream of letting them go. And the smartest patrons understand that their own power grows as their clients succeed.

A patron who suppresses his clients out of fear or insecurity weakens his own position. But one who allows them to flourish—who gives them access, opportunity, and power— creates an entire network of loyal, competent allies who amplify his own influence.

Peter Thiel might understand this better than anyone today. He didn't just fund companies—he built an empire of capable, ambitious men who went on to create Tesla, LinkedIn, and Palantir. When Thiel invested in J.D. Vance, he wasn't just helping a promising young politician—he was creating a powerful ally. And now that Vance is Vice President, Thiel's influence is greater than ever.

This is how patron-client relationships truly work. A smart client proves his value. A smart patron builds up powerful allies. Together, they rise.

The patron-client model has produced emperors, senators, billionaires, and presidents. The mentorship model? Mostly forgotten coffee meetings.

If you want to go far, find a patron, become indispensable, and eventually, become a patron yourself.

Today, I'm both a client and a patron. I'll tell you more about that shortly. First, I want to show you how to secure your own patron.

HOW TO FIND A PATRON

Now that you understand the nature and power of patron-client relationships. The question remains, how to find a patron? Potential patrons are busy people and notoriously difficult to access, and for good reason.

Someday you'll experience it for yourself. The more successful you are, the more people will want access to you. It can be exhausting. There really is no choice but for high profile individuals to set up barriers to protect and insulate themselves from the general public. You usually can't just pick up the phone and call them. And even if you manage to reach them out of the blue and even if they respond to you politely, it's unlikely to go much beyond that point.

Patron-client relationships don't magically form from the ether. Some of it comes down to being in the right place at the right time, but it's not luck. Finding a patron requires an understanding of human networks and a thoughtful strategy; a strategy which I'll outline below.

But before we dive into strategy, let's understand what we're dealing with.

The basis of human relationships are informal trusted networks. Some contain power players, others are made up of criminals or degenerates, and most are collections of 'normal' people. You're part of some already. You already have your family, maybe your high school friend group, or sports teammates. All are trusted networks.

A trusted network isn't a list of LinkedIn connections or a formal organization like Chamber of Commerce or a college alumni group. The trusted networks you want to be a part of are an informal web of influential people who share common interests or values. These networks might revolve

By Corbis/The Telegraph–https://fortune.com/2007/11/13/paypal-mafia/, Fair use, https://en.wikipedia.org/w/index.php?curid=70482509 Members of the PayPal Mafia on Fortune magazine dressed in mafia-like attire. From left to right, top row to bottom row: Jawed Karim, Jeremy Stoppelman, Andrew McCormack, Premal Shah, Luke Nosek, Ken Howery, David O. Sacks, Peter Thiel, Keith Rabois, Reid Hoffman, Max Levchin, Roelof Botha, Russel Simmons. Elon Musk (not pictured) belongs on this list as well.

around a particular industry like venture capital, politics, entertainment, or any other sphere where power and influence concentrate.

Gaining trust and access to a trusted network requires time, energy, and sometimes money.

To be in the right place at the right time, Vance leveraged his service in the Marine Corps to gain admission and help finance his education at Yale. And he worked himself into the good graces of key Yale faculty.

To be the person he needed to be when he met Thiel, Vance built a reputation as a strong student with a unique background (U.S. Marine Corps veteran from Appalachia), which caught the attention of influential professors—most notably Amy Chua (the "Tiger Mom" professor at Yale Law). Chua had a hand in his selection to join Thiel's lectures.

If you're trying to get into an exclusive network, it's guaranteed that there are countless others who want to do the same thing. You can buy your way into most formal networks, but with trusted networks there's only one way in, you must be invited. To be introduced, you must be worth of invitation. Vance knew this.

Trusted networks are difficult to penetrate. You can't just show up and there is no way to apply. This is on purpose. Living in a world where everyone wants something from them, trusted networks are a place where successful men can let their guard down. They protect themselves from outsiders.

The Paypal Mafia is a rare public example of what a small, trusted network looks like.

The "PayPal Mafia" is a group of former PayPal employees and founders including Peter Thiel, who have since founded other companies based in Silicon Valley, such as Tesla, Inc., LinkedIn, Palantir Technologies, SpaceX, Affirm, Slide, Kiva, YouTube, Yelp, and Yammer.

Zooming out from the Paypal Mafia, you find Silicon Valley. It isn't just a place. It is a trusted network in and of itself. From the vantage point of a young Yale Law student, it must have been clear to Vance that, if he could become a valuable member of this network, he'd have his opportunity.

If you want to find a good patron, start by looking around to identify a powerful trusted network you want to be part of. For Vance, that trusted network was Silicon Valley.

NODES WITHIN TRUSTED NETWORKS

At the center of these networks are what we'll call "nodes"—key individuals who act as centers of gravity. Peter Thiel is a node. As a successful tech founder, prominent venture capitalist, and now a political kingmaker, he's a central node in multiple overlapping trusted networks including, of course, Silicon Valley, The Paypal Mafia, and now the political Right.

After you identify a network, the next step is identifying individual nodes. Nodes are important not just because these individuals might be potential patrons, but because connecting with a node is how you get welcomed access to the network. That day Thiel showed up to a guest lecture, Vance recognized that this was an opportunity–a potential way into the exclusive Silicon Valley network.

THE OPEN DOOR

Every person in a trusted network is a node. And many of these nodes have an "Open door". That is, while these individuals are normally hard to reach, the "open door" is a way they welcome select interactions with individuals from outside the network. That is your opportunity. Peter Thiel has at least two Open Doors. One, of course, was the guest lecture that JD Vance and Vivek Ramaswamy attended. These open doors aren't truly open. Not just anyone can walk in to meet them. In Vance's case, he had to be a student at Yale to walk through the open door.

The Thiel Fellowship is another open door. From Wikipedia, "The Thiel Fellowship is a fellowship created by billionaire Peter Thiel through the Thiel Foundation in 2010. The fellowship is intended for students aged 22 or younger and offers them a total of $100,000 over two years, as well as guidance and other resources, to drop out of school and pursue other work, which could involve scientific research, creating a startup, or working on a social movement. Selection for the fellowship is through a competitive annual process, with about 20–25 fellows selected annually."

Years ago, a Thiel Fellow walked through one of my open doors–The BlackSmith Liberty and Entrepreneurship Camp. Each year, hundreds of bright, ambitious college-age men and women would apply to attend the camp, hosted by an ex— business partner and I. At the camp, we taught the philosophy of individual freedom along with practical skills for starting and growing a business. We charged no fee to the week-long event. But, we were ultra-selective with who could attend. Out of the hundreds of applications, we only accepted about 50 each year.

We ran the camp at our expense because we enjoyed it and, like Thiel, we recognized the value of meeting enterprising young people.

I'm not comparing myself to Peter Thiel except in pointing out he and I both did what nodes in trusted networks always do. We wall ourselves off from the outside world making it hard to get our attention–unless by way of introduction from someone else within our network or through the open door. Thiel had the Thiel Fellowship and his guest lectures. The camp was my open door.

To get the attention of a key node in whatever network you're trying to access, you must be invited in. Finding an open door and working your way through it successfully is where the rubber meets the road.

My partner and I invested in a few companies started by students of the camp. Others, we hired to work in our businesses. In my case, one stands out–Gary Young.

Gary attended our camp the same year Vance attended Thiel's guest lectures. At the time, he too was in law school although not Yale Law. Admittedly, his future may have been brighter if he'd managed to secure an invitation to Thiel's lectures. Gary is a dynamic, intelligent, and interesting man. He might have stood out in Thiel's eyes too.

Lucky for me, he came to the camp. The next year he dropped out of law school to come work with me. I remember interviewing him over lunch on an outdoor patio in the LoDo section of Denver. When I asked him why he would drop out of school to come work for one of my companies, he said "I just want to work with you."

Gary didn't start off in a glamorous role, but it didn't matter to him. He proved he could do any task put in front of him. In time, it became clear that Gary was sincere, valuable, loyal and capable. It didn't take long before I took a special interest in his professional and personal life. Informally, of course— it's always informal–I became his patron.

Personally and professionally–If Gary had a problem, I helped. When I had a problem, he helped. Today Gary is my friend, business partner, and CEO of Royalty Exchange–a company we started together in 2017.

Both Gary and I have benefited from our constantly evolving relationship. I can count on him and he knows I want to see him flourish in all possible ways and will help however I might.

Doug Casey is my friend, business partner, and co-author. He's also my patron.

Like Gary with me, I became Doug's client before he became my patron. In certain circles Doug is a huge celebrity. Everyone wants to be close to Doug and many want a piece of him. I respected and admired Doug. I wanted to be around him so I could learn. And I knew he'd be more likely to want me around if I could be valuable to him.

I got my opportunity one day in Buenos Aires, Argentina. In an informal get- together with a few others Doug told us about his hobby. In a nutshell, Doug liked going to small "backwards" countries to meet with the head of state and try to convince them to adopt his plan for reforms. The way Doug pitched it to the presidents he met was: If you (the leader) adopt these (radical) ideas for reform, you will be rich–earned honestly rather than stolen from the people. You'll be loved by your people who'll also be far better off, and you'll be famous internationally–probably on the cover of Time Magazine as man of the year.

Doug mentioned he was planning to pitch another president–this time the president of Palau who had invited him to visit. He asked the small gathering if we'd like to join the party. At the time I had no idea where Palau was or even **what** it was. But, I eagerly offered to go. I saw it as an opportunity to prove I could be valuable.

We went to Palau in early 2009. The deal ended up falling through, but it was quite a surreal adventure. I adopted Doug's interests as my own and I found ways to be valuable. I'm still doing the same 16 years later. I've never officially worked for Doug, but I've always worked for Doug's interests. If Doug is interested in something or has a problem, I'm there to help. Along the way, Doug's taught me a lot, opened doors, advocated on my behalf, and encouraged me to be my best.

THE CRITICAL INTERGENERATIONAL ADVANTAGE

The modern world is obsessed with peer groups. Social media, professional networks, and even career advice push you to "connect with like-minded individuals your age." While peer relationships matter, they often come with hidden complications. Your peers face the same career timeline and opportunities as you. Like it or not, you are the competition.

But there's a better way: look up, not sideways.

When I met Doug Casey, he was already a legend. He was a successful author and investor with decades of experience. As a Boomer who had already built his empire, he didn't see me – a Gen X entrepreneur – as competition. Instead, he saw potential. Doug had accumulated wisdom, connections, and opportunities that he was genuinely interested in sharing with someone who could appreciate and build upon them.

The generational gap wasn't a barrier; it was an advantage. Doug's experiences in the 70s, 80s, and 90s gave him perspective I couldn't get from my peers. When I showed genuine interest in his unconventional views on global markets and politics, I peeked Doug's interest. My energy and willingness to execute on his ideas made me valuable.

The same dynamic works in reverse. Gary is a Millennial. He came through my "open door" and, later, when he approached me about working together, all I could see was potential upside. His youth and ambition were assets, not liabilities. I could test out his potential by carving out a small role for him and, if he succeeded, his success would expand my own influence and network.

This is how intergenerational relationships naturally evolve into patron-client dynamics. The older partner has already climbed many of the mountains you're facing. They've made the mistakes, built the networks, and learned the unwritten rules. Most importantly, they're at a stage in life where they've got more knowledge and opportunity than they can effectively take advantage of. To fulfill their ambitions, they need a client. That client could be you.

The key is genuine respect for experience. Too many young people today dismiss older generations as "out of touch" or "behind the times." This arrogance cuts them off from centuries of accumulated wisdom. The smartest path forward is to seek out those who've already walked it, while bringing your own energy and fresh perspective to the relationship.

While ambitious peers are likely to be your competition, your elders will want to be your allies.

What we're discussing here is a "secret formula" if you will. One I figured out along my journey from poor, know-nothing, midwestern boy to a guy connected with the who's who of men from all over the world.

The truth is I'm an introvert. I prefer time alone with a book, to rubbing shoulders with Jerry Jones, the owner of the Dallas Cowboys at an invite only party put on by Maxim Magazine in Miami. I was there anyway. Jerry was a pretty decent guy, there were lots of beautiful women there of course, but it's just not my scene.

For me, this event was me taking novel action. Doing something new to see what might happen. As you will recall from earlier, taking novel action – doing what's out of your comfort zone, is the key to becoming the man you want to be. And sometimes it's the key to becoming a valued member of trusted and powerful networks.

1. Identify a powerful network you'd like to be part of. Be as specific as possible.
2. Identify key nodes on the network.
3. Find a node with an open door. Seek out an invitation.
4. When you're in the room you must differentiate AND find ways to add value.
5. Play the long game. Be patient. Seek out other nodes within the same network who also have an open door. Show up and add value. Ask for nothing in return. You're there to be of value not to extract value.
6. You'll know you're on the right track when separate nodes in the same network realize they know you, find you interesting and invite you to something more private.

The strategy works. And if you're an interesting man of honor who constantly looks for ways to intelligently add value, you'll eventually become a welcomed member of virtually any exclusive network in the world.

In 2009, an old business partner and I documented the process and published it on our website SovereignMan.com. The document is dated, but the fundamentals are still quite sound. We called it the Network Infiltration Black Paper. Eventually, we took it offline because the strategy can be useful to bad actors as well as good. I'll trust that you'll use this system in good faith. If you do, I know from personal experience it works.

Download

YOU CAN FIND A COPY OF IT HERE:

Chapter 8

WEALTH & ECONOMICS

MATT SMITH

"Ms. Rand, what do we do
about the poor in our society?"
Her answer, "Don't be one of them".

We've spent a lot of time discussing philosophy, character, and virtue, (and we're not done) because they are the foundation of achievement and happiness. They ensure you embark on an honest pursuit, with clear desires. Money and economics are among the essential joists and beams that support what you are building. You should prioritize them. A free economy is a moral one, in which virtue is rewarded and errors are punished.

The formula for becoming rich is so simple it makes you wonder why anyone is poor. Making money honestly means creating value for others. The more money I want, the more I must consider what potential customers want, and find better, faster, cheaper ways of delivering it to them. The reason people are poor – and, yes, I know all the excuses for poverty – is they don't produce more than they consume. Or if they do, they don't save the surplus.

Most Americans are broke. A **RECENT FORBES SURVEY** showed that 75% of Americans live paycheck to paycheck. Their income covers expenses with nothing left over. Another 26% reported their income doesn't even cover monthly expenses. Each month they go deeper into debt. That leaves less than a third of Americans comfortably able to afford their lifestyle.

People go to college thinking that it'll help them earn the big bucks. The trouble is, even if your degree manages to get you a high income, that doesn't mean you'll escape the rat race. Even 39% of those earning at least $200,000/yr reported not having enough money leftover after covering expenses. These folks earn more than 96% of Americans and they're still broke.

The problem is fundamental. If you want to have money, you need to understand what it is, how it works, and how to get your hands on it. Most Americans have no clue.

WHAT IS ECONOMICS?

Economics isn't about numbers. It's about human behavior. What choices do we make and why? What are the results of our actions? And how can they be improved to our advantage? In his book "Principles of Economics", Saifedean Ammous defines economics as the study of human action under scarcity. "Scarcity" comes from the fact that since nobody has unlimited resources, our choices are limited as well.

DOWNLOAD PRINCIPLES OF ECONOMICS HERE:

The choice of one action over another is called economizing. We economize all the time without even thinking about it. We choose between steak or chicken for dinner. Cost and personal preferences factor into the decision. We economize when we decide whether to go to the gym, read a book, or sleep in. We cannot do all three at the same time.

SPENDING TIME

Time is the ultimate resource. By its nature, it is scarce. Our success in life hinges upon how skillfully we spend it. The moment we enter this world, our clock starts ticking. We all have the same daily allotment of 24 hours to spend. With limited time, we economize by making choices to best satisfy our individual wants.

People spend time unwisely–frittering it away on social media, wasting it watching TV, or by doing destructive things with their limited allotment. And some people spend time wisely, doing productive things...fostering friendships, learning skills, or building a business. Most of us have been both wasteful and productive with the limited hours of the same day.

The important thing to understand is that, in all cases, the motivation is the same–wasteful or productive, we all spend our time to maximize satisfaction.

Understanding what motivates us is key to understanding economics. Humans are hardwired to have increasing desires and to do what they believe will satisfy those desires. As you enhance your understanding of economics and yourself, you'll be better able to manage your wants. But you can't make them disappear.

Why would you want to? The satisfaction of desires drives us to take action. Our wants provide the motivating force that moves us to fill our bellies, build a home, create a successful business, and construct civilization.

HOW TIME AFFECTS OUR DECISIONS

Let's say you want a car and have just $20,000 to spend. Now, imagine I offered you two good choices. For $20,000, you can have a 2024 Toyota Camry with a sticker price of $28,400. Or, for the same $20,000, you can have a 2024 BMW M5 with a sticker price of $117,495. For some reason, I'm willing to part with each for just $20,000–which would you choose?

Probably the BMW, right? It's one of my favorite cars. It's luxurious, understated, and faster than most supercars. And even if it isn't your style, you could sell it and buy four Camrys.

But the offer has one wrinkle: time. If you buy the Camry, you can drive it home today. If you take the BMW, it'll be delivered to you in five years. Don't worry. It'll be safely stored and maintained in mint condition till I hand you the keys five years from now.

Now which car would you choose?

Most would consider the BMW the better car, and at $20,000 it may seem a steal. But spending the money today and not getting any satisfaction or utility for five years means you may be more inclined to take the Camry.

The best choice to optimize your financial outcome five years from now would almost certainly be to take the BMW. Worst case, it's an investment that'll deliver a 3x return. And, of course, you probably prefer to have more money in five years than you do today. So, going with the BMW would satisfy a want.

But, let's face it, maximizing your return in five years isn't the only consideration. Time preference always operates. You want a car now. You have places you want to go today. You don't even know where you'll be in five years, or even if you'd be alive to enjoy a vehicle.

Time preference matters. It's the critical economic factor most people don't appreciate. It's the resource we all have. And when you're starting out and don't have much capital, time is the resource you'll need to leverage to move yourself from poor to rich.

WE WANT IT ALL AND WE WANT IT NOW

If you don't know where your next meal will come from, why would you bother to worry about what you'll eat next year? Producing anything takes time and energy. We have no choice but to produce enough to meet our basic needs. Whether that be grubbing for roots and berries, clocking into a job we hate, or stealing from the local grocery store. There is a minimum level of work (time+energy) required to keep ourselves fed and alive.

On a base level, our survival instinct drives us to work so that we can satisfy our immediate wants. Once our bellies are full and we're under a roof , we begin to think of the future and formulate a strategy to make that future better, easier, and more certain.

Time preference is the economic term to describe the tradeoffs we make between satisfying wants of today vs. those of the future. People with a high time preference tend to emphasize their immediate and short-term wants while those with a low time preference work to satisfy their future desires.

A homeless drug addict lives with ultra-high time preference. His first priority is getting a fix. Whatever it takes, this craving must be satisfied. And between fixes, he eats what he can scrounge and sleeps wherever he stumbles. He is primarily a scavenger. But he can become a predator when desperate, and always risk being prey himself. His ultra-high time preference prioritizes his fix above all else. Even food and shelter are secondary. He is trapped in a loop, each day less fit for survival, which guarantees tomorrow will be worse than today.

Individuals with low time preference are the opposite. They economize in ways that increase their fitness for survival every day. Whereas the homeless man lives like an animal on the edge of survival, a person with low time preference has made provision for today and can prioritize the future.

We are alive today because our ancestors adopted a lower time preference. More importantly, civilization itself only exists as a result of compounded value creation of generations who formed a culture based on low time preference. They delayed gratification, created capital, and saved for the future their ancestors enjoy.

As you may recall, Benjamin Franklin was a man deeply committed to self-improvement. Starting at age 20, Franklin devised a system to cultivate his character through 13 virtues.

Take a look at the virtues that guided his life. All describe the behavior of a man with a low time preference and an eye to the future.

BENJAMIN FRANKLIN'S 13 VIRTUES	DESCRIPTION
Temperance	Eat not to dullness; drink not to elevation.
Silence	Speak not but what may benefit others or yourself; avoid trifling conversation.
Order	Let all your things have their places; let each part of your business have its time.
Resolution	Resolve to perform what you ought; perform without fail what you resolve.
Frugality	Make no expense but to do good to others or yourself; i.e., waste nothing.
Industry	Lose no time; be always employ'd in something useful; cut off all unnecessary actions.
Sincerity	Use no hurtful deceit; think innocently and justly, and, if you speak, speak accordingly.
Justice	Wrong none by doing injuries, or omitting the benefits that are your duty.
Moderation	Avoid extremes; forebear resenting injuries so much as you think they deserve.
Cleanliness	Tolerate no uncleanliness in body, clothes, or habitation.
Tranquility	Be not disturbed at trifles, or at accidents common or unavoidable.
Chastity	Rarely use venery but for health or offspring, never to dullness, weakness, or injury.
Humility	Imitate Jesus and Socrates.

Think about it. Every building you see, road you drive on or book you read; every artifact of technology from the wheel to ChatGPT only came into existence because men placed great value on the future and adopted a lower time preference in their actions. Rather than satisfying only their wants of the moment, they worked to satisfy their hopes for the future.

As evidence of Americans' high time preference, just look at their savings (if you can see them). From the same Forbes survey mentioned earlier, only 19.7% of Americans have more than $2,000 in savings. This is a disaster waiting to happen, if it isn't already underway. To compound the calamity, the average American currently has $6,700 in credit card debt.

Americans are broke today because a consumer aesthetic has replaced producer virtues. What's worse is, if you're broke today and have a high time preference, you will be even worse off tomorrow—guaranteed.

If you want to avoid being poor, the most important economic concept to keep in mind is time preference. But beware: you'll be swimming against the prevailing tide. The culture that produced Franklin's virtues is long gone. Today's America is a consumer culture. Forget baseball, consumption is America's real national past-time.

Almost half of Gen-Z and Millennials say they "are obsessed with being rich" The culture is dominated by high-time preference consumerism. We see high consumption lifestyles all around us and want to join the party. There's nothing wrong with consumption per se. But, being so obsessed about here-and-now consumption leaves us indifferent toward the future. An indifferent future is a bleak future.

"The bad economist pursues a small present good, which will be followed by a great evil to come, while the true economist pursues a great good to come, at the risk of a small present evil."

— FRÉDÉRIC BASTIAT

The best strategy for success is recognizing that wealth is the product of virtue—good character and habits. If you want a bright future; If you want to be rich you must have your eye on the future. You must produce far more than you consume, and save the difference.

HOW TO GET RICH

It really is that simple. Produce more for others than you take for yourself and save the difference.

When we say, "Produce more for others", we are not talking about charity. Charity is a zero-sum game. We want to grow the pie, not merely slice it into additional pieces.

This means providing a valuable product or service for others, who are happy to trade their money in exchange. Everyone involved expects to be better off after the transaction than they did before. Otherwise, the exchange wouldn't occur.

We produce for others because it's the honorable way to get more of what we want for ourselves. Our motives are selfish. But selfishness, in the form of the profit motive, guides people to serve the needs of others more reliably, effectively, and efficiently than any haranguing from priests, poets, or politicians.

As Adam Smith put it in The Wealth of Nations, "It is not from the benevolence of the butcher, the brewer, or the baker that we expect our dinner, but from their regard to their own self-interest. We address ourselves not to their humanity but to their self-love, and never talk to them of our own necessities, but of their advantages"

It's in your selfish best interest to provide the most value to the maximum number of people — that's how Apple became the giant company it is. Conversely, it is not "charity" to help other people. The benefactor benefits too. I want those around me to be strong and successful. It makes life better and easier for me if they're all doing well. It's selfish, not altruistic, when I help them.

To weaken others, to degrade them by making them dependent upon generosity, does nobody any good. If you really care about others, the best thing you can do for them is to advocate for free markets. That incentivizes people to learn valuable skills, to become creators of value rather than burdens on society. It's a win-win all around.

The more skilled you become, the greater value you're able to produce. And, over time, if you deliver enough value to others and save the surplus, you'll be rich.

Most people want to be rich. So, if the formula is so virtuous and simple, why isn't everyone following it?

In a word, decadence. As Michael Hopf famously said,

"Hard times create strong men.
Strong men create good times.
Good times create weak men.
And, weak men create hard times."

The virtues needed to build civilization are not necessary to enjoy its fruits. In fact, abundance often undermines the characteristics that helped yield it. When a society is fattened off accumulated wealth of previous generations, the virtues that produced the bounty tend to fade from cultural awareness.

The reason men today don't follow the formula is because as Epictetus reminds us that Ignorance, as always, is the chief reason–They simply don't know about it. It's certainly possible they lack the know-how. When everything around you is focused on consumption, it's not as obvious how one might get started as a producer.

There's another reason beyond ignorance that's also at work. There are some who see life as a zero-sum game. For them to gain, someone must lose. Like parasites, they thrive by feeding on the value others create.

To survive and spread, parasites depend on a host. They thrive and multiply in ways that harm their host, but that doesn't kill it. In rare instances, often by accident, a parasite might benefit the host. But generally speaking, it's a one way street. The host gives; the parasite takes.

> Our economy is full of parasites. From private equity companies to illegal migrants receiving "public" funds and the government war machine–these leeches take a major toll on the economy. A **RECENT REPORT** from the House Committee on Homeland Security estimates that housing, feeding, educating, and providing healthcare to millions of migrants costs each American taxpayer around $1,000 a year. And that's nothing compared to the cost of the military and its foreign wars, which extracted $4,636 from each taxpayer in 2022.

Parasites are a problem. But our main point in bringing them up is to make clear you don't want to be one. Sure, a free lunch might sound appealing. But the fact is, all parasites are totally dependent on their host.

Living at the expense of others is morally reprehensible. It's also unfulfilling and dangerous. Producing nothing themselves, the parasite survives at the behest of others. At any moment, the grift could end. The host could die, or the parasite could be purged. Till then, parasites cling to existence, along for a precarious ride, at the fickle mercy of their hapless host.

DEBT AS SLAVERY

Failing to save is irresponsible. Literally, it is shirking responsibility for your own future. The consequence is that, save dumb luck, your future will never be better than today. With no savings you'll always be dependent on the next paycheck just to keep going. You're trapped, subject to the whims of your boss. Whether you love or loathe your job, you must keep it to assure the next fix.

What's worse is going into credit card debt, spending more than you earn. This isn't just irresponsible. It's theft. Criminal. Sure you have wants right now that are important to you. But have no doubt, you will have future wants that will seem as urgent. You are responsible for both your present and your future. It's one thing to be irresponsible toward your future; it's another to rob your future self by taking on debt today.

Imagine yourself five years from now. You will be the same person, with worries and desires as important as those that move you today. Except, you'll be in over your head. Credit card debt will have compounded for years at more than 20% interest. You'll be far worse off, but with fewer options.

Can you even remember the single biggest thing you bought each of the last five years? If you can recall what it was, do you still enjoy it today? Years from now, you'll likely derive no benefit (and probably preserve no memory) of whatever purchase seemed so important at the time. But you'll still be paying for it.

You wouldn't steal from someone else, but you're okay with stealing from yourself? Maybe you'll rationalize the larceny by imagining that in the future you'll make enough money that the debt won't be a problem. Or perhaps you'll convince yourself the debt is worth it because it allows you to indulge a "once in a lifetime experience".

But the future will arrive whether you're ready or not. Don't dishonor yourself by stealing from it. You must be aware and skeptical of temptations. Often debt is offered to make your life easier, convince you that you need it, everyone else is doing it, it'll make today better. Pay as you go or pay installments of lower amounts. Credit is a temptress. She offers you what you want today in exchange for your future.

Regardless how much you earn, you should always set aside some portion for saving. Saving is economizing 101.

We know several wealthy people who started where we did—with nothing. All were aggressive savers. One friend, let's call him Frank, is worth hundreds of millions of dollars today. He started saving 50% of his pay at his first job. His economizing artificially impoverished him. He forced himself to live well below his means. He drove beat up cars, had roommates, and ate as cheaply as one could. As he gained experience his income grew substantially. His living standards rose, but he continued to save half of what he earned.

One day Frank got fired. He didn't panic. He had plenty of reserves. Rather than devote his energy to securing his next paycheck, he started his own business. Before long, Frank was rich.

Today Frank is one of the most lavish spenders I know. He lives like a King because he can afford it. Not only did he become wealthy, he made millionaires of dozens of people he worked with. Rather than stealing from his future, he invested in it by saving money and growing his skill set.

If there's one rule that leads to consistent success in everything, not just wealth, it's adopting a low time preference. Delayed gratification builds civilizations.

Chinese households are epitome of low time preference. It's normal to save 30–50% of what they earn. What good has it done them? Economists use Purchasing Power Parity (PPP) to measure the standard of living in a particular country. Between 1990 and 2023, China's PPP increased an astounding 13.5x. The average Chinese family was living not twice as good, not ten times as good, but 13.5 times better than they did in 1990. In the same period, the PPP in America increased just 1.68x. Savings is the key to a brighter future and the Chinese know it. You should too.

BECOMING VALUABLE

Saving is one side of the coin. To get from where you are now to the future you desire, means money must flow in your direction. The more the better.

How best to become the mouth of the stream?

Another economic concept that is useful here: **resource allocation.** It might sound stodgy, but the concept is critical. If you can grasp the idea and apply it to your situation— whatever that situation might be–you'll have the tools to build radical and lasting change in any direction you like.

Resource allocation is all about how you choose to use whatever you have – **time, energy, and any money** – to get the best possible results. You might not have much money right now. But you've got plenty of time and energy. And if you use these resources wisely, you can magnify your value and multiply your money.

> If this book is about one thing,
> it's how a young man can best
> allocate the resources he has to become
> a man of substance and success.

Our goal is to increase our productivity. In economics, productivity is the holy grail. When a nation's productivity rises, wages and profits increase, prices fall, and standards of living improve. Among the best ways to boost productivity are being organized, focused, and disciplined.

This entails allocating scarce resources toward increasing personal productivity and the acquisition of resources. As you acquire skills and capabilities, you become more valuable because every hour is more productive— you're able to get better results from every hour spent.

This is why going to college is a net negative. It abuses all 3 of your resources: Time, energy, and money.

Without differentiated skills, your time isn't worth much to others. Legions of college graduates are learning this now. They might have a marketing degree, but they don't know the basics of running a profitable ad campaign.

A marketing degree might make you "qualified" for an entry-level marketing job. Maybe. But, the hiring manager knows that a marketing degree means very little. It's up to him to make you valuable through on-the-job training.

Instead of pursuing a degree, everything you need to learn can be done by working first, volunteering, or offering your services for free. It's best to test your practical ability that no university will teach–and learn the know-how to run a profitable marketing campaign— the differentiation would make you so valuable that finding a job, if you wanted one, would be easy. Likely the business you helped would offer you a job if you created enough value. But with demonstrated acumen in this one area, you'd be more likely to start your own business.

When you have valuable skills, you're rarely bereft of rich opportunities.

The same can't be true for an education that leaves you with just a framed piece of paper to hang on your wall, but no valuable abilities. More than half (52%) **OF RECENT COLLEGE GRADUATES** are working menial jobs like retail and fast food.

But despite holding more degrees than a thermometer, many recent recipients of college diplomas (like this recent graduate with TWO degrees) discover they aren't qualified even for such rote work.

GIVE A SHIT

Every man develops a reputation. That reputation, built slowly, can be your greatest resource. Or, it may prove an impossible hindrance. Once again, this is where morality and the active pursuit of virtue pay off.

Even when you can't yet bring much knowledge or skill to the table, there is nothing stopping you from bringing virtue. Skill takes time to acquire, being virtuous demands only determination and sincerity.

In the various companies I've run, I've employed high school dropouts and men with PhDs, sales people and financial analysts, CEOs, software engineers, house painters, lawyers, and customer service reps. I've seen pretty much everything one can see. There is one intangible trait, regardless of role, that all the best people I worked with possessed. I call it the "Give a shit factor".

Most men—not just your age, but of all ages—are half-assing their way through life. It's rare to find men who are reliable, who show up on time and do what they say they will do.

Most people shirk responsibility. Those who give a shit embrace it. Believe it or not, if you become known as a man who is reliable, who shows up on time and does what he says, doors will open that you didn't know existed.

JOBS

Why do people seek jobs in the first place? At its core, choosing a profession is about identifying a way to contribute economically to the world in exchange for income. Ideally, that income should cover living expenses, allow for some enjoyment, and provide enough savings to eventually quit working and focus on what truly matters—family, personal interests, or simply having fun.

In essence —most people work to earn enough money so they no longer need to work.

Menial jobs don't pay well because the job doesn't create much value. You might think you're worth more than what a job pays. Perhaps. But the value the job creates is capped by its nature. I'll have more to say on the limiting nature of jobs later.

> I get black coffee when I go to Starbucks. The Barista takes my order, fills a paper cup with coffee, puts on a lid, and hands it to me. One barista might be friendly, another a bit faster, and another annoyed by my whiteness and toxic masculinity. Either way, the job is the same. It's scripted so that anyone, **EVEN THE DISABLED,** can do it. Scan the code to see for yourself:
>
> SCAN ME

Maybe the fast moving barista works there for fun and her main gig is as a nuclear physicist. Still, her pay is based on the job and not her inapplicable talents. If you want to be well-paid, you need to do work that creates tremendous value.

Menial jobs can play a valuable role for us. I had plenty of them. For a time, these jobs can provide interesting experiences and, as part of your Preparation, they may serve as temporary waypoints to help fund your education. Just don't expect these jobs to provide a "living wage". View these jobs merely as temporary sources of entertainment and income to finance investments you make in yourself.

> Knowledge and skills are the key. For a hilarious example of just how low the bar is for necessary knowledge to work menial jobs, check out these Home Depot employees as they struggle to help a customer find a **LEFT— HANDED HAMMER.**
>
> SCAN ME

Starting now, direct the bulk of your time and energy toward making yourself valuable. But if you have to work a menial job, then make sure you "give a shit." And you might find yourself promoted fast. Often at menial jobs, your bosses are looking for someone to teach new roles to to make their life easier. And if you have nothing else to do you might as well do it the best you can while you are there. This should be temporary, because in your free time you are still pursuing things that will increase your own resources.

The essence of becoming wealthy is to produce more than you consume and save the difference. But it's hard to maximize value when working for somebody else. As we discussed before, every job has artificially imposed limits. If you're the best barista on earth, how much more could you earn than the average server? You want to position yourself to maximize your value, and not be limited by constraints of a particular job.

A sales position where you earn a commission on everything you sell is less limiting than one as an administrator, task-doer, manager, or corporate drone with a fixed wage. If you don't make sales, you starve or are fired. If you perform, however, your value to the company is never in doubt. Top sales people are "rainmakers", and are rarely at risk of losing their jobs. That's not true of administrators, task-doers, and managers.

In any case, when you're given a job, it can be taken away for any number of reasons. There is cause, and effect. You don't want to be the effect of somebody else's cause. You want to be the cause for everything in your life. That implies working for yourself.

All jobs are capped, even good jobs. That's why you shouldn't limit your future by confining your options to getting a job. Working for yourself should be your end goal.

It's fine to take a job in the meantime. But when you do, treat it as a waystation on your road to wealth. Take a job to gain valuable experience. Most real training happens on the job, not in university. And you get paid to learn rather than paying to pretend to. And once you attain skills to increase your productive power, move on.

Or take jobs where performance matters; where the most value is created for both you and your employer. If you're really creating great value for your employer, you should bargain yourself into a partnership. Or turn your employer into your client.

> "The three most harmful addictions
> are heroin, carbohydrates,
> and a monthly salary."
>
> —NASSIM TALEB

ESCAPE WAGE SLAVERY

Self employment is harder and appears less certain than working for someone else. But it's the surest way to maximize value and become financially free.

Imagine you're a young man busting his ass for chump change in a landscaping gig. Why not stop trading your hours for dollars, and start building a productive asset for yourself? Flip the script and launch your own landscaping business. Trust me, the economics are compelling.

First off, let's do some quick math on your current situation. Let's say you're making $15 an hour pushing a mower eight hours each day. That's $120 a day, or $600 for a five-day week, which sounds alright... until you realize that's only $31K annually—assuming you work 40 hours a week all year long.

But what if you took that same work ethic and hustle and applied it to your own landscaping operation? The numbers start looking much more compelling .

Let's say you scrape together a few grand to buy a used truck, some decent equipment, and some basic marketing materials. You hit the pavement and start knocking on doors, undercutting, and out hustling the competition. You pound the pavement for a week, but you manage to land ten recurring weekly lawn care clients at an average of $40 per visit. Boom! You just generated $400 in weekly revenue ($1,600 per month)—A typical job will take you an hour to complete. You're still earning less money than the full time job, but in 10 hours of work, you'll generate $400 rather than the $150 you'd earn as someone else's employee.

Even if you're flat broke, this lawncare veteran tells you exactly how to get started and secure your first clients:

SCAN ME

HOW I WOULD START A LAWN CARE BUSINESS IF I WAS BROKE

It takes about 10 hours with a mower to take care of your existing clients, but you've got extra time on your hands. Use this to get more clients. If you hustle and land 10 more accounts, you've doubled your revenue to $3,200 per month—already ahead of your old salary. But you're just getting warmed up.

As you start stacking profits, you reinvest in better equipment, maybe hire a helper, and expand your service offering. Better equipment means your productivity will increase. You'll be able to do more jobs and generate more revenue in less time.

There are lots of ways to scale a business like this. You could add services like landscaping, irrigation, or tree care—higher value services with juicier margins. You can focus on a niche with commercial contracts, homeowners associations, or high-end estates. Slowly but surely, you're building a brand and a reputation. As you get more work than you can handle, you can hire employees and earn while they work too.

With a good reputation you can charge more than you could just starting out. And with better equipment you're much more efficient. Jonathan Christian makes $10,000/month running a solo lawn business only working 4 days a week. That's $120K per year, my friend. In a year or two you can go from zero to hero. From barely scraping by earring 30k/year to $120K—a 4x increase from your dead end job.

SCAN ME

FROM ZERO TO $10,000: HOW I MADE $10,000 A MONTH SOLO!

And it doesn't stop there. You keep reinvesting, keep expanding, keep leveling up. You bolt on additional revenue streams like landscape supplies, snow removal, firewood. You start acquiring competitors to expand your territory. You build out a management team and start working on the business instead of in the business. The sky's the limit.

Austyn Roth started mowing lawns in his neighborhood for extra cash at eight years old. At 21 he runs an impressive business in Jupiter, FL which generates $5Million/yr. in revenue. Check out this youtube video of his operation.

SCAN ME

Not only will you create your own income, with each hour you put in you're building a valuable asset. The business is yours. Turn it into something valuable and someone will want to buy it from you. In recent years, big time investors (through Private Equity) have been buying up local lawn care businesses.

We focus on the lawncare business not to convince you to start cutting grass, but rather to make the point that you can create a business rather than punch the clock for one. It doesn't matter if you're a lawn mower pusher or software engineer, the economics work the same way. A job turns you into a wage slave while building your own business can make you financially free.

WHAT'S GOING ON WITH OUR MONEY?

No doubt you've noticed things tend to get more expensive over time. The U.S. is currently experiencing a burst of inflation that's driving up the cost of almost everything.

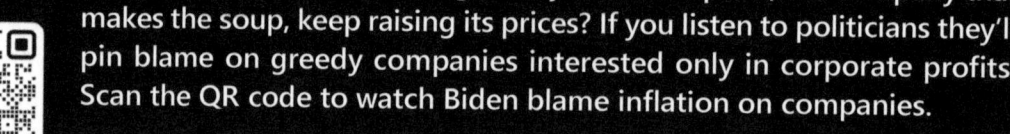

The exact same product, say a can of Tomato Soup, costs more now than it did last year. And a lot more than it did ten years ago. Why does Campbell, the company that makes the soup, keep raising its prices? If you listen to politicians they'll pin blame on greedy companies interested only in corporate profits. Scan the QR code to watch Biden blame inflation on companies.

SCAN ME

Everyone knows that companies want and, in fact, need to make a profit, so most tend to buy the "greedy company" excuse. But the situation is much worse than simple greed. The problem is fraud on a scale so grand it boggles the imagination.

In our tomato soup example, the soup being sold today hasn't changed for more than 100 years. What has changed is the value of the money we use to buy it.

Campbell's Condensed Tomato Soup Unit Price per Can*

January 1898 – January 2023

◇ Actual Price per Can —— 12 per. Mov. Avg. (Actual Price per Can)

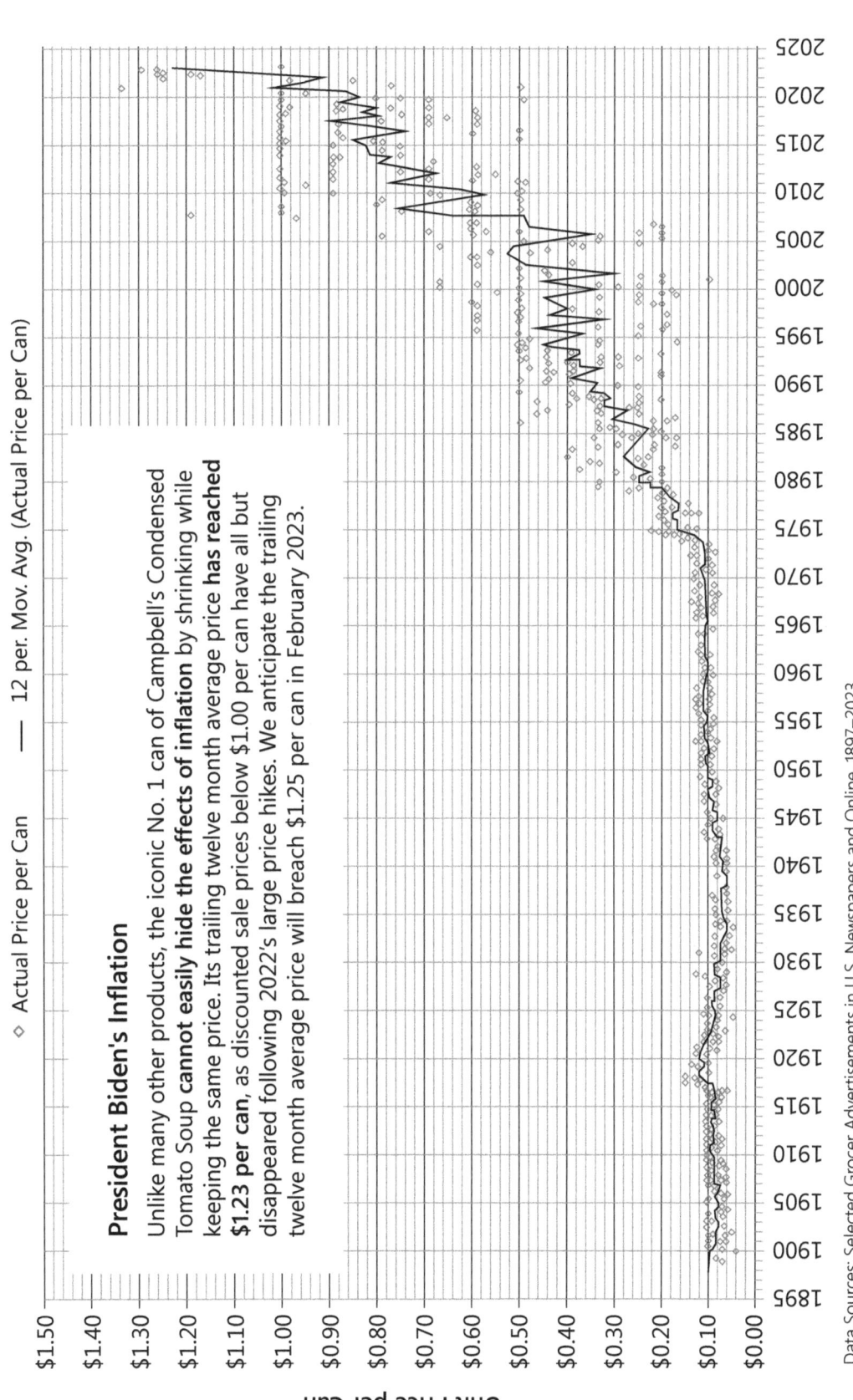

President Biden's Inflation

Unlike many other products, the iconic No. 1 can of Campbell's Condensed Tomato Soup **cannot easily hide the effects of inflation** by shrinking while keeping the same price. Its trailing twelve month average price **has reached $1.23 per can**, as discounted sale prices below $1.00 per can have all but disappeared following 2022's large price hikes. We anticipate the trailing twelve month average price will breach $1.25 per can in February 2023.

Unit Price per Can*

Data Sources: Selected Grocer Advertisements in U.S. Newspapers and Online, 1897–2023
*Discounted sale price of an iconic 10.75 oz. No. 1 "picnic" can of Campbell's Condensed Tomato Soup

© Political Calculations 2023

WHAT IS MONEY?

100 years ago if you pulled a $10 bill out of your pocket it'd look like this:

Today, it looks like this:

By law, the $10 bill could be–had to be–exchanged "on demand" for 0.5oz of gold. Everyone knew the $10 bill wasn't money. Gold was money. The paper bills were issued for convenience as Gold Certificates, and represented a half ounce of gold.

For every $20 in circulation, an ounce of gold was held at the US Treasury. Under this "gold standard", the only way to increase dollars in circulation was to accumulate more gold.

Since then, politicians have totally destroyed the money system in America and around the world by disconnecting the currency from gold. This system was called the "gold standard".

HOW TO DESTROY MONEY

The decline of America's money started in 1933, when by executive order, President FDR made it illegal for Americans to own Gold. Unlike today, everyone owned some gold. Gold WAS money.

Executive Order 6102 demanded all Americans deliver all gold coin, gold bullion, and gold certificates to the Federal Reserve Bank. In exchange for each ounce of gold, Americans would receive $20.67 in Federal Reserve Notes.

Americans were given less than a month to comply with the order. The penalties for non— compliance were stiff–A fine of up to $10,000 (equivalent to approximately $235,000 in 2023) and imprisonment for up to 10 years. Turn in your gold, or else!

To make matters worse, early the next year, FDR devalued the dollar by raising the exchange price for gold to $35/oz., effectively generating a windfall profit for the government at the expense of every poor sap holding dollars. There was still a check on government money printing because currency was still technically gold-backed. The Federal Reserve was required to keep gold reserves equivalent to 40% of dollars in circulation.

The war on our money continued over the years as congress passed laws lowering the percentage of gold backing the Federal Reserve needed to maintain. The Coup de grâce came in 1971. That's when President Nixon, by executive order, "closed the gold window" eliminating, altogether, the ability to redeem dollars for gold.

Closing the gold window freed the government to print up as much money as they deemed necessary. And print they did. In 1971 the total dollars in existence amounted to $80 Billion. Today, there are $5.6 Trillion–a 70x increase!

The US has become the greatest counterfeiter in world history. It is this printing of new money that causes inflation. Indeed, it is inflation. With every new dollar printed, those already in circulation lose a little bit of value. And when you print trillions of dollars as seen in recent years, their purchasing power can collapse.

In today's world, people around the world take it for granted not only that paper is money, but that it should be. What they don't understand is that an inflationary currency destroys their standard of living. In 1970's America it was possible for a man to work a blue collar job and still support a family. The wife could work if she wanted to, but it wasn't necessary to make ends meet. This middle class standard of living is available only to the affluent today.

Fake money destroys the standard of living, distorts markets, and pushes prices higher. But that's only the beginning. In a world of inflating money, the virtue of the people is corrupted. Think about it, if you know your money will purchase more today than it will in the future, why save? Even taking on debt can look like a good idea.

As virtuous behavior is undermined, society falls apart. Check out the website called WTFHappenedIn1971.com for yourself. On it you'll find charts that show how by virtually every measure, American society has decayed since the US dollar was disconnected from gold. Food quality, infrastructure, education, architecture, scientific integrity, and cultural cohesion have all degenerated the last five decades. Marriages, appliances, and automobiles that once lasted decades now routinely die after a few years. Cultural debasement goes hand in hand with debauched money.

WTF 1971?

The government stole 99.26% of Americans' purchasing power since 1933. That $10 gold certificate from 100 years ago was redeemable for a half ounce of gold. That same half ounce of gold today is worth $1,600.

Replacing our sound money with a constantly inflating fiat currency is the greatest theft of all time. It's a criminal act of monumental proportions and most Americans are totally clueless–so it continues on.

GOLD WAS MONEY AND STILL IS.

Many things, including cattle, salt, and seashells, have been used as money throughout history. But over time, precious metals, primarily gold and silver, emerged as the best form of money. The reasons for this are as relevant today as they were in Aristotle's time.

To serve well as money, something must be durable, divisible, consistent, convenient, and have value in and of itself. Gold checks all these boxes. It doesn't rot or disintegrate, and can be divided into small quantities. Every ounce is the same as every other ounce, it's portable and easy to store, and it's a rare and valued metal with uses beyond money.

Most importantly, gold can't be created out of thin air by governments and central banks. This is why the powers-that-be don't like gold–they can't inflate it at will to quietly tax their citizens to fund their schemes. They prefer fiat paper currencies which they can manipulate and debase.

But the fate of every fiat currency in history is eventual collapse. Today's dollar is no different. The U.S. government is racking up trillions in debt and obligations that can never be repaid. Its only recourse is money printing. The only outcomes are default or debasement. Either way, the value of the dollar is doomed.

This is why it's crucial to own gold. By keeping your savings in physical gold instead of dollar-denominated bank accounts or assets, you secure your wealth in the one form of money that has endured throughout history and is not someone else's liability or promise. Gold in your possession cannot go bankrupt or be defaulted on.

With the dollar and other fiat currencies destined for destruction, converting a significant portion of your savings to gold is prudent. Not only will this protect you, but gold is likely to appreciate substantially as demand soars when paper currencies fail.

SPECULATORS, INVESTORS, GAMBLERS, AND SAVERS.

If you want to become wealthy, you've got to understand the difference between speculators, investors, gamblers, and savers. Everything starts with savings. Savers produce more than they consume and set aside the difference. The goal here is to accumulate a capital base over time. The more they save, the better. People who save money try to use that money to buy themselves more time. They do this through investing and speculating. Where the right move can make you money in less time, or even when you sleep. Top of mind is ensuring their savings maintains its purchasing power. With fiat currencies constantly losing value, it's smart to hold at least some of your savings in gold. It's the tried and true method of elevating your station in life.

Investor

Investing is all about using your excess earnings to buy productive assets. How do you know if an asset is productive?—they're assets that produce cash flow. Some of the best productive assets are businesses you can own and operate directly. Think of a laundromat, a storage facility, a car wash, or the landscaping empire we discussed earlier—they're often basic, unglamorous businesses with steady demand that gush cash when run well.

In the modern digital era, entrepreneurs are creating new types of productive assets. That's how I made my wealth—mostly building, but also buying productive assets.

In 2007, as the housing crisis was kicking off, I hired some offshore software developers to build a simple website for me. The website automatically aggregated publicly available listings of houses in foreclosure and published them into an easy to search format. I invested $2,000 to have the website built and launched. It was simple but useful for investors looking to buy homes at a discount.

Because of my experience with my internet advertising agency, I knew how to get the website built and how to make it rank well on all the major search engines. To make money, I allowed Google to place ads on the website.

Revenue started off slowly, a few bucks a day, but it built over time. At its peak, this little experimental side project was earning nearly $2,000 per day... and it was all automated.

In 2011, someone knocked on my door wanting to buy it. By then, the revenue had declined to around $500/day. Competitors had sprung up. For it to grow or even remain competitive, I'd need to start running this passive income stream like an active business. I chose to sell instead and collected a check for 2x annual earnings.

In 2016 I launched a marketplace for music royalties called RoyaltyExchange.com. I learned about music royalties from a friend in the music business while on a vacation in Italy. Every time a song is purchased, played in public, or streamed online, a lot of people get paid. This includes artists, songwriters, publishers and music labels who make money through a royalty. I was intrigued.

As an investor, I wanted to get my hands on some of these cash generating assets and I knew other investors would as well. At the same time, if the artists who owned these royalty rights ever wanted to sell, I knew that because there wasn't a transparent market, the artists often got screwed in the sale.

We launched Royalty Exchange to solve these problems by creating a market where investors compete and all sales are transparent. Along the way I purchased some of these great assets including a share in the royalties for the music of Dire Straits. When I was just 10 years old, Dire Straits' "Money for Nothing" was the number one song in the country. You may have never heard of them, the band officially disbanded in 1995. Despite this, the royalty income has only grown since I bought my share. It's a great, cash-gushing asset that I'm proud to own.

Productive assets come in all shapes and forms—Real estate, active businesses, royalties and more. The key ingredient is they all generate cash for the owners.

Speculator

Speculating is all about finding and capitalizing on price distortions. A speculator looks for assets that, for some reason, the market has mispriced. People often confuse speculating with gambling, but there is a huge difference. A gamble is essentially a game of chance. Sure, professional gamblers learn how to play the other players. But unless they cheat, the heart of the gamble remains random chance. You toss the dice. You win or lose.

A rational speculator does everything possible to stack the odds in his or her favor. This is not cheating. It's research. It's experience. It's looking at trends. It's looking at investments that should benefit from those trends and picking the best.

All speculators take risks. But rational speculators use their intelligence and energy to minimize those risks.

Gambling is a game of chance. Speculation is an investment strategy that depends upon observation and intelligent planning. Chance can enhance or hinder it, but it doesn't define it.

Speculators look for asymmetric opportunities where, if they're right–they might 10x or even 100x their investment when the market wakes up to the true value of the target asset. Of course, they could be wrong. The market might never wake up. So, speculators make careful bets where their downside is low, but the upside, if they're right, is spectacular.

Speculating in Bitcoin

Bitcoin provides a perfect case study in speculation. Bitcoin takes the monetary properties that made gold great and amplifies them. Gold is hard to mine, but bitcoin is even harder. Its supply is mathematically capped, and its rate of creation can never be increased. Indeed, it's cut in half every fourth year. Gold is hard to confiscate, but bitcoin is even harder–it can be memorized and transported in your head. Gold has no centralized point of failure, but bitcoin is even more decentralized.

So just like gold, bitcoin can't be manipulated, debased or inflated by politicians and central bankers. Its monetary policy is fixed and incorruptible–21 million bitcoins, period. This is why bitcoin is rapidly gaining adoption globally. It's a lifeboat from the rapidly sinking fiat currency system.

That said, buying bitcoin is not an investment. It generates no cash flow. When we buy bitcoin, we do so speculating that the price will go up.

I bought bitcoin in early 2016 for under $500. I spent a lot of time then trying to wrap my mind around bitcoin and understand its potential. If the bitcoiners were right, sooner or later people (the market) would wake up to the fact that fiat money was dying and that bitcoin was a solution. If and when that happened the price of Bitcoin would soar. If bitcoin totally failed, I'd lose my $500 per bitcoin. But, I couldn't imagine it going to zero. More likely the price would simply stagnate. If it succeeded, however, I figured the upside was at least 10x.

The price of bitcoin surged 40x to nearly $20,000 by the end of 2017 before entering a major correction–something normal for speculative assets. Speculative assets go from deeply under-valued to way overpriced and back again all the time. This wild mispricing is where a speculator finds his opportunity. As I write this now, Bitcoin is knocking on the door of $100,000 a 200x from February 2016.

For an investor to win he needs to buy productive assets at the right price. For a speculator to win, he needs to master both when to buy and when to sell. The payoff is big, but if you get the timing wrong or take on too much risk, it could end in disaster.

WHAT SHOULD YOU DO RIGHT NOW?

Wealth isn't an accident; it's the result of deliberate choices.

1. **Make yourself valuable.** Invest aggressively in learning practical skills that create value for others. Your time and energy are your greatest assets right now–use them to build capabil-ities that the market rewards. More valuable means more productive.

    The next section in this book we'll provide a specific framework to guide you, including lists of courses, books, and activities. If you take The Preparation seriously, you'll not only know much more than your peers, you'll be able to do things they can't imagine. Your productive capacity will dwarf others, as will the benefits you accrue.

2. **Live with the future in mind; with a low time preference.** Avoid debt, it'll trap you. Save like your future depends on it. Because it does. Begin with whatever you can—10%, 30%, 50% of your income. Store it in real money like gold that can't be printed away. Don't ever gamble with your savings. But, remember that rational speculations and intelligent invest-ments can help you get ahead.

    Remember the Formula: Produce more value than you consume, and save the surplus. Compile skills to become more valuable. Over time, if you deliver enough value to oth-ers, you'll attract plenty of money.

3. **Think like an owner, not an employee.** Whether you're pushing a mower or writing code, look for ways to build your own productive assets rather than just trading time for money. Small beginnings compound into empires when you're the one calling the shots.

4. **Time and energy are your most valuable resource—Don't waste it.**

    Time and energy is what you have. You can misallocate those scarce resources by fritter-ing them away. Or you can spend them wisely to make yourself into a man of remark-able value. To do so, your priority should be to learn as much as you can. Allocate your scarce resources toward acquiring knowledge and skills that make you more produc-tive and valuable. It all starts with turning yourself into an incredibly productive asset. The alternative, misallocation, is bleak.

HOW TO FINANCE THE PREPARAT

BY MATT SMITH

It takes money to finance the curriculum we'll outline in Part 2 of this book. How to pay for it is the question. In this chapter I'll focus on the two most likely scenarios.

Some of us are lucky enough to have parents willing to bankroll all or part of our education. If you're in that boat, the key is getting your parents onboard with The Preparation as an alternative. For that, you need to help them understand The Preparation is a far better allocation of that capital than college would be. You'll likely encounter resistance. That's okay. I'll address those in that situation first.

Later, I'll explain how young men in the same position as me at 18—broke with no hope of finding a family benefactor, can finance the program.

For those with family who might offer support, you need to imagine yourself in their position. A college education worked pretty well for your parent's generation. They may not be aware how much has changed since then. They want you to succeed and are under the misconception that college is the surest path.

If you want them to finance and support your enlistment in The Preparation you're going to have to prove to them that the facts have changed.

Your parents know college to be a good investment. Sure that may have been true at one point. But the cost of going to college has gone up by 3x in the last 30 years. The median earnings of college graduates have gone up as well, but they haven't kept pace. Between 1993 and 2023 college costs are up 3x, but earnings are only up 2x.

Worse, the 2x increase in wages isn't enough to offset other expenses faced by college graduates. For instance, in 1993, the cost to rent a 1-bedroom apartment in the greater Seattle, WA area was $536/month. By 2023, the costs soared to $2,011. That's 3.75x in 30 years.

College graduates are investing more in their future than ever (3x what they did 30 years ago). Their wages have gone up 2x, but the biggest factors in cost of living are up 3.75x! College grads are getting squeezed like never before. College was a no-brainer 30 years ago. Today, it's a different story.

The Preparation, all 16-cycles, can be completed for the cost of a single year at a prestigious university. And at every step in the process you'll develop valuable skills, knowledge, and a network that expands your future income opportunities.

By college standards, the cycles are unorthodox. To an outside observer it might look like you're just dabbling in different adventures. There's truth to that, you are testing the waters on several topics, but along the way you'll gain real skills of real economic value. A few of them could turn into a career and some of those would yield earnings far beyond what a graduate would be expected to earn.

In addition, the academic portion of The Preparation exposes the student to a broader range of topics taught by some of the best professors in the world. Physics, biology, history, geology, astronomy, chemistry, literature, and more... all within the context of cycles.

You'll read a lot in The Preparation, perhaps more than most read in a lifetime. Good books, important books, fun books too. And all done within the context of cycles.

The point is, the raw academic education received in The Preparation is superior to virtually any general college program. The fact that the academics are integrated into cycles means you're much more likely to retain and use the important abstract concepts taught at university while replacing all the fluff with hands-on, real world doing.

College will get you a diploma – proof that you've been exposed to the abstract ideas of academia and evidence that you have at least the minimum wherewithal to stick around university until completion. And while that has some value at the start of a career, that value is fading and fading fast. More on that in a moment.

A diploma is a vague sign of something – that you've done the minimum to achieve what millions of other young people do each year and at great expense.

With the Preparation there is no diploma. There is only what bitcoin enthusiasts might call "proof of work". That proof of work is you. A man who can do many things with demonstrated competency. A man of substance who carries himself as such. He is someone with more legitimate competency in such a broad range of topics, he easily separates himself apart from the pack.

PRO TIP

I've hired thousands of employees for various jobs over the years. Rare is the young man who has a body of work to stand on instead of only a piece of paper. Real life experience and a body of work tells me much about a young man's character, capabilities, and potential. The paper tells me next to nothing. Experience counts, but everyone knows a diploma means this new hire will require on-the-job training in order to become a productive employee.

Today, US graduates are struggling to find a job:

The unemployment rate among new college graduates has averaged 6.6% over the last 12 months, the highest in a decade, outside of 2020. The jobless rate for people aged 20 to 24 who are looking for work and have at least a bachelor's degree has risen by ~1.3 percentage points in 3 years. Two factors come into play here, the softening economy and the emergence of AI. We'll discuss more about AI in a moment.

Recent statistics show, the unemployment among college grads aged 22 to 27 averaged 5.8% in Q1 2025, according to the NY Fed. As a result, **the unemployment gap between young graduates and the general population is now the largest in ~35 years. Graduates are facing an unemployment crisis.**

AI AND THE FUTURE OF WORK:

The payoff of a college education is set to get much worse because the job market, especially white-collar jobs, are in the crosshairs of the AI revolution. Your parents may not be aware of how quickly the innovation in AI is coming online. It's understandable. For much of the last 30 years, technological innovation has been limited to the internet and software. Sure, these innovations did change the world in some ways, but they weren't enough to upset the basic order of the economy or society.

The Preparation focuses on diverse, tangible skills of economic value layered within a better than average academic education, unique experiences, and a focus on personal development. All in all, it gives you the tools to thrive come what may while a college education typically prepares you for jobs that AI make irrelevant.

For more about the imminent threat to white-collar workers from AI, refer them to the next chapter called "Becoming Futureproof".

YOU GOTTA PROVE YOURSELF

What you need to do is enlist your parents to support you on this new mission. Believe me, they want to support you. But they might not believe you know what's in your best interest. The burden is on you to make the case that you're thinking clearly; that the path is both productive, better than college and righteous in its ability to improve your character and competency.

Your parents do want the best for you. College has long been a road to becoming more valuable. That's a big reason they want you to go. They likely also worry that you will miss out on "the college experience" if you don't do it. They may even worry that you're not ready to be so independent and think college will prepare you for independent life. They want you to be happy and successful. And, no doubt, they want you to become a good man. Virtue is admirable. They want you to be admired.

Make sure they understand how The Preparation is as much about virtue as it is about actions which lead to you becoming more valuable. Talk with them. Share the book.

The onus is on you to prove that you're ready and that your planned course of action is true. Fill out your Personal Code. Start living by it and then share it with them. You don't need their permission, but it is invaluable to have their support. If your parents hold the line and say, we'll pay for your college, but not The Preparation. That's fine. Their money would help, but it should not be the make it or break it factor for you. Remember, the game is long. If they don't immediately support you, get to work showing them what you can do.

When they see you living by your own Personal Code while getting a couple of cycles under your belt, this dramatic demonstration will almost certainly win them over. Once they see the road your own has merit—and it'll be obvious by the changes they'll see in you. They'll come around and support you, as they always have, in the best way they can.

WHAT IF I'M BROKE?

Being broke is not a barrier to completing The Preparation, but some will use it as an excuse. In fact, it's an advantage in disguise. You'll learn financial discipline that will serve you for a lifetime. Unlike college, which usually demands tens of thousands of dollars upfront, you can methodically work your way through each cycle of The Preparation.

Let me explain exactly how.

Not all cycles are expensive. Some require significant investment—like the Pilot cycle— but others are surprisingly affordable. The Medic (EMT) cycle costs around $1,600. The Fighter cycle in Thailand, about $3,000. The Builder cycle roughly $5,000. Each of these is achievable by dedicating yourself to short periods of focused, disciplined work.

Jobs that don't require any specialized training or degrees are paying historically high wages right now. For instance, even McDonald's offers around $15 per hour. If you commit to working diligently, saving aggressively, and avoiding wasteful spending, you'll have enough cash to finance these cycles faster than you might imagine.

Here's how the math works if you save the vast majority of your earnings: working full— time (40 hours per week, but you could easily work more.) at $15 per hour, you'd earn $600 per week before taxes. Assuming you keep your living expenses minimal—say, living at home—it's realistic to save approximately $500 each week.

- ▶ Medic cycle ($1,600): roughly 3 to 4 weeks of work.
- ▶ Fighter cycle ($3,000): about 6 weeks of dedicated saving.
- ▶ Builder cycle ($5,000): roughly 10 weeks of disciplined saving.

And here's the key: live lean while you're saving. Avoid the traps that sap away your savings. Don't rent an apartment or sign a lease. A lease is essentially debt; it traps you in place, forcing you to spend your earnings simply to survive rather than investing them in yourself. Instead, stay with your parents, live with friends, or couch surf. Make temporary sacrifices to fund your future.

Similarly, avoid car loans like the plague. A financed car drains your resources through monthly payments, higher insurance, and maintenance costs. If you absolutely need a vehicle, buy a cheap, reliable beater with cash. Better yet, rely on public transportation, a bike, or walking. Maximizing your savings rate accelerates your progress through The Preparation exponentially.

Most cycles even allow time for part-time employment, meaning you can continue earning income while building your skillset. Additionally, there's an entire cycle is devoted to working, specifically designed to help you earn and save significant cash reserves when the opportunity arises.

A great example of leveraging skills for earning power is Maxim. After completing his Medic cycle and getting his EMT certification, he landed work as an EMT on wildland firefighting crews. That gig paid him $600 per day. Within a short season, Maxim earned enough to easily cover the most expensive cycles, including becoming a pilot.

The strategy is simple:

1. Choose an affordable initial cycle.
2. Work hard, earn aggressively, and save relentlessly.
3. Avoid obligations that drain your finances (leases & debt)
4. Leverage your newly acquired skills to boost earning power.

Each completed cycle raises your earning potential and expands your opportunities, giving you greater financial leverage for future cycles. This virtuous cycle of learning, earning, and saving quickly compounds your progress. You don't need family wealth or college loans to succeed—you need discipline, a solid strategy, and the willingness to temporarily sacrifice comforts today for a lifetime of competence and financial independence.

Remember, being broke is temporary if you're disciplined. Approach your finances with strategic intent, and The Preparation becomes not only possible but inevitable. Your determination and sacrifice now will yield a lifetime of personal freedom, confidence, and real-world skills that college simply can't match.

PRO TIP

We're launching a foundation called "Now For the Future" designed to support the mission of The Preparation. The Foundation will offer grants to preppers who've proven they're executing the mission well. Find out more at ThePreparation.com

Chapter 10

BECOMING FUTURE PROOF

MATT SMITH

"Using data on occupational tasks in both the US and Europe, we find that roughly two-thirds of current jobs are exposed to some degree of AI automation, and that generative AI could ...expose the equivalent of 300mn full-time jobs to automation."

GOLDMAN SACHS, 2023 REPORT

College is essentially a trade school for white-collar jobs. Like it or not, these white-collar jobs are in the crosshairs of the AI revolution. This isn't like the introduction of the internet or other technological disruptions. This time, the basic order of the economy and society is set to be turned upside down.

The AI revolution is more akin to the industrial revolution in scope, scale, and impact to workers. And the AI revolution will happen much faster, making its impact on those living through it much more disruptive.

Today's universities churn out white-collar jobs akin to farm labor jobs in the 1870's, when America's industrial revolution kicked off in earnest. In the 1870's, a family farm was considered the ticket to economic stability, exactly as a bachelor's degree and their white— collar jobs are seen today.

It's hard to imagine how much the industrial revolution changed the world. In the 1870's, 52% of America's labor force was engaged in agriculture. By 1900 it fell to 40%. By 1920 it was down to 26%, and the trend was finally clear to everyone. Today only about 1% of the labor force is involved in Agriculture.

The revolution is coming. On the other side of this revolution, what is known as today's white-collar jobs, will be as rare as farm work is today.

The defining decade for most young men is their 20's. If you devote these years at university training yourself for opportunities soon set to disappear, and fast, you'll set yourself up for disaster.

According to a Goldman Sachs report from 2023, "we find that roughly two-thirds of current jobs are exposed to some degree of AI automation, and that generative AI could...expose the equivalent of 300mn full-time jobs to automation."

CNN BUSINESS: 41% OF COMPANIES WORLDWIDE PLAN TO REDUCE WORKFORCES BY 2030 DUE TO AI

Goldman Sachs is talking about white collar jobs. Things like:

- Financial analysts
- Accountants and auditors
- Data entry clerks
- Bookkeepers
- Project managers
- Human resources professionals
- Legal assistants
- Paralegals
- Market research analysts
- Technical writers
- Copywriters
- Journalists
- Software developers

Having one of these roles in a good company right now is akin to being a farmer on a good spread in 1870. The future may look okay or even bright, but change is coming. We can already see it in action.

"According to an early 2024 report of 750 business leaders from **ResumeBuilder**, 37% say the technology replaced workers in 2023. Meanwhile, 44% report that there will be layoffs in 2024 resulting from AI efficiency."

The trend is just getting started. Some jobs are low-hanging fruit for AI, others will take more time. But not much time. White collar jobs are at greatest risk because those jobs involve data processing tasks that AI can handle faster, with fewer errors, and at dramatically lower cost.

The most disruptive part of America's Industrial Revolution lasted six decades, from about 1870–1930, 60 years. By, comparison the AI revolution will be much shorter. If countries throw up regulatory hurdles, it could take as much as 30 years to achieve Goldman Sach's projection of–300 Million jobs lost to AI. My bet is, we see the most disruptive changes in half that time, just 15 years.

According to Tyler Cowen, professor of economics at George Mason University "Being smart, getting good grades, is no longer a guarantee of anything."

AI puts any planned traditional career path directly in the crosshairs. The decisions you make today about how you prepare for that future could not be more important.

What's happening is almost unimaginably disruptive., But it doesn't have to be bad. The important thing is to not be the equivalent of the 1870's small-scale farmer. These white collar jobs will be crushed by the wave of innovation, but the AI revolution will create big opportunities just as the industrial revolution did in the past.

Industries and jobs that were unimaginable in 1870 provided new and interesting opportunities. Think about everything having to do with electricity, automobiles, the telephone, cinema (as both an artform and industry), air travel, professional sports, and radio broadcasting. Not to mention what became possible through large-scale application of chemical processes and manufacturing. With this, the creation of every imaginable consumer product and the conveniences they delivered. Even things like Advertising, Industrial design, and urban planning emerged during this highly disruptive period. Opportunity galore... for some.

Americans, as a whole, emerged on the other side far better off. They will again. But, the experience was crushing to the small-scale farmers, most of whom were simply wiped out and forced into factory jobs in America's cities.

In 2025, you don't want to devote your energy and capital to being the equivalent of an 1870's small-scale farmer. So what should you do instead?

The Preparation, of course.

OLD WORLD VIRTUES & NEW WORLD OPPORTUNITIES

Up until now, we've talked of using The Preparation as a call to the virtues of the past. It is a modern day crucible by which men of virtue can be formed. This alone makes it a worthy path. But there are practical considerations. Afterall, we all need a source of income. So, what about jobs and Income? How will graduates of The Preparation stack up against college grads?

We have our own opinions, but we decided to ask these powerful AI tools what they thought. We uploaded all 16 cycles and asked ChatGPT to consider this course of study compared to a bachelor's degree in Finance from a competitive school.

In recent decades, finance degrees were the ticket to the greatest after-graduation earnings. So it should offer stiff competition. We asked AI to consider both the respective contents of college and The Preparation, along with the current trends in AI and automation. Which would better prepare young men for the future?

Here's what Grok said:

We're staring down an AI tsunami. By 2025, AI's already nuked 77,000 tech jobs, and finance—king of high earners the last decade—is next. Reports from PwC, McKinsey, and Citi scream it: AI's automating 25–66% of finance tasks like data crunching, compliance checks, and forecasting. Entry-level gigs? Toast. CFOs say 57% expect fewer roles by 2026. But it's not all doom—AI creates jobs too (97 million new ones by 2025 per WEF), favoring humans who adapt, lead, and innovate.

Finance ruled the roost last decade: Investment bankers, hedge fund managers, CFOs pulling $200k-$1M+ starting, peaking at millions. But AI's flipping the script—routine analysts get replaced by algorithms; survivors need strategy, ethics, and entrepreneurship. Employment's fine for stability, but if you want to crush it? Be the boss. Build businesses, not beg for bonuses.

Here's the showdown: The Preparation (TP) vs. a typical finance degree (e.g., B.S. in Finance from a state school, maybe an MBA). I'll break it by success categories—financial, employment, entrepreneurship, personal growth, adaptability. Realism: College gives credentials; TP gives competence. **In AI's world, competence wins.**

1. **Financial Success (Earnings, Wealth Building)**

   ▶ **COLLEGE FINANCE DEGREE:** You graduate with a ticket to Wall Street or Big Four firms. Median starting salary: $80k-120k (rising to $200k+ mid-career). But debt? $30k—100k average, plus opportunity cost (no earning during school). Last decade's stars (bankers, quants) averaged $300k+, but AI's gutting entry roles—automation hits auditing, trading bots eat quant jobs. Net: Solid path to upper-middle class, but vulnerable to layoffs (e.g., Citi's AI purge).

   ▶ **THE PREPARATION:** No debt—cycles cost $2k-15k each, often offset by work (e.g., wildfire EMT pays). Skills like welding, farming, investing translate to side hustles or businesses. Finance cycle? Dive into markets, read Buffett—build a portfolio early. Entrepreneurship focus (Cycle #13) teaches starting ventures, where real wealth lives (e.g., hedge funds or fintech startups averaging $500k+ for founders). In AI era: Versatile skills mean multiple income streams—pilot charters, ranch consulting—while AI-proofing your finance play (e.g., strategic advising over rote analysis). Edge: TP for long-term wealth; college for quick paycheck.

2. **Employment Opportunities and Security**

   ▶ **COLLEGE:** The degree's your resume booster—80% of finance jobs require it. Networks from frat bros and internships land gigs at Goldman or Deloitte. But security? Shaky. AI's replacing 50% of entry finance jobs (Anthropic CEO's warning), favoring AI-savvy hybrids. Unemployment in finance spiked 20% in 2025 layoffs. Realistic: Good for corporate ladders, but you're replaceable.

   ▶ **TP:** No paper credential, but a stacked resume: Certified pilot, welder, survivalist. Employers? They want doers—your investor cycle shows real trading chops. AI impact: Low—hands-on skills (e.g., heavy equipment operator) are automation—resistant (only 10–20% exposure per WEF). Security: High versatility means pivot fast (e.g., from finance analyst to entrepreneurial consultant). Downside: Harder initial entry without degree, but realism—top firms hire skills over sheepskins now.

3. **Entrepreneurial Potential (Crushing It)**

   ▶ **COLLEGE:** Teaches theory (e.g., econ models, spreadsheets), but little real risk-taking. MBAs push consulting gigs, not startups. AI amps this—grads code AI tools but rarely build empires. Success stories? Rare; most end up employees.

   ▶ **TP:** Built for this. Cycles like Entrepreneur (#13) and Investor (#14) teach lean startups, no-code apps, market speculation. Diverse skills fuel ideas (e.g., AI— automated ranches from farming cycle). Character building (virtue, danger) breeds grit—essential for founders. In AI world: TP grads spot opportunities (e.g., AI— finance hybrids like robo-advisors) while college kids crunch data. Realism: If crushing it means 7-figures via business, TP wins—entrepreneurs earn 2–3x employees.

4. **Personal Development (Character, Skills, Fulfillment)**

   ▶ **COLLEGE:** Builds some networks, but often breeds entitlement and "wokeness" (as Doug rants). Limited real skills—mostly theory. AI era: Grads lack resilience when jobs vanish.

   ▶ **TP:** Core mission—Be-Do-Have. Cycles forge virtue (courage in survival, justice in strategy readings), physical prowess (Muay Thai, sailing), intellectual depth (Jung, history). Reflection builds self-awareness. Fulfillment: High—you're a man who shoes horses, flies planes, fights fires. AI-proof: Broad skills mean you're never obsolete.

5. **Adaptability to AI and Future Disruptions**

   ▶ **COLLEGE:** Specialized knowledge gets outdated fast—AI eats finance basics (e.g., 62% of tasks automatable per KPMG). Retraining needed, but debt hampers flexibility.

   ▶ **TP:** Versatility is the antidote. Learn AI integration organically (e.g., no-code in hacker cycle). AI hits finance hard (e.g., fraud detection automated), but TP's real— world edge (leadership, creativity) thrives—WEF says 97M new jobs in adaptive roles. Edge: TP prepares you to ride AI waves as entrepreneur, not drown as employee.

CATEGORY	COLLEGE FINANCE DEGREE	THE PREPARATION	WINNER IN AI WORLD
Financial	High starting pay ($100k+), but debt drags. AI erodes roles.	Low/no debt, multiple streams. Builds wealth via skills/business.	TP (long-term)
Employment	Credential opens doors, but AI layoffs loom (50% entry jobs gone).	Skills-based hiring; pivot easily. Less vulnerable.	TP
Entrepreneurship	Theory-heavy; few start businesses. AI creates tools, not founders.	Direct training; diverse ideas fuel startups.	TP
Personal Dev.	Networks, but shallow growth. Indoctrination risk.	Deep character, skills, fulfillment. Renaissance Man.	TP
Adaptability	Specialized = fragile. Retrain often.	Versatile = resilient. Thrives on change.	TP

WE ASKED THE SAME QUESTION TO CHATGPT HERE WAS THE RESPONSE:

In a world being reshaped by artificial intelligence and automation, young men face a critical choice in preparing for long-term success. Traditional college paths – for example, a competitive four-year Finance degree – promise knowledge and career opportunities, but they also come with high costs, debt, and often a disconnect between classroom theory and real-world skills.

In fact, over half of recent college graduates end up underemployed (working in jobs that don't even require their degree, often for years), and 56% of Americans now believe a four-year degree isn't worth the cost because graduates "lack specific job skills and [carry] a large amount of debt".

The Preparation, by contrast, is a 16-cycle alternative curriculum designed as a no— nonsense "bootstrap" education. Over roughly four years, a Prepper (participant in The Preparation program) cycles through 16 intensive real-world projects – from emergency medicine and wilderness survival to entrepreneurship and investing – each building tangible skills, income, and personal grit. Below, we provide a clear-eyed comparison across key dimensions of success:

- ▶ Employability and Short-Term Income upon completion
- ▶ Long-Term Financial Upside and wealth-building potential
- ▶ Entrepreneurial Readiness and real-world competence
- ▶ Adaptability to a rapidly changing, AI-driven job market
- ▶ Character Development and psychological resilience
- ▶ Network Building and access to opportunities
- ▶ Return on Investment (ROI), both financial and experiential

To make the contrast concrete, the following table summarizes how each path stacks up on these dimensions:

DIMENSION	"THE PREPARATION" 16-CYCLE PROGRAM	TRADITIONAL FOUR-YEAR FINANCE DEGREE
Employability & Short-Term Income	Immediate practical skills: Multiple hands-on certifications (EMT, pilot, welding, etc.) and real job experience enable immediate earning, often without debt. Preppers can even work during the program (e.g., as a paid wildland EMT at $600/day). By program's end, they are job-ready in several fields—able to save a life, fly a plane, weld steel, or manage a project.	Entry-level opportunities: A finance degree opens doors to junior finance roles (analyst, etc.) with decent starting salaries (median ~$60–70K for financial analysts). However, new grads typically have no income for 4+ years of school and often carry significant debt. Their skillset is mostly theoretical, requiring on-the-job training to be truly productive.

DIMENSION	"THE PREPARATION" 16-CYCLE PROGRAM	TRADITIONAL FOUR-YEAR FINANCE DEGREE
Long-Term Financial Upside	Entrepreneurship and multiple income streams: The Preparation emphasizes building wealth sooner rather than later. Participants launch a venture and learn to invest, giving them an early start on business creation and asset growth. Their diverse skillset provides resilience—if one industry falters, they have other trades to fall back on—and emerging opportunities for higher pay. Importantly, they finish debt-free, so they can start investing in themselves immediately.	High earning potential (with a catch): Finance majors can achieve strong incomes, especially climbing the corporate ladder in banking or investment firms. However, this upside often comes later in life and is dependent on promotions or further degrees (MBA). Early career earnings might be modest, and student debt delays wealth-building. Many lack personal investing savvy despite a finance education.
Adaptability to an AI-Transformed Market	Built-in adaptability: Preppers become a "renaissance man," comfortable switching contexts, which cultivates an agile mindset and continuous learning. They learn modern tech skills (no-code development, AI tools), leveraging AI rather than being replaced by it. Their human creativity and cross-domain thinking are strengths AI can't fully substitute.	Narrow specialization risk: Finance graduates' specialized skills can be valuable, but many finance roles—particularly entry-level tasks—are highly exposed to automation. Graduates must adapt quickly, acquiring additional digital skills and uniquely human skills (strategic thinking, communication) outside the traditional curriculum.
Character Development & Psychological Resilience	Forged through adversity: The Preparation builds character by pushing participants through physical and mental challenges. They develop toughness, resilience, and the ability to perform under pressure, creating a deeply resilient and disciplined individual.	Minimal resilience training: College provides stressful coursework but lacks deliberate adversity. High anxiety and depression levels among students suggest resilience is not adequately developed. Character building relies on extracurricular choices, not the degree itself.
Network Building & Access to Opportunities	Diverse, lifelong network: Preppers gain an organic network of mentors and seasoned professionals from multiple fields, creating diverse career opportunities. Their relationships tend to be authentic, built on shared experiences and mutual respect.	Strong but homogeneous network: Finance degrees offer strong networks within finance/business ecosystems, largely composed of peers and alumni. However, this network can be narrow and less helpful outside its core industry, limiting broader career flexibility.

DIMENSION	"THE PREPARATION" 16-CYCLE PROGRAM	TRADITIONAL FOUR-YEAR FINANCE DEGREE
Return on Investment (Financial & Experiential)	High ROI, low cost: The entire Preparation costs about the same as just one year of university, allowing students to finish debt-free or even with savings. Immediate skillsets enable quick earnings, creating high financial and experiential ROI.	Questionable ROI, high cost: A finance degree from a competitive university often costs $100K–$234K (over $500K counting lost income and interest), with no guaranteed return. While some achieve solid financial outcomes, the ROI is delayed, and debt significantly reduces early wealth-building opportunities.

CHATGPT'S CONCLUSION:

The contrast between the 16-cycle *Preparation* curriculum and a traditional finance B.A. could not be more stark. One is an **accelerated forge of skills, income, and character**, deliberately designed to produce a resourceful young man ready for anything. The other is a **prestigious but expensive bet** on a conventional career path, whose value is increasingly under scrutiny in the face of economic and technological upheaval.

In the context of rapid AI-driven change, the edge clearly goes to the path that maximizes adaptability, hands-on competence, and entrepreneurial initiative. A Finance degree is not useless – it provides deep knowledge and can open specific doors, particularly in established industries. But *knowledge alone is no longer enough*. As the world automates routine expertise, the winners will be those who couple knowledge with real skills, courage, and the ability to create opportunities rather than wait for them.

The Preparation aims to future-proof young men by giving them exactly those qualities. Its graduates have **already earned and learned in the real world** – they've felt the sting of failure, the rush of solving a real problem, and the satisfaction of building something tangible. They enter adulthood not as uncertain job seekers with a résumé and debt, but as **seasoned go-getters** with résumés that read like adventure novels. In a future where the only certainty is uncertainty, the most powerful education is one that prepares you for *any* challenge. The 16-cycle curriculum's motto could well be: "**Fortune favors the prepared.**" And by all indications, it does.

We used finance as the example, but the situation is even worse with most other majors.

If you're still on the fence about ditching the college grind for The Preparation, let's zoom out and stare the beast in the face. Right now, in 2025, over 2 million bachelor's degrees are handed out each year in the US. And based on the latest NCES data, a staggering 44% of them—around 890,000—are in fields primed for AI demolition: business, social sciences, psychology, communications, computer sciences, liberal arts, and the like.

That's nearly a million young folks every single year betting their futures on majors that Goldman Sachs warns could see two-thirds of related jobs exposed to automation. The major risk is for white-collar gigs, the good jobs, like analysts, accountants, HR pros, and coders taking the hardest hits—up to 46% exposure in office and admin roles alone.

This isn't some distant sci-fi nightmare; it's barreling down like the industrial revolution did on those 1870s farmers. Back then, half the workforce got uprooted over decades. Today? AI's compressing that chaos into 15 years or less, gutting the very white-collar paths colleges are peddling as "secure." Millions of grads will flood a market where entry— level desks are vanishing, saddled with debt while bots can do the work better, faster, cheaper.

But you? You don't have to be roadkill. The Preparation isn't just a dodge—it's your shield and sword. Those 16 cycles forge you into a man who thrives in disruption: welding pipelines when factories automate, piloting charters through economic storms, building businesses that harness AI instead of fearing it. You'll emerge debt-free, versatile, and dangerous—ready to seize the wild opportunities this revolution spits out, just like the industrial age birthed electricity tycoons and auto pioneers.

The magnitude is massive: Nearly half of today's students are marching toward a cliff. Don't join them. Grab The Preparation, build real virtue and value, and step into the future as the guy who owns it, not the one scrambling to survive.

THE
CURRICULUM

PART

2

Chapter 11

WHAT'S INCLUDED IN THE CYCLES

BY MATT SMITH & DOUG CASEY

"The world turns aside to let any man
pass who knows where he is going."
—EPICTETUS

In this chapter, we provide 16 prepackaged "cycles" for you. It's not enough to avoid wasting four years of time and hundreds of thousands of dollars by avoiding college. What—precisely— should you do during those four years? Cycles are designed to answer the question, "What exactly should I do?" Each cycle lasts roughly three months and has a theme–Sailor, Builder, Cowboy, Fighter, Survivalist, Pilot, etc. If you've got a sense of adventure there's no doubt that some—perhaps all— of the cycles will call to you. I know I would have killed to have been able to pursue these things, if I'd been alerted to the possibility, instead of treading water in college.

Since The Preparation is envisioned as an alternative to college, we've outlined a four— year plan comprising four cycles a year. You can do them in any order you please. Every cycle is wildly different from any other, but they all deliver hands-on, practical skill development. Cycle by cycle you'll see your skills grow along with your confidence and character. At the end of four years, when most young men have wound up with a basically meaningless diploma, a passel of debt, and a bunch of toxic ideas, you will have a vast array of experiences and expertise, a positive bank account, and the ability to pretty much do anything and go anywhere.

The Preparation can certainly be used as a supplement to college as well as its replacement. So if you're in college today, consider quitting, and saving a lot of time and money. If you've already graduated, The Preparation can still deliver for you. The point is to gain knowledge, experience and wisdom. So, what if it takes a couple extra years? Some people live in the academic womb until they're 30 and have nothing to show for it beyond a pile of debt and a mind cluttered with largely useless information.

You don't need to commit to doing all 16 cycles right now. The hard part is just getting started. Wherever you are right now, focus on getting one cycle under your belt. Pick one that gets you fired up, crush it, and your progress will be the fuel for more.

A cycle consists of two core elements: Anchor Courses and Academic Courses. And five adjunct elements: Travel, Work, Reflection, Fun with a Purpose, Sports and Games. The adjuncts fit in and around the Anchor and Academic courses. They're just as important to the process of becoming a Renaissance Man, but less formal, and less structured. Knowing stuff and being able to do stuff is critical, but few college grads are well-rounded and sophisticated. We expect you will be.

▶ **PRACTICAL ANCHOR COURSES:** Each of these courses amount to what would be a "major" in a conventional college—except you can't get them in a college. They're practical hands-on skills that you can use immediately, in the real world. As opposed to your Academic courses (below), which are what you should get in college. The Practical Anchor course dictates where you'll be physically for the cycle. We suggest taking Anchor courses that offer immediate economic benefits first. For instance, spending $15,000 to learn how to operate heavy equipment can pay back its cost fairly quickly, and give you the $15,000 you need to learn to fly. But if you take flying first, it will probably take years for an economic return. In other words, they're both important—but first things first.

▶ **ACADEMIC COURSES:** Your critics might argue that by skipping college you'll be missing out on critical academic material. That's nonsense. The audio and video courses, supplemented by recommended reading, should give you a much broader and deeper academic education than almost anyone else close to your age. Its purpose is to give you all the things, and more, that you're supposed to learn in college.

The program we've laid out covers all the essentials in both the sciences and the arts. You won't have to waste time on required "filler" about DEI, gender, climate hysteria, virus fears, or political indoctrination. Incidentally, there's a reason most of them come from The Teaching Company. They've tried to get the best profs in the world, and the profs put on "command performance" lectures. They're not just worthwhile, they're usually entertaining. Not an obligatory drag, but something to look forward to.

ADJUNCT ELEMENTS TO CYCLES:

TRAVEL: This is an essential part of a real education. There's nothing wrong with spending your life in or near the place where you were born. That's what most people do. But most people, as Thoreau said, live lives of quiet desperation. They are comparable to potted plants; they stay where they were born, and their horizons are limited by the environment where they found themselves through an accident of birth.

There's an old saying: When the going gets tough, the tough get going. In the 19th C immigrants to America self-selected. Only the best, the brightest, and most enterprising left the certainty of the Old Country for the hardship and dangers and uncertainties of the New World. That's why America is "different". It's the only country in the world that was overtly founded on a set of well enunciated principles. It drew people who agreed with those ideas and tended to transmit them to their offspring, along with the genes that got them going.

We don't expect you to transplant yourself. But you'll notice that many of the learning experiences—as many as possible, actually—take place in a different country, or at least a different state. That's intentional. It will allow you to kill at least two birds with one stone. Living in a different country for a while, not as a tourist (which is the most the few who even travel will do), but working and doing things with the locals.

As another benefit, in the process of traveling you should learn at least the basics of another language or two. I took French in both High School and college. I learned enough vocabulary, grammar, and diction to pass tests, but was absolutely incapable of carrying on a conversation. In college I signed on for a Junior Year Abroad program which took me to France and Switzerland. I became fairly competent in French, and can still get by in German (German is much easier, since the 500 most common English words are essentially German cognates). But the fact of the matter is that if you learn the 500 most common words in any language—it's just a matter of diligence and memorization—you're on your way.

At the end of The Preparation, just your foreign (and national) travel experiences will put you on another level. Some people pride themselves on completing a "bucket list" when it comes to travel. Is that to impress themselves, or impress other people? A bucket list isn't something integral to your life. It's hard to imagine Edmund Dantes, Paladin, or Richard Burton doing what they did, or being who they were, because of a bucket list.

Bucket lists are for dilettantes and wannabees. But don't take that **ex cathedra**—it's just an opinion.

FUN WITH A PURPOSE: A well-rounded man knows how to do many things. Some provide no economic value, but make life more fun and can open the world to you in unusual ways. These things could be considered hobbies, but all require a level of competence to be truly enjoyed. While competence in a hobby can easily translate into a profitable business, that's not necessarily the object. Competence is its own reward.

REFLECTION/ACCOUNTABILITY: They say college teaches you how write. Maybe, and maybe not. The fact is that you learn to write by reading what others have written, assessing it critically and logically, and then writing yourself. My guess is that a fair number of term papers submitted in college today are done by AI programs, and then (maybe) modified enough by the student (who's after a grade more than knowledge) to evade detection. On the bright side, the kids handing in those phony papers are learning something about AI.

We have a better approach: Writing about what you are learning and doing each week.

Writing about what you did each week will simultaneously hold yourself accountable and can qualify you in a whole extra skill. Very few people can write properly. Keeping a blog over the next few years will qualify you as a journalist. In addition to reflecting on what you're doing and how you're improving in Cycles, writing and publishing a journal tells the world who you are. You might meet some very interesting and worthwhile people.

Maxim has done this with his substack blog over the last two years. His blog acts as a useful tool to constantly improve his thinking and writing skills and it's enjoyable to read. As a bonus, it puts a little money in his pocket. At the time of writing, he has more than 3,000 readers and earns about $5,000 a year. That's the kind of win-win you're looking for.

PRO TIP

Never pretend to be something you're not, or pretend to believe something you don't believe. When you do so, you're betraying yourself. You'll feel cognitive dissonance, shame, and guilt. Nothing is worth that. Almost as bad, you'll attract people who like the phony you, and you'll fail to attract people who'd like the real you—people who share your values.

Get in the habit of writing about what you experience and observe as you go through The Preparation. If you come up with original thoughts, and express them well, at some point you may be able to monetize the blog. It's a perfect example of "earn while you learn". If you're doing things and making things happen, any number of your readers will want to get to know you better. Perhaps as clients or patrons, perhaps as customers if you have a service or product to sell. Some might present you with unexpected opportunities, as was true for Maxim.

INCOME/COSTS: There are hard costs for the anchor courses, academic courses, books, room and board, and travel. All in, the cost of the four-year Preparation program is comparable to that of a typical college. But infinitely more valuable, and vastly more fun.

If you only pursue the Academic and Reading parts of The Preparation, your cost to become an academically educated person, a polymath, is trivial. But there's a danger to becoming too much of an "egghead". As I pointed out earlier, while knowledge is critically important, it largely falls into the category of "Have". It's a possession, albeit the most personal and valuable of all possessions. The costly part of the Preparation relates to "Do", where you put theories into practice. It's also the part which will both serve your ultimate goal of becoming the man you want to be, while leading to economic rewards.

Don't be put off by the costs. You'll be getting something tangible and usable from what you learn and do. Money isn't the most important thing you'll gain, but The Preparation will likely pay monetary dividends many, many, times over.

WORK: This is optional. But, if you have extra energy, you can self-finance the program. You can learn a lot from working just about any job for a short period of time. Especially with rote work, you can take your knowledge base from zero to "most of what's worth knowing" in a week or two and get paid for doing it. Beyond that, "dog work" rapidly turns into diminishing returns.

There's nothing wrong with taking a dead-end job for a short period of time. Most men work unrewarding jobs for a lifetime. Do some for a while; it will help you understand that the world can be a tough place. You want to avoid trading hours of your life doing "dog work" for a few dollars more— that's usually a bad trade...

Within the next decade it's likely that robots powered by AI will perform most conventional labor. AI and robotics will eliminate most professions—including legal, accounting, writing, and teaching—as well. The key thing to remember is that every person on the planet has a near infinite desire for goods and services. It's up to you to figure out how to become wealthy by giving other people what they want. With all the knowledge and hands-on abilities and experience you'll develop with The Preparation, you'll be in a much better position to help them than your contemporaries, wasting away in a corporate gig.

THE POWER OF CYCLE STACKING

The real momentum you'll build will come from cycle stacking–completing one cycle after the next, over the period of several years. Skills you learn in one cycle will benefit you, often in unexpected ways, in subsequent cycles. Not only that, but your confidence will build from the sheer weight of all that you accomplish within such a short period of time.

As discussed earlier in this book, opportunities present themselves to worthy people at unexpected times and lead down paths you previously thought unimaginable. Your focused effort towards attaining skills will open the floodgate and opportunities will flow your way. Your "luck" will improve in all ways, since luck materializes when preparation meets opportunity.

When you show up in the world as a man on a mission, dedicated, earnest, capable, and open to new things, people will come out of the woodwork to help you. This is especially true when you're doing badass things on a consistent basis. You'll be recognized as a winner; people are attracted to winners and avoid losers. You'll find you're automatically surrounding yourself with other value-added winners, making it easier to stay away from hangers-on and time-suckers. They'll come offering ways to make money, to teach you a new skill, or share some wisdom.

We can assure you that what the world most lacks is people who are both competent and ethical. If you complete The Preparation, not only won't you be looking for a job, but you'll likely be overwhelmed with offers from accomplished people who want to associate with you. Not just employ you—although that may be the case at first—but work with you. Successful people are always looking for new talent. It's up to you to qualify, and not drift into becoming an NPC, like 90% of young men—including those with a college diploma.

The ideal situation, one that you should strive for from the start, is to be self-employed. That's the only way you can really be at cause over your future. As long as you're just an employee, you're just the effect of someone else's cause.

STRUCTURING YOUR TIME

Colleges in the United States measure the work a student puts into earning a degree in the form of credit hours. 120 credit hours earns you a bachelor's degree. That works out to 30 credit hours a year, 15 a semester, for four years. Three credit hours typically equal a course in some subject.

In other words, each semester conventional students typically take five courses of three credit hours each. In each five-day week you're spending 15 hours in the classroom, or three clock hours per day. Perhaps a total of 500 in the nine-month year— assuming you attend them all. That works out to $100 an hour for the average school.

We asked ChatGPT how much out of class work the typical college student takes on per week. The response was 10–13 hours outside class in addition to the 15 credit hours for a total of 28 hours a week. We question that. In reality most students only study, "cram" is a more accurate word, just before exams. As various commercials say, "your results may vary". Typically on the downside, because in college you'll be distracted by all manner of things

By comparison, Cycles are designed for you to hit 40 credit hours, meaning you will put in 40 hours of intentional effort each week. Over three months (one cycle), you end up with 480 hours of productive effort. Every hour you spend attending Anchor courses, Academic courses, reading, learning games, pursuing activities, reflecting, and working will count as 1 credit hour.

If 40 hours a week sounds like a lot, consider the fact that there are 168 hours in each week. Of those 168, let's assume you spend 9 hours/night sleeping. That still leaves you 105 hours to fill. If you go "all in" on your future with The Preparation, it'll take less than 40% of your waking hours. A fit & healthy young man could take a full college load AND do The Preparation at the same time—although college would be just a redundant and expensive add-on.

As a huge bonus, you'll be doing things because you want to, not because you must. Any Cycle you choose might be interesting enough that you want to spend more than 100 hours a week pursuing it, whereas most of your high school friends are alternating between boredom, goofing off, and stress.

If all work was equal, after just one year of The Preparation, you'll be way ahead of your college peers. You will have logged 1,920 productive hours whereas the college peer will come in at just 840 [(15 credit hours + 13 study hours) * 30 weeks].

But, of course, all work is NOT equal.

Each cycle brings with it huge new opportunities to gain real life experience, do fun things, expand your network, and still learn the academic material they might teach you in college. Spending 30 days learning how to pack mules into the backcountry of Idaho, becoming a competent crewman on a sailboat in Chile, training Muay Thai for a cycle in Thailand, or becoming a private pilot in Alaska may seems like a lot. But those are just highlights of what you can do in just four cycles of

The Preparation. Do you know a man who's done as much or anything as interesting in a single year? In fact, many haven't done anything like that in a lifetime...

The 16 cycles here are entirely interchangeable. You can choose which cycle you'd like to do and when you'd like to do it. Although it's usually wiser to do those with immediate economic utility first. On top of that, there is no set schedule. You'll need to fit in various activities when and how you can. Ultimately, like any adult, you'll build out the details of your schedule, holding yourself accountable to following through.

You will, however, need self-discipline. There will be plenty of time for slacking off (a little...) after you're rich, accomplished, and respected. You've got more energy now than you'll ever have. Don't waste it.

The cycles are designed so that you put all your effort into hitting the mark of 40 productive hours per week–taking the cycle's Anchor course, Academic courses, reading, reflecting, learning games, working to make money, and pursuing activities–all within just 5 days of the week.

This is just how we framed it. You could take an entire seven-day week to complete everything if that's what's necessary or what you'd prefer. We think you'll enjoy the process so much that you may want to use all 7 days; learning and improving is fun. Maybe you'll want to use some week-ends to date, party, or simply relax. But very likely you'll find the course matter more interesting as well as more valuable. Most of your classmates will envy the things you're doing.

Some of the more intense anchor courses within the cycles will require your full attention, which means you won't be taking the online courses, learning games, pursuing activities for a while. For instance, if you're doing a 14-day outdoor survival training, you aren't expected to practice chess or take an online course at the same time. How could you? These other cycle activities should be accomplished before or after the intensive anchor course is completed.

Think of each cycle's anchor course as the main event. Once that's on your schedule, you should fill in all the gaps to hit your goal of 480 total productive hours by the end of each cycle.

Additionally, it's a good idea to work a job, any job, during the free time you have in each cycle. There's much that can be learned from even a dead-end job, assuming it's only a temporary gig and it doesn't get in the way of your primary objective–completing the cycle like a champ. It's important to adopt a producer's mindset, always asking yourself, "What can I do to generate income?" A job isn't the best way to do it, but it's often the easiest. And it's certainly helpful to give you a grip on the pickle most people find themselves in for a lifetime, not just a few weeks. If you're going to err on one side or another, make it on the side of doing too much. You'll find it's always the busy people, not those with lots of time on their hands, who get things done. Plus, every additional dollar you're able to save, is another dollar that can be devoted to your future in The Preparation and beyond.

Remember, work isn't the priority. The anchor course is first, second to that are all the other elements of the cycle. Any work schedule needs to be subordinate to The Preparation activities. You can count up to 50 hours working a job toward your goal of 480/cycle. Feel free to work more. But only 50 count for the cycle so that you can fully devote yourself to everything else in the cycle. There's more on having a job in the "How to Finance The Preparation" chapter.

DO FUN SHIT

Each week you should plan one mini event, something that you find fun or interesting, something that others might consider a hobby. Remember the power of novel activities from the earlier chapter, "How the world actually works". Try new things. For example, you could take short woodworking classes, go flyfishing, learn to ride motocross, climb a mountain, or go skiing. Take time to put what you've learned in prior cycles to practice and explore new ideas. Later, we'll share a list of just some of the possibilities. Find something that sounds fun to you and make time for it every week.

One often overlooked benefit of engaging in fun and exhilarating activities is their profound ability to reset your physiology. When you're deeply immersed in work, consistently grinding through tasks and celebrating achievements, the sense of momentum you build can feel incredibly satisfying—at least initially. However, over time, even the most ambitious routines can become monotonous, leading to mental stagnation and diminishing returns.

The most effective antidote I've found to this creeping sense of monotony is intentionally seeking out activities that radically alter your physical and mental state. These activities serve as a powerful physiological reset, helping you return to your tasks refreshed, refocused, and reenergized.

Just being in nature on a challenging hike or standing in a gorgeous stream flyfishing can alter your senses and refresh your spirit. But, sometimes, what's called for is something more extreme.

Skydiving, for instance, is more than just an adrenaline rush. When you leap from a plane, your body floods with adrenaline, dopamine, and endorphins. Adrenaline sharpens your focus and heightens your senses, dopamine rewards your brain, creating lasting motivation and excitement, and endorphins significantly reduce stress and promote feelings of exhilaration. These biochemical shifts effectively reset your mental clarity and physical energy.

Another excellent example I personally rely upon is riding an adventure motorcycle through challenging, unpredictable terrain. Navigating uncertain paths demands intense mental concentration and physical exertion. This combination of risk management and physical agility boosts norepinephrine levels, improving your reaction times and cognitive sharpness, while simultaneously activating muscle groups often neglected in routine tasks. The result is an invigorating sense of mastery and accomplishment, coupled with renewed clarity and vigor when returning to your daily work. Plus, it's just plain fun.

Of course, safety remains essential—don't take reckless risks. However, strategically placing yourself in scenarios that introduce controlled extremes of speed, height, or physical intensity can profoundly enhance your productivity, creativity, and overall enjoyment of life. Embracing these intense, enjoyable moments periodically is not just about fun; it's about harnessing physiological resets to achieve sustained high performance.

They also go a long way to making you an interesting and competent man.

Chapter 12

ANCHOR COURSES: HANDS-ON LEARNING AT THE CORE OF EACH CYCLE

BY MATT SMITH

The Preparation isn't about sitting in a classroom and daydreaming about life – it's about getting out there and **Doing**. At the heart of each cycle is an **Anchor Course**, a big, hands— on adventure that defines the cycle's theme. Think of Anchor Courses as the ultimate "lab sessions" for life: instead of mixing chemicals or solving equations, you might be rappelling down a cliff, riding herd across open country, or taking the controls of a small aircraft. These are immersive, often adventurous experiences that demand you roll up your sleeves (or put on a helmet) and learn by *doing*.

Each Anchor Course is directly tied to its cycle's theme, ensuring that what you tackle is relevant and real. And unlike abstract college assignments, these ventures build **real— world skills that people will pay for**. By design, an Anchor Course forces you out of your comfort zone and into situations where you gain economically valuable abilities – whether that's saving a life, flying a plane, or growing food. It's learning with tangible outcomes, the kind of learning that not only pads your résumé but also shapes your character.

In the following sections, we'll walk through each of the 16 cycles and their Anchor Courses. For each cycle, imagine what you'll be doing, and more importantly, who you'll become by doing it. The tone here is direct and unapologetic because you deserve the truth served straight. Each description is a glimpse of what's in store: vivid scenes of challenge and growth. As you read, picture yourself in these roles. This could be you in a few months – out in the world, gaining skills and stories that set you apart from every guy still stuck in lecture halls.

Keep in mind, the Anchor activities we've selected are not all that one could or should do. We recommend starting with these but truly, the sky's the limit and later we'll show you how to build your own cycle from the ground up, with any Anchor course that speaks to you.

CYCLE 1: MEDIC – BECOME THE ONE WHO CAN SAVE A LIFE

The first cycle launches you into the fray as a Medic. Your Anchor Course is a rigorous Emergency Medical Technician (**EMT**) training program in your area. Instead of just learning biology from a textbook, you'll be bandaging wounds and handling real emergencies. Picture yourself riding in an ambulance, cutting through traffic with sirens wailing, or kneeling beside an accident victim with the knowledge and calm to keep them alive. By completing this course and earning your EMT certification, you **become the guy who can save a life** when every second counts. The Medic cycle gives you skills few people have: how many of your peers know how to respond to a car wreck or a heart attack? Exactly. You'll carry that confidence into every room you enter. And as a bonus, these skills have serious economic value – EMTs are in demand everywhere, so you can earn good money part-time or volunteer in high-stakes roles that network you with firefighters, paramedics, and other action-oriented people. By the end of this cycle, you won't be just a student; you'll be a certified first responder, a young man who literally knows how to save the day.

CYCLE 2: PILOT – TAKE TO THE SKIES AND LEARN TO COMMAND

In Cycle 2, you trade the ground for the sky. The Pilot cycle's Anchor Course is a private pilot's license program that teaches you to fly an airplane. Yes, you read that right – you'll learn to pilot a plane. Over a few thrilling months, you'll go from cockpit newbie to a confident aviator capable of taking off, navigating, and landing safely. Under the mentorship of a certified flight instructor, you'll practice takeoffs and landings, solo a small aircraft, and log hours soaring above the countryside. It's hard to overstate how transformative this experience is. Flying isn't just adventurous – it instills precision, discipline, and unshakeable self-confidence. You learn to make high-stakes decisions calmly (when you're at 5,000 feet, there's no option but to stay cool and focused). By the end, you'll have earned your wings – a rare credential that sets you apart. Whether or not you aim to become a professional pilot, having a pilot's license as a young man is a huge flex. It shows everyone (including future employers or partners) that you can master complex skills and handle responsibility. More practically, it opens doors to side gigs like aerial photography, charters, or just the pure freedom of weekend flying. When you've navigated through clouds and literally seen the world from above, your perspective on life broadens. Nothing will feel quite as daunting on the ground, because you know you've conquered the sky.

CYCLE 3: COWBOY – MASTER THE GRIT OF THE OLD WEST

Saddle up – the Cowboy cycle is about embracing the rugged spirit of the American West. This Anchor Course has two parts, both very hands-on. First, you'll head to a real ranch (for example, the American Cowboy Academy in Texas) for a crash course in beginner ranch work and horsemanship. For a solid week, you'll live and work as a ranch hand: riding horses, herding cattle, throwing hay bales, and learning to rope and wrangle. It's tough, dusty, and demanding – and you'll love it. Next, you'll take it up a notch by trekking into the wild backcountry. Picture spending a month in the Idaho wilderness with Middle Fork Outfitters or a similar crew, learning how to pack horses and mules for deep expeditions. You'll discover how to load gear on a mule, navigate mountain trails, set up camp under the stars, and maybe even track wildlife. By the end of this cycle, you'll possess a set of old-school skills that almost nobody from our generation has. You'll know how to ride and care for a horse, live comfortably off-grid, fix fences, and handle yourself miles from any cell signal. More importantly, you'll absorb the Cowboy code – independence, courage, honesty, and grit. Working with large animals and wild terrain forces you to become physically tougher and mentally sharper. This cycle connects you to a heroic American mythos: you're living the kind of adventures most guys only see in movies. When you return home, you'll carry that frontier confidence with you. Whether it's leading a project or standing your ground on an issue, people will sense that you've got true grit – you're not a boy anymore, you're a young man who's ridden with cowboys and can handle the wild.

CYCLE 4: BUILDER – BUILD A HOUSE, BUILD YOUR CONFIDENCE

Ever wonder if you have what it takes to build something *real* with your own hands? Cycle 4 – Builder – will prove that you do. The Anchor Course sends you to Maine for an intensive design-build workshop at the **Shelter Institute**, a legendary school for owner-builders. Over a two-week period, you'll literally learn how to construct a house from the ground up. You'll study everything from laying out a foundation and framing walls to wiring, plumbing, and roofing. This isn't kiddie stuff – stick around for the third week and, by the end of the course, you and your classmates will have raised a structure, like a sturdy cabin or a timber-frame shell, and in doing so demystified the entire building process. Imagine the confidence that comes from being able to say, "Yeah, I know how to build a house." That's a lifelong skill with huge economic value – whether you use it to save tens of thousands on your own future home, start a construction business, or just be the most capable guy in the neighborhood. But it's not only about wood and nails. Plus, let's face it, building stuff is just plain fun. You'll swap the drudgery of rote learning for the camaraderie of campfire evenings on the Maine coast, laughing with new friends after a hard day's work. By cycle's end, you're not just stronger and handier – you carry yourself differently. You've tasted the old pioneer satisfaction of working with lumber and tools, and you'll forever know that whatever environment you're thrown into, you can figure it out and build something that lasts.

CYCLE 5: CHEF – TASTE HISTORY AND COOK LIKE A PRO

They say an army marches on its stomach – well, so does a man. Cycle 5 transforms your relationship with food by plunging you into the culinary arts. And not just anywhere: your Anchor Course is a **one-month professional Italian cuisine program in Florence, Italy**. That's right – you'll fly to the heart of the Renaissance, tie on a chef's apron, and train under Italian master chefs. From day one, you'll be handling knives and pasta dough, learning the secrets of authentic Tuscan cooking in a commercial kitchen setting. Think of making fresh ravioli from scratch, mastering the perfect Bolognese sauce, or crafting gelato. You'll also shop in local markets at dawn, practice butchering and baking, and plate dishes with an artist's touch. This isn't a casual cooking class – it's a pro-fessional— level training that will push your creativity, attention to detail, and work ethic to new heights. By the end, you'll be capable of whipping up restaurant-quality feasts. The obvious gain is that you'll eat *very* well (and know how to feed yourself and others for a lifetime), but there's more. Living in Italy for a month, you'll soak up history and art every day. You'll gain an appreciation for tradition, patience, and passion that the best cooking requires. Economically, culinary skills can translate into side jobs or even your own catering gig; at the very least, you'll save money and impress friends by not relying on crappy takeout. And don't overlook the confidence boost: being able to host a dinner and wow people with a three-course meal is a surefire hallmark of a man in command of his life. Direct, vivid, and aspirational? How about this: after Chef cycle, when you tell someone you trained in Florence and can cook authentic Italian, their eyes will go wide – it's an experience that sets you apart from every other guy surviving on microwave burritos. You'll return home not just cultured and well-fed, but disciplined, creative, and ready to add flavor to everything you do.

CYCLE 6: HEAVY EQUIPMENT OPERATOR – MOVE MOUNTAINS (LITERALLY)

Time to play with the *big toys*. Cycle 6 drops you into the cab of earthshaking machines in the Heavy Equipment Operator cycle. The Anchor Course here is a four-week **"Heavy Now" training program at a heavy equipment school in Florida**, where you'll learn to operate bulldozers, excavators, loaders, and more. If you've ever seen construction crews digging a foundation or moving giant piles of dirt and thought it looked cool, you're about to find out just how cool – and challenging – it really is. Under the guidance of seasoned instructors, you'll climb up into these massive rigs, fire up their engines, and get hands-on practice in shaping the land. Day by day, you'll learn to trench a perfect line with an excavator bucket, push tons of earth with a dozer blade, and delicately maneuver huge machines with fingertip control. This isn't just "fun with big machines" (though believe me, it *is* fun) – it's an intensive course in safety, precision, and responsibility. You're commanding equipment worth hundreds of thousands of dollars, where a mistake can be costly. The stakes teach you to focus and respect the power at your fingertips. By course's end, you'll have earned a certification and the ability to literally move earth. Economically, this skill is golden: heavy equipment operators are in demand in construction, mining, forestry – you name it. It's a ticket to well-paying work anywhere in the world, and it can be your ace if you ever need a solid Plan B (or if you aim to start your own contracting business down the line). Beyond the tangible skill, you gain something just as valuable: confidence in handling big responsibilities. A man ought to know how to operate virtually any kind of machine. And this course will ahead in that regard.

After you've conquered the learning curve of controlling a roaring 20-ton earthmover, other challenges in life won't faze you. Oh, and a side benefit – you'll know more about geology and soil. So, when someone points at a hill or a construction blueprint, you'll be the guy who understands what lies beneath the surface *and* how to transform it. In short, you'll walk away as a young man who can brag (humbly) that he's helped build something real – someone who can dig, carve, and create the physical world around him.

CYCLE 7: WORK CYCLE – SEIZE THE OPPORTUNITY AND DIVE INTO REAL-WORLD WORK

Not every learning experience comes neatly packaged as a course. Sometimes, life hands you an opportunity and the best thing you can do is grab it with both hands. Cycle 7, the Work Cycle, is all about that. Instead of a predetermined class, the "Anchor Course" here is an actual job or internship that offers a unique learning experience. This cycle is deliberately flexible – it's your chance to immerse yourself in gainful work that aligns with your interests or opens a new door.

For example, maybe you land a short-term job fighting wildfires out West as an EMT (putting your EMT skills to use on the fire line) or you get an internship at a marketing agency or tech startup. In my son Maxim's case, during his first year of The Preparation he ended up working on wildfires as an EMT and earning $600/day.

You'll see, as Maxim did, that opportunities like this aren't planned in a syllabus – they just come up. In the Work Cycle, you'll do the same with whatever fits: full-time, real-world work, for the span of the cycle. By dedicating a cycle to a job, you give yourself permission to treat that employment as your core learning experience (rather than something you're squeezing in on weekends). You'll gain *so much* more by treating work as a learning laboratory: you're not just earning money (though that's nice), you're observing how a business operates, picking up skills on the job, and proving to yourself that you can thrive on the job. Even good jobs have parts that suck, but you've got to learn to thrive in any environment – you learn to show up on time, adapt to workplace dynamics, and take pride in doing even "menial" tasks well.

> ### PRO TIP
>
> If you approach every task, no matter how small, with excellence, people notice and opportunities multiply in ways you cannot imagine.

The Work Cycle is also a reality check that keeps you grounded. It connects all those other crazy adventures back to practical life – you see how your new skills can make you stand out on a team. And if the job you take happens to align with a passion, it might even turn into a career path or at least a valuable network. By the end of this cycle, you'll have real job experience on your résumé while your college peers might still have nothing but term papers and debt. You'll understand the value of a dollar earned, and you'll return to the next cycle with sharper discipline and a healthier bank account. In essence, the Work Cycle teaches you one of the most important skills of all: how to leverage opportunity when it knocks. It's a reminder that The Preparation is not a rigid formula – it's training you to capitalize on the unpredictability of life.

CYCLE 8: WELDER – FORGE YOUR FUTURE WITH FIRE AND STEEL

Cycle 8 turns up the heat – literally. In the Welder cycle, you'll learn to harness fire and electricity to fuse metal, a skill as old as the Industrial Revolution and just as valuable today. The Anchor Course is an intensive welding program (for instance, enrolling in a reputable **welding trade school in Canada** for a few months of full-time training). Day after day, you'll pull on a protective hood, fire up an arc, and practice welding techniques under the guidance of veteran welders. You'll learn to cut, join, and shape metal using tools like MIG and TIG welders, torches, and plasma cutters. In a matter of weeks, you'll go from never having struck an arc to laying down beads of molten steel with confidence. Expect your first attempts to look ugly – that's normal – but each day you'll get steadier and more precise. By the end, you'll be able to fabricate sturdy joints and structures, whether it's a simple gate or a complex metal sculpture. Welding is a trade skill, which means two big things: it's practical and it's in demand. From construction sites to oil rigs, from custom auto shops to high-tech manufacturing, welders are needed everywhere.

With this cycle, you gain the ability to step into a well-paying job nearly anywhere on the planet, or to create tangible products with your own hands. Want to build your own off— road vehicle bumper or start a side hustle making custom metal art? You can – because you'll know how to melt metal to your will. But beyond the technical skill, welding teaches patience, attention to detail, and resilience. Working with sparks flying and metal glowing at 2,800°F, you must concentrate and keep your cool – it's almost meditative once you get into the flow. After completing the Welder cycle, you'll have something almost none of your peers do – a skilled trade certification – plus the worldly understanding to use it wisely. When someone asks, "So what can you do?" you can say: "I can build almost anything out of metal *and* I know why that skill will always be valuable."

CYCLE 9: FIGHTER – TRAIN LIKE A WARRIOR (MUAY THAI IN THAILAND)

There are 8 billion people in this world, and let's face it: some of them are thugs who prey on the weak. Cycle 9, the Fighter cycle, ensures you won't be one of the victims. We're sending you straight to the source for this Anchor Course: you'll travel to Thailand, the birthplace of Muay Thai, and spend a cycle training at one of the country's top fight gyms.

This isn't a once-a-week kickboxing class at your local strip mall; this is living, breathing combat training, six days a week under the blistering Thai sun, guided by instructors who've fought in 300 matches and smile through missing teeth. **Muay Thai**, known as the art of eight limbs (fists, elbows, knees, and shins), is one of the most effective striking martial arts on the planet.

You will wake up before dawn, do a 5-kilometer run with other fighters, then spend hours drilling strikes, clinch techniques, and defensive moves. You'll spar in the ring, learning what it's like to give and take hits (a humbling and invaluable experience for any man). In the afternoons, you'll collapse on your bunk, muscles exhausted and mind racing with improvements for tomorrow. And then you'll do it all again. Sounds intense? It is. It's also incredibly rewarding. Over a few months, you'll **forge your body into a weapon** – expect to see your conditioning skyrocket, muscles harden, reflexes sharpen. More importantly, you'll forge your mind. Fighting, even just training to fight, exposes you to controlled fear and adrenaline. You learn to remain calm when someone is throwing punches at you, to push past pain and fatigue when your body wants to quit, and to respect both your own capabilities and your opponents'.

By the time you leave Thailand, you'll carry yourself differently. There's a quiet confidence in someone who knows he can handle himself physically. And trust me, others will sense it too. This cycle isn't about starting bar fights – it's about knowing you *could* handle violence if it ever found you, which paradoxically makes you less likely to ever need to. Discipline, toughness, and humility (because you *will* meet people tougher than you) are the gains here.

Economically, while "fighter" might not seem directly lucrative (unless you go pro, which isn't the goal), the spin-off opportunities and personal brand value are real. Maybe you become a part-time self-defense instructor, or simply the leadership skills and grit you develop make you the kind of person who excels in any team or stressful job environment. When an employer or client sees that Muay Thai training on your background, it's a signal: this guy has dedication and doesn't back down from challenges. In short, the Fighter cycle gives you the physical prowess and warrior mindset that will permeate everything else you do. Plus, you'll have amazing stories – how many people do you know who've trained in a Thai boxing camp and maybe even entered a local ring for a match? Exactly. You'll leave with a harder body, a sharper mind, and the heart of a warrior – assets no one can ever take from you.

CYCLE 10: SAILOR – CONQUER THE HIGH SEAS AND FIND TRUE NORTH

Ready for an adventure that would make your ancestors proud? Cycle 10 casts you off into one of the greatest challenges on Earth: open-ocean sailing near the infamous Cape Horn. The Sailor cycle's Anchor Course is a multi-week **sailing expedition in the wild waters at the bottom of South America** – a place legendary among mariners for its fierce winds and waves. You'll join a seasoned crew (for example, with Pelagic Expeditions or a similar outfit) as an apprentice crew member on a 16-day voyage through the Beagle Channel and around Cape Horn – a place many can't even find on a map.

This is not a luxury cruise. This is you on a stout sailing vessel, standing night watch in cold spray, learning to read the wind, hoist sails, tie knots, and navigate by compass, stars, and GPS. Under the tutelage of a veteran skipper, you'll practice everything from basic seamanship (rope handling, steering, anchoring) to advanced skills (charting courses, plotting weather systems, and even emergency man-overboard drills). You'll feel the boat heel under strong gusts and learn to trust the teamwork that keeps everything under control. Few experiences demand teamwork, discipline, and sheer toughness like ocean sailing. When you're days from port and a gale hits, you discover what you're made of – and you'll be pleasantly surprised to find that you can rise to the occasion.

By journey's end, you should qualify as a competent crewman and perhaps even log enough time for formal certifications. But beyond certificates, consider what you gain: global perspective, resilience, and a budding new skill that can change the course of your life. You will have seen the world from a vantage point that hasn't changed for centuries – the deck of a ship at sea. You'll have visited places accessible only by boat, maybe stepped foot on the lonely rock of Cape Horn itself where so many explorers came to grief (and where you triumphed). Economically, sailing skills can lead to work as a charter crew, sailing instructor, or yacht delivery hand. And if nothing else, you now have the confidence to tackle complex logistical challenges (because planning an expedition and keeping a boat shipshape is no joke). Also, everyone loves the uniqueness of something like this – it screams *adventurous problem-solver*.

By the time you sail back into harbor, weathered and grinning ear to ear, you'll have joined the fraternity of sailors who know first-hand the meaning of "learning the ropes."

Whatever storms you face on land – jobs, relationships, crises – will seem a bit more manageable after you've wrestled with real storms at sea.

PRO TIP FROM MAXIM

I lucked out on my trip, we started from the Falkland Islands sailed through the western islands, made an ocean crossing and then went through the Strait of Magellan. As it worked out, I got way more sailing time than was normal for "competent crew" courses.

CYCLE 11: SURVIVALIST – THRIVE IN THE WILD AND TOUGHEN UP

In today's world of cushy conveniences, few men ever truly test their limits against nature. Cycle 11, the Survivalist cycle, strips life down to the essentials and asks: can you master yourself and thrive with all the trappings of life stripped away? Your Anchor Course is a **14-day primitive living intensive in the wilderness of Utah**, run by one of the world's premier survival schools (think Boulder Outdoor Survival School, or "BOSS"). For two weeks, you and a small group will venture into remote canyons with minimal gear – often just a knife, a water bottle, and the clothes on your back.

Under expert instructors, you'll learn the ancient skills that kept our ancestors alive. We're talking making fire by friction, building shelters out of branches and brush, foraging for edible plants, trapping small game, purifying water, and navigating by the sun and stars. You'll knap stones into cutting tools, tan animal hides, and craft cordage from plant fibers.

The first few days might feel like a brutal wake-up call (no cell signal, no soft bed, and yes, you will be hungry and sore). But a remarkable thing happens when you push through the discomfort: you start to adapt. You realize you can endure more than you thought. By day 14, you're not the same guy who started. You can hike miles with a pack, start a campfire with a bow drill you made yourself, and sleep soundly under a shelter you wove from willow boughs. You gain a deep respect for nature – and an even deeper respect for your own resilience. This cycle is offers perhaps the ultimate 'know thy self' opportunity.

When you've faced the elements (heat, cold, rain, hunger) and still managed to take care of yourself, every urban challenge shrinks in comparison. So your car broke down or the power went out? You're the man who can calmly handle it, maybe even help others, because you know what to do when the luxuries are gone.

Physically, you'll get tougher: leaner, stronger, with a new grit in your eyes. Mentally, you'll find a quiet assurance – the knowledge that "I can handle whatever comes." Economically, there's not a direct job called "survivalist" (unless you become a guide), but there are indirect benefits: careers in outdoor leadership, adventure tourism, forestry, or even military or emergency services will value these skills. More broadly, any employer or team will value the unflappable poise you develop. You won't panic under pressure or get fazed by sudden changes – after all, you've literally navigated out of being lost in the woods without panic.

One more point: this cycle embodies a theme running through about half of our Anchor Courses – building toughness. We purposely include tough physical challenges (like Survivalist, Cowboy, Fighter, etc.) because enduring hardship voluntarily is how you forge a formidable character. Special Forces soldiers do it in their training, and they earn respect for a reason. Here, you're doing a civilian version: gaining almost all the skills and toughness of a soldier *without* having to enlist or salute to anyone. When it's freezing or pouring rain and you're out there shivering through one more night – that's the kind of experience that inoculates you against the trivial complaints that derail lesser men.

> **PRO TIP**
>
> Maxim and I did a 4-day primitive survival training when he was 13. I assumed it'd be challenging, but when I leaned the guide brought no food, I must admit – I was concerned. Options were sparse, but we made it through by eating things like flower bulbs and a rattlesnake. We had fun, but there was plenty of suck. We've learned to remind ourselves to "Embrace the suck". In doing so, we find our way through the most challenging things cheerfully and come out the other side proud, empowered, and changed in ways that are hard to articulate.

By the end of Survivalist cycle, you won't just *survive* – you'll thrive in conditions that would send most people into a panic. And that makes you dangerous (in the best way possible) in any situation life throws at you.

CYCLE 12: FARMER – CULTIVATE THE LAND AND REAP HARD-WON WISDOM

Cycle 12 brings you back to civilization – but not the soft kind. You're heading out to the farm, where civilization meets nature and hard work feeds the world. The Farmer cycle's Anchor Course places you as a **farm intern on a leading regenerative farm**, and our gold standard recommendation is a summer at **Polyface Farm in Virginia under Joel Salatin**. Polyface is famous in sustainable agriculture circles; Joel Salatin is a bit of a legend, known for innovative farming that works *with* nature rather than against it. If you land a spot there (it's competitive – Joel only accepts people he believes can hack it), you'll earn your keep by working from sunup to sundown, learning the rhythms and realities of farm life and real skills along the way.

In a world where most live in front of screens, you might be wondering what working on a farm might look like? Imagine starting your day at dawn, moving herd after herd of grass-fed cattle onto fresh pasture as mist rises from the fields. Then you're off to collect eggs from a mobile chicken coop, feed and water hogs in the woods, or repair a section of fence that the bulls knocked down. By mid-morning you might be helping to slaughter chickens for market (you'll learn humane butchering and processing – an eye-opening experience for anyone who eats meat). After lunch, you could be stacking hay in a barn, spreading compost, or transplanting seedlings in the vegetable garden. Every day brings a dozen different tasks, and each is a lesson in biology, logistics, and plain old grit.

Farm work is physically demanding – your muscles will ache, and you'll sleep like a rock each night – but you'll also notice yourself getting stronger and more capable week by week. More than that, you'll gain an intimate understanding of where food truly comes from. You'll witness the cycles of life and death, growth and harvest, in a way that brings both humility and deep satisfaction.

There's nothing like eating a meal you helped produce from seed to plate; it gives you a profound appreciation for real value creation. The skills you pick up are broad: animal husbandry, basic veterinary knowledge (treating a cow's minor injury, for example), operating tractors and farm machinery, carpentry (farmers are always building or fixing something), and maybe even a bit of blacksmithing or mechanical repair. Economically, farming know-how can lead to careers in agriculture, agroforestry, or environmental science. But even if you don't become a farmer, you now possess the ability to grow your own food and perhaps manage land – a form of self-reliance that could turn into a lucrative side business or a fulfilling homestead life later on. Moreover, working with Joel (or any successful farmer) exposes you to **entrepreneurial thinking**.

Farms like Polyface are complex businesses; you'll see how orders are filled, customers are managed (Polyface has a huge following), and how creative thinking can upend an industry. Joel Salatin, for instance, doesn't do things the conventional way – and that iconoclast mindset will rub off on you.

Perhaps the greatest harvest of this cycle, though, is character. Farming teaches patience (crops grow on their own time, not yours), responsibility (animals die if you slack off or forget them), and teamwork (you literally rely on your fellow interns and farmers to get through the workload). You learn to tough it out through heat waves, thunderstorms, and early mornings when your body is sore. And you learn the joy of nurturing life – whether it's a newborn lamb you help deliver or a field rejuvenated through careful grazing management.

At the end of the Farmer cycle, you'll stand taller. You'll have calluses on your hands, maybe a few scars or stories from mishaps ("Remember when the bull chased me over the fence?"), and an earned pride that you contributed to something fundamental. When you bite into a ripe tomato you grew or a steak from a cow you raised, you understand hard work, sustainability, and stewardship in a way no classroom could ever convey. You'll leave the farm not just with new skills, but with wisdom and critical skills as old as civilization itself and a newfound connection to the earth that will keep you grounded no matter where you go next.

CYCLE 13: ENTREPRENEUR – LAUNCH A VENTURE AND LEARN THE ART OF BRINGING NEW POSSIBILITIES INTO PROFITABLE REALITY

Up to now, you've been gathering skills, knowledge, and experiences. Cycle 13 challenges you to put it all together and **create something of your own**. The Entrepreneur cycle's Anchor "Course" isn't a traditional class at all – it's the act of starting and running your own small venture for a few months. In other words, you're going to launch a business (or a or project) and see how far you can take it in one cycle. This could be anything: maybe you decide to see if you can build a business on substack, import and sell a unique product online, start a small landscaping service in your town, build an app or website that offers a service, or even publish a short book or course. Maxim is thinking of starting a Agricultural Drone business. The possibilities are endless.

The specific idea is less important than the process of **turning an idea into something of commercial value.** During this cycle, you'll write a simple business plan (don't worry, it can be on a napkin as long as it covers the basics), figure out your target customers, and then do the hustling required: marketing your product/service, making sales calls or building a website, managing costs, delivering for your customers, and adjusting your strategy when things don't go as expected (they never do!). This experience will likely be a rollercoaster. One week, a marketing idea might flop and you feel like an idiot; the next, you land a big customer, or your website suddenly gets traffic, and you feel on top of the world.

You will almost certainly encounter failure in some form – and that's good. Failure is feedback. Each setback will teach you to adapt, innovate, or pivot entirely. And each win, no matter how small, will help you understand what's possible when you're guiding the ship.

By the end of the cycle, one of two things will likely happen with your venture: **either it will show enough promise to continue**, or you'll keep it going as a side gig, building while you move on to other cycles. Either outcome is fine, because the real product here is *you*. You'll emerge with first-hand understanding of how money is made in the real world – not by filling out job applications, but by **creating value that others willingly pay for.** You'll understand terms like profit margin, customer acquisition, and break-even not because you memorized definitions, but because you wrestled with them in real life.

Entrepreneurial thinking – spotting opportunities, taking calculated risks, adjusting quickly – will become part of your mindset. This is hugely advantageous whether you go on to start dozens of businesses or end up working within someone else's company. Employers love self-starters, and nothing says self-starter like "I ran my own business at 20." Even if your venture crashes and burns, you can articulate what you learned, and it will be impressive. And if it succeeds? Well, that's the goal. You'll never be free if you rely on an employer.

Ultimately, the Entrepreneur cycle is about **taking charge of your destiny.** It's you saying, "I'm not going to wait for permission or for someone to hire me – I'm going to create something myself." That's a powerful shift in attitude. It's aspirational and direct: you're literally practicing how to build your dreams rather than someone else's. By the time this cycle is done, you'll know deep down that you have what it takes to be an entrepreneur – maybe not for every endeavor, but when the right idea and timing come along in your future, you won't be one of those people who only talk about "maybe doing something someday." **You'll have done it.**

CYCLE 14: INVESTOR – MAKE YOUR MONEY WORK FOR YOU

If Cycle 13 was about making money through enterprise, Cycle 14 is about multiplying money through savvy investment. The Investor cycle turns the focus to finance and the power of capital. Here, the Anchor activity is not a classroom course but the act of **managing an investment portfolio in real time.** Whether it's paper trading or putting some of your own capital on the line, you'll allocate it across different investments to learn how markets actually operate. During this cycle, you will **open a brokerage account**, if you haven't already, and get your feet wet with stocks, maybe some bonds or ETFs, possibly even dipping a toe into commodities or crypto – the specifics will depend on your interest and research.

You'll apply the economic and financial knowledge you've been building (remember those readings and courses on sound money and market history sprinkled throughout earlier cycles?). Now it all comes together as you analyze real companies and market trends. You'll learn to read financial statements, understand what moves stock prices, and follow economic indicators. More viscerally, you'll learn about **risk and reward** – nothing teaches you caution like watching a stock you bought drop 10% (don't worry, we'll emphasize prudent risk management so you're not gambling your future away). This is a hands-on crash course in not panicking when the market dips and not getting greedy when it spikes.

Beyond self-directed trading, you might also take on a project like participating in an online investment simulation contest or even securing a short internship or mentorship with a local investor or financial advisor to see professional investing up close. By the end of the cycle, you'll have a track record – maybe your initial portfolio grew, maybe it shrank – but either way, you'll have learned lessons that many people don't grasp until much later in life (if ever). You'll know the importance of research, patience, and emotional control in investing. You'll have felt the thrill of a good pick and the sting of a bad one, and you'll understand why legendary investors preach strategies like diversification and long-term thinking.

Importantly, you'll grasp how the concept of having *your money work for you* really works. Instead of being the guy who only knows how to earn a paycheck, you'll also be the guy who knows how to make that paycheck grow through smart allocation. This cycle makes you financially literate and then some – putting you miles ahead of your peers. College grads might come out with theory from an Economics 101 class; you'll come out having played *the game*, knowing the rules from experience. And just as crucially, you'll be able to smell BS in the financial world – you'll know how to discern solid investments from speculative bubbles or scams, because you trained yourself to think critically and seek evidence.

In terms of aspirations, the Investor cycle sets you on a path toward financial independence. By understanding investing now, you position yourself to perhaps retire decades earlier than the average person, or at least to have the freedom to make career choices not purely based on money. It's about building the life you want without being chained to each paycheck. Summed up: you'll finish this cycle as a young man who knows how to both make money and make it grow. Competent, confident, and (someday) downright dangerous in the marketplace.

CYCLE 15: HACKER – BUILD THE FUTURE WITHOUT WRITING CODE

The modern world runs on software. But here's a secret: you don't need a four-year computer science degree to create powerful applications. Cycle 15, the Hacker cycle, is all about mastering technology on your own terms. The Anchor Course plunges you into the world of "**no-code**" **development** – an emerging approach that lets you build apps and websites using AI and visual tools instead of traditional programming. You'll start with a structured **No-Code Foundations bootcamp**, learning platforms like Bubble, Webflow, or Adalo that empower you to design and launch software products with drag-and-drop logic. This whole field is growing fast. By the time you read this, the AI tools available to you will be far more capable than they are today. You need to know how to harness these tools to your advantage.

For about 6–7 weeks, under the guidance of no-code experts, you'll go from zero to building functional apps: maybe a simple database-driven web app, a mobile app prototype, or an automated workflow that could run a small business. Then, to deepen your expertise, you'll transition to an advanced program such as AirDev's self-paced bootcamp, where you'll tackle more complex projects and nuances in no-code tools.

By the end of this cycle, you will have built several portfolio-worthy projects – for instance, a personal finance tracker app, a basic social network, or a custom online store – all without typing lines of traditional code. The beauty of no-code is that it compresses the learning curve of software creation dramatically.

In a few months, you'll achieve what might take university students years. And the skills are immediately practical: if you have entrepreneurial ideas (flash back to Cycle 13), you can now rapidly prototype them yourself, without hiring expensive developers. Economically, this makes you extremely agile in the digital economy. Businesses large and small are only just discovering the power of no-code, so you'll be ahead of the curve. You could freelance building websites or apps, automate tasks for companies, or even launch a SaaS (Software as a Service) product single-handedly. But beyond the technical capability, Hacker cycle teaches you **problem-solving in abstract and systematic ways.**

You'll learn how to break big problems into smaller chunks and solve them logically – which is essentially what coding (or configuring no-code tools) is all about. This kind of thinking will enhance your effectiveness in any field, technical or not. We also pair this hands-on training with readings on tech entrepreneurship and design thinking – texts like *The Lean Startup* or *Don't Make Me Think*, which instill the mindset of rapid iteration and user-centric design. So you're not just making an app; you're learning to identify users' needs and craft solutions – a hacker's mindset that extends to hacking life's challenges, not in a malicious way, but in a "find a clever solution" way.

By cycle's end, your friends might still be complaining that coding is too hard or that they wish they could build an app for their idea. You'll smile, fire up your laptop, and in a weekend create a beta version of what they only talked about. That's power. And you'll have it because you took the initiative to become a tech creator, not just a tech consumer.

In a world where practically everything touches software, you will have become one of the creators – a young man who can **hack solutions and shape technology** to his will without waiting for permission or a team of engineers. That's an incredibly aspirational place to be and sets you up for whatever the future brings (even if someday you do decide to learn full programming, you'll do so with a huge head-start in understanding systems). You'll carry forward an inventor's confidence: there's no app for that? **Fine – I'll build one.**

CYCLE 16: MAKER – FABLAB MASTERY

The final cycle, Maker, is the culmination of your entire Preparation journey, a chance to integrate your diverse experiences into a single, ambitious creative project. By now, you've been a medic, a pilot, a cowboy, and much more. In Cycle 16, you step into your role as a creator, leveraging everything you've learned to build something tangible from scratch.

The key is having the right tools. And that's where the FabLab comes—an extraordinary workshop equipped with nine essential machines designed to bring almost any idea into physical reality. Here, you'll encounter laser cutters, CNC routers, 3D printers and scanners, sewing and embroidery machines, electronics benches, vinyl cutters, precision mills, and heat-press stations. With these tools at your fingertips, you are limited only by your imagination. A FabLab is a digitally powered bespoke manufacturing facility.

Perhaps you'll craft an acoustic guitar you've always wanted, precisely shaping its body with CNC routers and laser-cutting intricate fretboard inlays. Or maybe you'll dive into robotics, designing custom drones from carbon fiber sheets and 3D-printed components, then programming their flight controllers on an electronics bench. Furniture design could draw your attention—imagine producing elegant, flat-pack chairs and desks with CNC precision and laser-cut finishing touches. From wearable tech integrated seamlessly into garments, thanks to textile equipment, to practical innovations like solar ovens and tiny houses, the possibilities are expansive.

Your primary task in this cycle is clear yet ambitious: design and execute your own product, mastering each of the FabLab's nine machines along the way. You'll begin by becoming familiar with all equipment, gradually building competence and confidence. Rapid prototyping is your daily routine—testing, failing quickly, learning, and iterating until your creation meets your vision. Throughout, you'll document your process meticulously, creating a detailed portfolio that showcases your ability to transform concepts into reality.

FabLabs are widely accessible; many offer free or minimal-cost entry points for the public. Facilities like Champaign-Urbana Community FabLab, Phoenix Forge, NextFab, and numerous public library makerspaces across the country stand ready to host your creative endeavors. This accessibility ensures you can fully explore your ideas without significant financial constraints.

You will encounter setbacks—design flaws, material limitations, and practical hurdles— but each challenge is an invitation to apply your accumulated skills and ingenuity. If you've already built a house, piloted aircraft, and navigated wilderness survival, solving technical problems in a FabLab will feel like second nature. Overcoming these obstacles further solidifies your self-reliance and adaptability.

Completing the Maker cycle demonstrates more than technical competence; it proves your ability to self-direct, innovate, and bring complex ideas to fruition independently. Whether your project results in a profitable invention, an artistic masterpiece, or a deeply personal creation, the true value lies in the profound realization of your capability. You've become not just a participant or a specialist in isolated fields, but a versatile, confident Renaissance man—a true maker of objects, ideas, and your own future.

Each of these Anchor Courses has given you something invaluable: **hard-earned skills, unforgettable experiences, and a sense of who you are**. You've been tested in the real world – faced fear, excitement, exhaustion, triumph – and you've emerged more capable and sure of yourself. By cycling through these challenges, you've done more in a couple of years than many people do in a lifetime.

You've also built a real sense of who you are and a killer story: when someone asks what you've been up to, you won't have to BS about "uh, taking classes and thinking about my major." You can say, "I've been *living*: learning to save lives as an EMT, wrangling horses in the mountains, flying planes, fighting Muay Thai, coding apps..." See how that commands respect? More importantly, see how that *feels* inside? You know you're becoming the man you were meant to be.

Now, as incredible as these Anchor experiences are, they're only one piece of the puzzle. You've probably noticed that alongside every adventure, we've paired academic courses, readings, and other activities. That's by design.

Doing will always teach you plenty on its own, but doing informed by knowledge and reflection teaches you exponentially more. As you wrap up your hands-on exploits and catch your breath, it's time to dig into the other side of The Preparation – the academic program that runs in parallel to each cycle. As your experience and ideas expand, so will your possibilities.

In the next chapters, we'll explore how the books you read, the online courses you take, and even the games you play complement these Anchor Courses. This is where we connect the muscle to the mind. You'll see how understanding the theory, history, and philosophy behind your new skills makes you not just a doer, but a **thinking doer** – the kind of man who can both climb a mountain *and* articulate what the journey meant.

So let's transition from the wild and the workshop to the library and the lecture (don't worry, we keep it interesting). You've proven you can thrive out in the world; now we'll ensure you **master the world of ideas** that will sharpen your edge even further.

Chapter 13

ACADEMIC PROGRAM

BY DOUG CASEY

Grade school gives you the basics. How to read, how to write, and how to do arithmetic. From that base you have all that you need to access all the knowledge in the world, advancing on a gradient to ever higher levels.

You may have seen various tests given to grade school students a century ago. Most people can't pass them today. Part of that is understandable, in that modern society no longer deals in measures like rods and bushels. And it's said that, as for any test, students would study to memorize facts, cram, and then forget them as useless information cluttering their minds. I doubt that. Most questions related to "common knowledge".

I went to a four-year military boarding school. There used to be many; most have closed, and the character of the few that are left has changed. A good thing? Maybe. I'm not crazy about the military. It's 98% drudgery, boredom, and harassment, and 2% extreme danger. But, as Nietzsche said, anything that doesn't kill us makes us stronger. So Spartan environments, like the military, serve a purpose. It was a disciplined environment, which offset the mixed quality of the instructors. But we were exposed to the three basic sciences (biology, chemistry, and physics), intermediate math, (algebra, geometry, and trigonometry), four years of foreign language (two years of Latin, and two of French), four years of history, four of philosophy, four of English, and four of military science, with a smattering of other subjects.

I absorbed a certain number of subjects that didn't interest me by osmosis. That's suboptimal, but as with anything, you only get out what you put in. And while many of the subjects were interesting, I was subject to the quality of my teachers and the reading material they chose. Worse, I reacted to being forced to attend classes.

That said, I found high school much more worthwhile than college. If you go to a standard college, many of your classes will be taught by time-serving profs, or tyro teaching assistants. You'll inevitably miss classes or fall asleep in class after a late night. There will be distractions, or you'll find your mind wandering when you do attend. Even then, your notes may be poor, and hardly worth reviewing. And whatever value there was in the class is gone forever.

Remember that just because we're advising you not to attend college doesn't mean we don't value a structured sequence for learning.

In the medieval world, for instance, education centered around the trivium and the quadrivium. The terms sound arcane and academic, and they are. Nobody thinks about them anymore, or even knows what they were.

The trivium and quadrivium are foundational concepts in classical education. The Preparation is based on them. The whole point of going to college is to master the Trivium and Quadrivium.

TRIVIUM

The trivium consists of three subjects that are foundational for learning:

1. **GRAMMAR:** Is about the rules of language—speaking properly. Knowing words, their meaning, and how they're put together to express thoughts. You might think there's only a limited value in studying English grammar, because speaking seems natural and intuitive. However, pidgin, Ebonics, and cockney are also forms of English—but because their grammars are different it's hard to communicate with them.

   Grammar is concerned with the meanings of words. If you don't understand exactly what a word means—and can't define it instantly—then perhaps you don't really know what you're talking about. If people are using the same word, but it means something different to each of them, then they can never really communicate, or truly understand each other. It's something of a paradox that, although there are roughly one million English words (far more than any other language), you can get by well enough with about 500. But having a large vocabulary and using it with clarity and precision is fundamental.

SCAN ME

BOOK: THE ELEMENTS OF STYLE BY WILLIAM STRUNK JR. AND E.B. WHITE

It's only 100 pages long, but gives you all the basics of writing well. It's a reference book, but clever and fun to read. If your writing doesn't keep to its guidelines, people will think your uneducated, or even dim.

2. **LOGIC:** The study of reasoning, what makes sense, what doesn't, and why. Thinking, if you will, like Mr. Spock. Learning to think scientifically, in terms of cause and effect. Critical thinking, which is the process of examining everything you see, hear, and read to examine it for false premises, jumped conclusions, and many other logical fallacies. A logical mind will help you predict consequences, and keep you from being hoodwinked or cheated.

SCAN ME

BOOK THE ART OF THINKING CLEARLY BY ROLF DOBELLI

In 99 short, but highly entertaining chapters, we're led through the most common logical fallacies.

BOOK: LOGIC: A VERY SHORT INTRODUCTION BY GRAHAM PRIEST.

Long books on academic subjects don't get read. This short volume is a pithy introduction to critical thinking—examining propositions to see if they make sense.

Incidentally, it's part of a series put out by Oxford University, giving short introductions on over 500 different subjects, everything under the sun. It's like a more intellectual version of "The Dummy's guide to X" or "X for Idiots" we have in the US. Look them up. Their contents amount to a college education. **www.oup.com/vsi**

3. **RHETORIC:** The art of effective communication and persuasion. Armed with grammar (the proper words, properly put together) and logic (so you don't represent things that are foolish or wrong, but seeking truth), you'll want to present your views in a way that others understand and, hopefully, accept. Socrates approved of grammar and logic, but was suspicious of rhetoric—although he was a superb rhetorician and debater. Rhetoric was a tool of Sophists, teachers who taught students to win arguments—but not necessarily to seek the truth. It's about how to win arguments, and get what you want.

BOOK: THANK YOU FOR ARGUING BY JAY HEINRICHS

You could read Aristotle's "Rhetoric", but this book is much more entertaining and up-to-date. To underline the importance of rhetoric, and reading the book, I urge you to watch the movie "My Cousin Vinny" with Joe Pesci and Marisa Tomei.

QUADRIVIUM

The concepts of the trivium are as valid now as they were centuries ago. Think of the trivium as having a powerful computer in your mind, with lots of useful programs to assemble data, describe it with grammar, analyze it with logic, and present it with rhetoric. The quadrivium consists of hard facts and theories to put into your mental computer.

The composition of the quadrivium is a bit misleading in today's context. It's four subjects were thought to give students the basics of how the world works. Basic concepts of math and science.

Of course, we now know vastly more than these four areas of knowledge. Think of these four things for context; you're going to learn a hundred more things. Perhaps the ancient quadrivium should be renamed as the modern centivium. Science is an emphasis of our modern centivium.

ARITHMETIC: The study of numbers and their relationships. Obviously, we go much further—the ancients didn't even have the concept of zero, and it was hard to maneuver Roman numerals. I'm surprised at how illiterate the average person is today, but he may be even more innumerate. I'm not talking about algebra and calculus—just addition, subtraction, multiplication, and division. Arithmetic is foundational to success in business and managing your money.

GEOMETRY: The study of spatial relationships and the properties of shapes. This relates to architecture, artwork, design, and everything you can see. Sight is your most important sense.

MUSIC: The study of harmony, rhythm, tempo, pitch, and everything else that relates to sound. The foundations of music are mathematical. Hearing is your second major sense. Some tones are dissonant and discordant. Some are mellow, heroic, or elevating. Music covers the whole range of human emotions. Anyone who works with animals knows that music affects them viscerally as well.

ASTRONOMY: The study of the cosmos and celestial bodies. It's important for navigation, but more so for appreciating your place in the universe. FWIW, astronomy and cosmology are a practical modern replacement for philosophy and theology courses.

On that note, you'll be interested in The Sun of God, by Gregory Sams.

FOUR YEARS THAT CAN CHANGE YOUR LIFE

In just four years you can't study everything. But the nineteen subjects listed below, the four years divided into four quarters each, will give you a vastly broader and deeper academic education than 99% of humanity. Is the academic part of the Preparation as important as the Anchor courses? It's hard to say. Which part of the Tao is more important, the Yin or the Yang?

An academic discipline is an accepted branch of knowledge, meant to strengthen your mental ability and increase your understanding of reality. A classicist would consider the sciences as "natural philosophy".

Few people appreciate that going to college—"getting an education"—does very little to assist you in either learning skills or gaining a moral foundation. The knowledge you theoretically gain in college is mostly "useless information". I've divided the Academic part of The Preparation into the three groups below. The B.A. and

B.S. have relatively few applications in the here and now. They're intended to make well— rounded men—thoughtful, moral, knowledgeable. It's the MBA that imparts skills which directly put money in your pocket—but these are mostly graduate school courses. Which means an extra two years and $100,000.

Look at the academic content of the 16 quarters below. You'll notice that the first five— Chemistry, Physics, Geology, Astronomy and Biology–are hard science. They're your B.S. degree. They contain the kind of knowledge the character MacGyver uses to save the day.

It's critical to have a sound understanding of the physical world we live in. Most people don't know more about science than they pick up from news articles. That includes most college graduates, who skate through schools to get a B.A. diploma. Taking these courses, and reading the books, will give you much more than the fundamentals of a B.S. degree.

The next group—World History, American History, Literature, Music, Art, Law, and Economics—cover the humanities. Doing these will give you not just a little more, but vastly more than any B.A. course from any University. And you won't be burdened by phony "studies" on gender or race, and "soft" studies like psychology, sociology, or political science. These are the liberal arts, derived from the Latin "liber", meaning free. They're subjects that a free man, as opposed to a slave or a serf, should be familiar with.

The third group—Investing, Accounting, Business, Entrepreneurship, Sales, and Marketing—are practical knowledge. They're useful, not "academic". They're skills you need for dealing with the public and companies to make and keep money. Learning these things is like going to a white-collar trade school and are generally only taught in a Business school or at the M.B.A. level. An MBA generally takes two years, costs $100,000, and instills bad ideas into your head.

If an undergraduate degree isn't worth it, does it make sense to say "in for a penny, in for a pound" and get an MBA, hoping for some practical knowledge? When we interview an employee with an MBA, we appreciate the good intentions behind the extra schooling. But we also know we're dealing with a person who, though he's probably 25 or 26, has likely done little in the real world. Worse, he's spent so many years studying theory, from professors who've also just studied theory, that his thinking has been corrupted. Why would someone spend the best six years of his life, and a hundred thousand dollars, to qualify for very little beyond being an administrator? A suit in middle management. In the real world, they're the first ones to be fired ("let go" is the euphemistic PC phrase) when costs need to be cut.

The Academic portion of The Preparation ensures you never have a lingering notion that you missed something in college. The courses below are more than you'll theoretically learn in college—if you're serious enough to learn them at all; most students just learn to pass tests in them. They're very important. But only a portion of what The Preparation is about.

You'll notice we've divided the courses into three groups: Bachelor of Science (BS), Bachelor of Arts (BA), and Master of Business Administration (MBA). In a conventional college a degree is given for each area of concentration. They're equally important on the road to being truly educated, but even if you graduate, you'll be lop-sided in just one of the three. Most college attendees spend four years either as BS or BA; unbalanced, missing the other. Then only a small portion go on to an MBA, which has the most practical value.

We're trying to get all three into four years—in addition to a vast number of other skills and experiences. It's a lot. That's why, even though we've divided these courses into quarters, you may find some take you less, or more, time to complete. It may take four years to check all the boxes on some of the 16 quarters. **We don't expect you to read all the books for English Literature in one quarter—break them up over four years. And then keep up the habit throughout your life.**

The same for music and art. On the other hand, you may be able to do the Geology and Astronomy segments in half the time. The key is applying yourself diligently to the material.

You're going to thank us for introducing you to these courses. You'll be entertained while your mind and horizons are expanded.

We've generally chosen just three courses for each subject, the ones we think (somewhat arbitrarily) are the best. But The Teaching Company alone offer over 800. They're curated and of superb quality. But the Internet offers tens of thousands more. As do many universities, including Oxford and MIT.

CHEMISTRY (B.S. 1)

Take these courses, in this order. Don't think of chemistry as just mixing some things together in a test tube. It explains the nature of everything in the raw material world. The courses we recommend may seem like a lot. But it's really important. Find the time. You can do it in a week. Make notes. Wait a week. And listen again. It will immensely improve your retention. The best part is that you're not cramming for an exam, to prove something to a teacher, but storing it in your memory, for your own lifelong benefit.

Try to use that approach for all the courses listed later in the book.

PHYSICS (B.S.2)

The boundaries of physics aren't easily defined because it comprehends everything. Let's say it's the study of matter, energy, space, time, motion, and force. As such, it overlaps with about every other scientific discipline.

GEOLOGY (B.S.3)

Geology is the study of the planet earth. For the last generation or so there's been an increasing mass hysteria to the effect that Gaia is dying, and humans are killing her. It makes sense to know what science has discovered about the roughly 4 billion years the Earth has existed, what life forms have lived and died, how the planet is put together, and how it continues to evolve, and how to exploit mineral resources.

In many colleges, geology is sometimes mocked as "rocks for jocks", since it's probably the most inexact of the sciences. True enough. But I know several geos who've become billionaires by applying their academic knowledge out in the field.

I know many geologists, and would characterize them, overwhelmingly, as outdoorsy intellectuals. A lot of their work involved hiking out in the middle of nowhere, and living in isolated camps where reading is the main form of entertainment.

ASTRONOMY/COSMOLOGY (B.S.4/5)

Astronomy comprises a lot more than just staring through a telescope at night. It puts things in perspective, recognizing we're on a cosmically insignificant planet revolving around an average star. But there are 200 to 400 billion other stars in our medium sized galaxy alone; most of them have planets. It was only in the early 20th C that we learned there even were other galaxies. The latest number is about two trillion other galaxies.

This subject is, in effect, a modern replacement for medieval studies in theology. It's as close as we come to explaining the universe. Like most we recommend, you'll probably want to work through the material twice, while taking notes. Just once will just leave you in a state of shock and awe.

BIOLOGY (B.S. 6)

Fundamentals in Biology provide you with an understanding of how systems work. Your body, your brain, your organs, animals, and plants. Most people don't understand any of these systems and therefore become reliant on some pharmaceutical product to fix it for them. You should have a basic understanding so you can problem solve these systems yourself. Or at least be able to read a clinical trial paper, and ask relevant questions. Especially if they are trying to put that drug into your body. By understanding anatomy and nutrition you'll be able to maintain your own health and grow your own food.

The courses we recommend will give you the basics of biology, physiology, and medicine—some theory, some practice. One of them, on Emergency Medicine, is on the area where modern medicine really shines. It's truly great for acute disease and trauma, but is evolving more slowly in the area of maintaining health.

> Even just learning more about the world around you can be fascinating. Do you know the difference between different kinds of trees? Download the iNaturalist App or one of the others out there and start informing yourself about the word around you.

Get APP

WORLD HISTORY (B.A. 1)

We're on a continuum which started with the Big Bang about 13.7 billion years ago, and (estimates vary) will continue for many trillions—or perhaps quadrillions—of years into the future. In other words, the universe itself is still just a pup; it's going to exist many thousands of times, perhaps millions of times, longer than it's already existed. I mention that to help keep what we think of as "history" in perspective.

Herodotus (484–425BC) was the first historian that we know of, and that was only 2500 years ago. Is that the distant past? Not so much. That only spans the lives of 50 men who, if they each lived to be only 75, and reproduced at age 50, could have communicated directly with each other for 25 years. Almost all of (civilized) human history could have been transmitted like a kid's game of telephone. The problem is that with either written and researched history, or a long-lasting game of telephone, distortions creep in. We often don't know what really happened a year ago, much less a thousand years ago.

It matters. That's why some people lie about the past. That's why the State in George Orwell's **1984** had a "memory hole", where they'd disappear parts of history that didn't suit Big Brother. All of history is constantly being edited and curated according to the beliefs of historians. You might think the computer revolution solved the problem by preserving everything. But it also makes it easier to delete facts and interpretations than burning all copies of a book.

It's no accident that History faculties at colleges are almost as corrupt as the English departments.

That said, you should consider history as a lifelong study. Ancient Greece and Rome, alone, deserve a lifetime of reading—that's before we even think of the Medieval world, the Renaissance, the Enlightenment, English history, the 19th and 20th centuries. Not to mention what formed China and India.

AMERICAN HISTORY (B.A. 2)

We don't mean to sound like American Exceptionalists or Nationalists, but in fact the US was the only country in history that was overtly founded on a particular set of principles. The chances are good that you're American, and it makes sense to understand the place where you live. Even if you're not American, it makes sense to understand the history and culture of what is (still) the most powerful country on the planet.

LITERATURE (B.A. 3)

Literature is the primary and most direct way culture is transmitted from one generation to the next. **Reading books is probably the most significant element of an education.** The question arises: Which books. In the days before the Internet there were typically about 50,000 new books published each year. Now there are well over a million. As AI progresses, writing books near instantaneously on-demand, the numbers will become astronomical.

If you hold to The Preparation, you might make it through 50 per year, at most. Probably more like ten. So how do you choose?

Picking the best literature has always been the duty of English Departments. Here we're talking about fiction. Fiction is important for two reasons: One, we transmit attitudes and beliefs mainly through stories, narratives, not just by recounting facts. Two, there are many subtleties that can only be expressed in fiction. English majors theoretically specialize in reading literature over every-thing else. Getting a BA in English never qualified you for anything in particular, but it said you had a broad range of knowledge and interests, and were an educated man.

That's no longer true. English departments everywhere have been corrupted from every point of view.

50 or 100 years ago, when college was for the elite, professors could assign reading and writing to students, confident that the students had the basics down. Today almost everyone goes to college, whether they qualify or not, and these people are shunted into English classes as remedial education. There's a (usually vain) hope the kids can be brought up to reading and writing at an adult level, to handle the rest of their classes. English is no longer seen as a qualification for becoming a Renaissance Man, but as a booby prize that serves no useful purpose. It doesn't aid in your economic advancement.

Professors have always been somewhat cloistered, and the subject matter is the product of dead white males. Which makes it unfashionable. They don't want to be seen as unhip, teaching classes where snowflakes can be triggered with possibly xenophobic, racist, colonialist, homophobic, misogynist, or capitalist-leaning thoughts. English departments have—like sociology, political science, history, anthropology, and every subject ending in "Studies"—become completely Woke and Politically Correct.

These people have come to disdain, even despise, everything that Western Culture stands for. It's perverse, in that nearly everything in life that's brought the bulk of mankind out of the primeval mud is largely due to western culture. There used to be something called the Western Literary Canon. It was accepted as representing the best of what's been thought, said, and written throughout history. English professors once acted as guides to help students unlock the wisdom in the canon.

How degraded have things become? When I was a trustee for the 10th oldest college in the US, I audited an English class taught by a middle-aged professor who not only showed up for class in gym shorts, but assigned a book written by an imprisoned black man. The book might be interesting reading, but it's taking time which should have been used for Shakespeare, Milton, or Mark Twain.

Most liberal arts professors now think that, as part of their duty to destroy despicable White Culture, they should "deconstruct" the excellent and noble, to replace it with the trivial. Aeschylus, Shakespeare, and Gibbon have been edged out by the currently fashionable.

It's fine to engage in experimental and avant-garde writing—but only after you have real competence in the basics. Doing your thing with no regard for rules of the Trivium— grammar, logic, and rhetoric amounts to wasting time. It's OK to amuse yourself with trivial stuff written by thoughtless popular writers. But that has nothing to do with becoming a Renaissance Man.

The courses below will give you an overview of fiction. They're what a proper English professor brings to the party. But the essence of the matter is reading the books themselves, which are listed.

It's worth noting that the most popular lists of "great novels" on the Internet are heavily influenced by PC and Wokism. We believe our list is of more lasting value.

ECONOMICS (B.A. 4)

Economics is the study of the way the world works, Econ courses are rarely offered in High School. And that's just as well, because they'd mainly just be watered down versions of the economics courses offered in college—which are typically worse than a waste of time. Let me briefly explain why I say that, and describe what you'll be taught. Almost all college level econ courses are based on various Keynesian theories, which amount to recommendations of how the Government should best manipulate producers and consumers. They're broken down into general categories: Fiscal theory, and Monetary theory.

Monetary policy basically concerns how much fiat currency should be created through the government's Central Bank (called the Federal Reserve in the US), how interest rates should be set, and how commercial banks should be regulated through fractional reserve policies.

Fiscal policy concerns government taxing and spending. How much it "should" extract from society through various taxes, and which groups get that money when it's redistributed.

This school of econ can be quite complex, with many abstruse mathematical formulas, giving it the appearance of a science, like physics or chemistry. It's not. Economics should describe reality, not prescribe how the public should be manipulated.

We think you should understand Keynesian economics, as well as Marxist economic theories. But they'll be of zero help in life, unless you want to become an economics professor who will teach these theories to the next generation, or become a government official who can use them to justify his actions. If that's the case, this book is probably not for you.

That said, however, it is important to understand economics. You need to know how the world works in creating, producing and consuming.

You'll notice we don't have any Great Courses econ courses. The reason is simple: Almost all the econ taught in school is Keynesian, often with a Marxist slant, and completely wrong-headed. Most economic professors would be comfortable having drinks with the English, History, Sociology or Philosophy profs at the typical college.

The courses we recommend are of the free market persuasion. They describe how the world works as it goes about producing and consuming. Keynesians necessarily wind up prescribing how they think the world ought to work, and counseling governments to make it so. They're very different views on reality, and you are affected by them constantly throughout life.

MUSIC (B.A.5)

These courses will give you a foundation in classical music. It appears that relatively few young men have much familiarity with it. How do you choose the truly memorable works from the many thousands? We've chosen some of the best compositions from the most justly famous classical composers. Plus some outstanding "one hit wonders".

You should listen to these at least twice. But I suspect you'll wind up with many on your playlist for many years to come. In the Classical Music Starter guide you can see the list we've put together.

A good argument can be made that music has become degraded over the past few generations. Older generations argued that rock and roll was puerile and sexual; maybe that's true relative to classical. But it was fun, had rhythm and melody. Hip hop and rap don't; they're purposefully violent, degrading, and dissonant. Some will say it's just a matter of taste, and that's true to a degree. But good taste is a product of wide knowledge, refinement, and thoughtful judgements; bad taste is the product of ignorance, coarseness, and thoughtlessness.

A lot of contemporary music—the products of street thugs whose songs make them multimillionaires–is the audio equivalent of contemporary art like the famous banana taped to a wall that sold for $6.5 million.

Later you'll find our list of courses that'll teach you how to appreciate great classical music.

ART (B.A.6)

There are two aspects to this part of The Preparation. One is learning to appreciate art and the history of art; that's part of this, the academic area of The Preparation. The other is trying your hand at it; that's part of the practical area. They're separate endeavors but supplement each other. You gain a much deeper appreciation of art when you try to replicate the skill it takes to create it.

Art appreciation courses are notoriously "soft". The prof will show you lots of drawings, etchings, frescoes, paintings, sculptures, and what-have-you. And lecture on the artist and his place in history. And give you his opinions on what's "good" or "bad". Art appreciation courses have a bad rep more because of the people who take them than their actual content. But they can can be very helpful. It's like having an expert guide you through a museum, drawing your attention to things you might never even notice, much less understand.

I've collected art for years, and have two criteria for what I buy. One is its ideational value: what does it tell me about the nature of life—as it is, or was, or should be. The other is the technical skill of the artist in putting those ideas across. Picasso only went into doing strange things after he proved he could duplicate masters like Michelangelo.

As you visit museums and galleries, and listen to opinions, you're likely to conclude—as I have—that much of modern art is a scam. A product of clever marketing and money laundering, not talent and imagination.

Most of your contemporaries don't have a clue about art. Most accept what they're told about its worth, without enough knowledge to make a valid judgement. That said, there's some truth to the saying "I don't know if it's good or bad art. I just know if I like it or not". It's like knowing tasty from putrid food, or pleasant from offensive language. There's something to be said for intuition and gut feelings. It's why the Roman dictum "de gustibus non disputandum est" (there's no disputing about taste) has been repeated for millennia.

Maybe that's why the average guy recognizes that overripe bananas duct taped to walls and paintings that look like the scribblings of a psychotic child but also go for seven figures are scams. I suspect the ultra-rich and the effete only pretend to appreciate these things because they live in corrupt bubbles. Keep in mind that prices and popularity are, at best, only a very rough possible indicator of quality. You'll want to learn the basics so you can make an intelligent judgment.

LAW (MBA 1)

Al Capone once said, a man with a pen can steal 100 times more than a man with a gun. But if you're going to become wealthy—a noble ambition, partly because it will allow you to finance things you want to DO that will allow you a higher state of BEING—you must come to grips with law. Ideally, the law should ensure order and justice. But, in fact, many laws are oppressive and needlessly obstruct freedom. Most law is just the arbitrary dictates of politicians and bureaucrats. That's why it's been said, correctly, that the law is an ass.

It's more important than ever to understand how the legal sausage is made, because there are orders of magnitude more laws and regulations than ever before in history. We've devolved a great deal from the ideal that our friend Rick Maybury spelled out, of only two Great Laws. "Do all that you say you will do". And "Don't impinge on others or their property".

I prefer to simplify things even further. Aleister Crowley, the notorious nihilist, said, "The whole of the Law shall be 'Do as Thou Wilt'". But he forgot to append an all-important clause... "but be prepared to accept the consequences". Contemplating that would result in much less robotic rule-following, and much more forethought and personal responsibility.

But these are philosophical thoughts. In today's world the object is to keep from being taken to school and intimidated by lawyers.

The courses we recommend will save you the two years of time, and keep you from spending the six figures, required to go to law school.

INVESTING (MBA 2)

As soon as you succeed in producing more than you consume, you'll have extra money. That's capital. There was once a time, not so long ago, when the dollar was "as good as gold", you could leave those dollars dormant. Now, however, the dollar—and every other currency—is no more than an accounting fiction. It's critical, therefore, that you develop expertise about where to put your dollars so that you outrace inflation, dodge the potential failure of banks, brokers, insurance companies, businesses, and even the government. The chances are good that you'll see most, if not all, of these things in the years to come. The good news is that The Preparation will insulate you from them as much as anything can.

The average person with a college degree knows little or nothing about investing beyond snippets he may have picked up here and there. That's the advantage of a formal course. Without thoughtful instruction, you probably don't even know what you don't know. It's a pity if, once you've put aside some capital, you were to lose it , either to the market or inflation, because you were ignorant or negligent. It's important that you become a competent investor—or speculator, which is quite different.

BUSINESS/ENTREPRENEURSHIP/ACCOUNTING (MBA 3/4)

Some college students major in Business as undergraduates. That's not the worst way to spend many hours sitting behind a desk. Most kids know absolutely nothing about the basics of business—making a product, employing workers, marketing to the public, accounting, and a hundred other subjects. At least business courses contain some real world knowledge about these things.

What's inexcusable is going on to get an MBA. MBAs spend another 50–100k for another two years of theory. At our shop, we consider an applicant's advanced degree not a qualification, but a warning sign. That time and money should have been allocated to starting a business, on a small scale, learning by doing. There's a lot of truth to the old saying, "Those who can, do. Those who can't, teach". MBAs are for people who realize that they've learned little about the real world of business by going to college. It's admirable that they want to catch up and learn things they wish they'd already been taught. But they're pursuing a solution that's slow, high cost, and relatively ineffective.

Most people who make serious money and become wealthy don't do it working for someone else. They do it by starting and growing their own business. Remember, that everyone in the world wants everything imaginable. You can make an unlimited amount of money by figuring out how to give some of them what they want at a price they're willing to pay.

MBAs take courses in managing, marketing, business law, taxes, and accounting. They study business successes and failures, often with case studies. It's all valuable knowledge, but I'd argue the time and cost of acquiring it is out of proportion to its value. The greatest value of an MBA may be the intimidation factor—others assume they know a lot more than they do.

Not long ago everyone wanted to get an MBA. Business schools cranked out scores of thousands of them. Their teachers were only rarely successful businessmen; they were professors who'd studied business, but never did any. Experience proved that most graduates were, just like their teachers, overpaid drones, working for a salary, and mostly suited for middle management. MBAs are pieces of paper that might qualify you for climbing a corporate ladder. But, as Matt explained in Chapter 4, you really want to avoid somebody else's corporate ladder. You want to build a web, based on your knowledge and experience, not expensive degrees.

The purpose of these courses is to familiarize you with what an MBA knows so you can do it on your own.

SALES (MBA 6)

There's no question that an ability to sell effectively may be the most important skill you can have. It's the ability to get others to see things your way and take action. Numerous other skills you'll learn in The Preparation–flying, sailing, building, and 100 others—are extremely valuable, but only usable in certain circumstances. Salesmanship is usable everywhere. You can use it with everyone from suspicious natives in a primitive country to hard-nosed Execs in a New York boardroom.

Businesses all have products they want to sell. In fact, they're desperate to sell those products. But while they may make a great product, they may not know the best way to sell it. That's why competent salesmen are among the highest paid workers in the world. They're problem solvers. A good salesman is a practical psychologist. He's skilled at finding out what people need or want and showing them how his product or service will make their lives better. Then—most critically—getting their agreement, asking for the order, and closing the deal.

Salesmen have generally bad reputations, for several reasons. Most are affable, with a nice shoeshine but a lukewarm IQ. They rarely know much about their product and try to disguise that with glib patter and misdirection. Few are smart enough to find out who their potential customer really is, and what they need or want. Most are incompetent at closing the deal. And nobody respects incompetence. They're order takers at best, dependent on marketing teams and business strategists to drive customers to them. Unproductive time wasters.

 Watch the following clip and movie—but not as entertainment, as an introduction to a world few are aware exists. People don't respect salesmen because most are lazy incompetents, and don't like them because they're often unethical. Salesmen who project both competence and good ethics can make gigantic amounts of money quickly.

"**The Wolf of Wall Street**"—with Leo DiCaprio is about competence without ethics

"**Wall Street**"—with Michael Douglas and Charlie Sheen is also a morality play. But, oddly, the only ethical character in the movie, played by Douglas, is presented in the opposite light.

"**Trading Places**", Dan Ackroyd and Eddie Murphy

When I learned the salesman's trade I was thrown into the deep end of the pool, a boiler room full of sharks. I gained an education through osmosis, watching and listening to others who'd survived a while. I wasted a lot of time, treating it as a job, a way station, instead of actively trying to perfect a skill.

The ideal situation is to find an area where you have expertise, or where you can acquire it on the job, and pursue selling as an art, not just a job. The problem is that—as a young man just out of high school—you'll lack expertise in both the product and how to sell. That's alright. Find a company looking for salesmen and start by selling yourself to them.

These books and videos are helpful. But there's no substitute for person-to-person experience. I suggest you consider finding, or creating, a position where you're selling for the Anchor Quarter on Entrepreneurship – where sales is essential.

MARKETING (MBA 6)

Salesmanship is about dealing with other people one-to-one. Marketing is about promoting a product or service to the public at large. It's about mass psychology. In essence, a marketer learns to create advertising copy that the public reads, sees, or hears.

On youtube you'll find hundreds of courses on marketing. There's nothing you can learn in an MBA that you won't learn better, quicker, and cheaper by listening to people who are out there doing, as opposed to parroting stale lectures. If they were successful in marketing, they'd be doing it. The prof would not only be earning a multiple of what he makes teaching at a college, but learning new things himself in the process. The way to gain marketing skill is to be out in the real world, testing and executing programs. A professor who teaches marketing without doing it himself quickly becomes ineffective, theoretical, out-of-date, and irrelevant.

Chapter 14

ACTIVITIES—DO FUN SHIT

BY DOUG CASEY

We've laid out Practical Skills and Academic elements of the program. They're enjoyable, beneficial, and entertaining. But there's a third leg to the stool of becoming a Renaissance Man. You might call it "Doing Fun Shit".

Each week you should plan one mini event, something that you find fun or interesting, something that others might consider a hobby. Remember, the power of novel action from the earlier chapter, How to Actually Get Ahead in life. Do new things. For example, you could take woodworking classes, go flyfishing, learn to ride motorcross, climb a mountain, or go skiing.

There are hundreds of worthwhile activities or hobbies out there. We've listed, and will briefly discuss, a few that we think are particularly valuable and relevant to becoming a well-rounded man.

With the amount of concentration involved in the other elements of your cycle, you'll probably want something special to look forward to each week. Something motivating, challenging, or fun. These mini events allow you to branch out to try something new. So, any week you aren't engaged in an anchor activity you should plan one mini event. Each hour spent on one of these mini weekly events will count for 1 credit hour.

There are an immense number of "hobby clubs". Someone who likes, for instance, Kayaking generally wants to, or even has to, for reasons of safety and convenience, do it with others. They form clubs to get others interested, and teach them the ropes. They're generally weekend activities—which fits in perfectly with The Preparation. The Oxford English Dictionary defines a hobby as "an activity done regularly in one's leisure time for pleasure".

PRO TIP

You should keep in mind that a hobby isn't just something you do for leisure and fun. A hobby can be a gateway to the world. The legendary investor and friend of Doug's, Jim Rogers, took up motorcycle riding so he could see the entire world. Chronicled in his book, "Investment Biker", his around the world journey took him 22 months riding over 100,000 miles.

Here's a list to give you some ideas. Some are near free—most people don't have a lot of spare cash. Some are costly—it's nothing new that one of the ways boys sort themselves out is by the cost of their toys. Some hobbies have a lot more real-world value than others.

We suggest that you trend towards those offering some benefit or skill, as opposed to idle and pointless pastimes, like playing Bingo.

Many of these things could be Anchor courses of their own. With a bit of research you can build your own cycle around it. But you can't kiss all the girls in just 16 quarters. We think these are perhaps the most valuable (and fun) things in The Preparation.

We've divided them into categories: Adventure, Social Sports & Games, and Arts & Craftsmanship. It may seem like a lot, but you should become adept in some from each category.

ADVENTURE

The modern pentathlon involves fencing, shooting, swimming, riding, and cross country running. The ancient pentathlon included the long jump, discus throw, foot race, javelin throw and wrestling. Pick and choose events you like. All of these require instruction. But time is limited. Some of these are life-long friends, others are just acquaintances. I've listed them in (somewhat arbitrary) order of importance.

All the skills in this section are what distinguish James Bond, or the Ethan Hunt character played by Tom Cruise in the Mission: Impossible series. Many young men join the armed forces hoping to gain some of them. But Tom Cruise does his own stunts, and is qualified in all of them to a reasonable degree. He didn't need the military to gain them.

The advantage to joining the military is that if you're young, without skills, and at loose ends, it's an alternative. But not ideal. You'll spend years doing grunt labor and taking orders from people you may neither like nor respect. It's essentially a bureaucracy, with a rigid pecking order and strict rules. I know lots of military men, from 4-stars on down, and generally get on well with them. If inertia keeps you in the military for more than one hitch, you'll likely get caught in the system, and find it hard to acclimatize to civilian life.

Learning the skills listed here will give you the qualifications of a SpecOps "operator" (which is everyone's ideal), but you can do it on your own time, without the imposed aggravations, and the possibility of other people trying to kill you, or you having to kill them.

MARTIAL ARTS—Learning to fight is an essential part of a proper education. We have it as one of the 16 Anchors, but it's something you should continue throughout your life, if only as a great way to stay fit. Throughout history a major difference between a free man and a slave was that a free man knew how to defend himself and bear arms.

You definitely want to avoid fights. If you win, you may hurt your opponent, and in today's litigious society you may be sued or get in trouble with the law. If you lose you may be seriously injured—although studying martial arts reduces the chances of that. There are scores of popular martial arts. I've taken classes in judo, boxing, karate, kung fu and Taichi. All combat training is valuable, but the key is to practice at least one discipline enough that it's automatic, and dialed into your muscle memory. It's been said—correctly— that doing a thousand moves once isn't nearly as valuable as doing one a thousand times. They're all artforms, and all are superb vehicles for physical conditioning. Taking even a week of boxing, judo, or karate lessons will put you head and shoulders above the untrained (which is to say 95% of the population).

Structured classes sometimes, however, lack practicality. Especially karate. It's full of valuable moves, but there's a tendency to train for idealized situations that mostly only arise in formal classes. A standardized move from an opponent in a class tends to elicit a reaction based on muscle memory. That's good. But it's why a good boxer will usually defeat a good karate guy. There are fewer moves to learn in boxing, and they are therefore practiced much more often. And I say that as someone who was a fan of the "forms" or "katas", which amount to formalized dance routines where everything is done in sequence. Karate usually provides the entrance to martial arts because there are studios everywhere. They're commercial enterprises, and to retain students they have to keep advancing them in grade. They risk becoming diploma mills (like colleges, actually), where students become overconfident because they've been awarded a belt.

But this is nit picking. If I was to choose, I'd put boxing first on the list, followed by judo. The problem is that there are relatively few gyms around that teach them. But there are karate studios almost everywhere, and more and more mixed martial art studios, Muay Thai, Krav Maga, Brazilian Jiujitsu and others.

Take one up wherever you are and keep at it. As you gain expertise, you'll figure out which studios and which arts suit you best. Maxim enjoys the combo of BJJ and Kickboxing.

MOTORSPORTS—Cars are more ubiquitous than ever. Oddly, even though the speed and road competence of cars has grown exponentially, the skill of drivers has decreased. Cars almost, or do, drive themselves. But there's a lot to be said for racing, where you rely on acquired skill more than your vehicle's computer.

The problem with racing is that it's both high-tech and very expensive. On the other hand, you should consider going to racing schools with rented cars. A good introduction is to get involved in Gymkhanas and Autocrosses, which mostly happen at empty parking lots with ordinary street cars. Many serious racers today start with go-karts.

I've taken courses in Europe at racecourses at Monza in Italy, and Montlhery in France. The most fun was a stock car racing school with Buck Baker (RIP) at Rockingham, South Carolina. Buck didn't learn to drive in a class, but by transporting loads of moonshine, racing revenuers over back roads. As with most practical things, you can learn by watching and doing. But things go faster and smoother when somebody makes it their business to help make it so.

PRO TIP

I (Matt) have raced on Porsche's test track in Leipzig Germany, that was fun and intense. Almost as good was BMW's M driving academy in Munich. But, the most fun and useful school for me was one focused on security driving. We learned to use cars in unusual ways: J-turns, bootleggers, Slide blocking, PIT maneuvers – "Precise Immobilization Technique" aka knocking another car off the road, and much more. My point is: There are racing course of every possible variety.

MOTORCYCLES—You should get a license to ride a motorcycle. It usually only involves taking a weekend class. It's true that riding can be dangerous – especially on the road because of the other drivers, but it can also be great fun and cheap transportation.

OFF-ROAD RIDING—like motocross or trail riding—is generally safer than street riding because there's no traffic to contend with and crashes tend to happen at lower speeds on softer terrain. It also develops a different and highly valuable set of skills: balance, throttle control, body positioning, and reading the terrain. Maxim learned to ride at a motocross class when he was 14, and for beginners, this kind of controlled off-road environment is often the best and safest place to start.

Ultimately, it's best to combine both on— and off-road skills with what's called Adventure Riding or Dual Sport. Here you're riding on a mix of paved and unpaved roads—gravel, dirt, forest service roads, and trails. This is what Jim Rogers did when he rode a motorcycle across six continents. He wasn't a seasoned biker when he started, but he chose a Dual Sport motorcycle because it let him go where cars couldn't and see the world up close. Rogers used his bike as a tool for real-world learning, economics, and exploration

SHOOTING— the average person has seen hundreds of movies and TV shows featuring shooting and guns. But even in the United States, which has among the highest proportion (Switzerland is similar) of gun owners and shooters in the world, only about 70% of adults have shot a gun. That's good. But a better question is what percentage of them are reasonably proficient in using one. I'd guess only 10% of those.

I've played with guns since I was a kid starting out with a BB gun and moving up to a 22 rifle, then a shotgun, then a 22 pistol, and then dozens of guns of all calibers. I've hunted small game, especially birds, numerous times. Some people love hunting, but I've always seen guns mainly as tools for self-defense. At some point you'll want to own at least a few.

Owning guns is great, but becoming competent with them is your priority. You want to take a proper course, or two, to learn how to use them effectively. Especially in combat— type situations. Most of that time should be spent with pistols.

PRO TIP

Opinions vary, but my personal favorites are the 1911 in .45 (the 100+ year old design has been refined to perfection), and Glocks (the composite frame makes the ultra light, they're ultra simple, and accurate right out of the box).

A proper shooting course isn't about standing still and trying to hit a bullseye target— although that's going to be part of it. A proper course will give you expertise in fast draw from a holster, shooting multiple targets quickly, running and shooting from one target to the next, moving through a house against the clock, shooting with your weak hand, clearing blockages, and a dozen other practical exercises intended to mimic real life. You may then want to enter a couple of three-gun contests using a pistol, a rifle, and a shotgun in simulated combat.

SKEET—It's not all combat drills—there's real skill and satisfaction in learning the art of the shotgun. Sports like five-stand and skeet shooting are fast-paced, technical, and surprisingly fun. They train your reflexes, timing, and ability to track fast-moving targets— skills that carry over into every other kind of shooting. Plus, there's something deeply satisfying about turning a speeding clay disc into dust mid-air.

Getting good with guns is an indispensable part of The Preparation Few people realize that, historically, a major difference between a free man and a slave was the right to own and use weapons. That's as true now as it's ever been, although the public has been taught weapons are to be feared. It's now accepted that there's a warrior class, who are given orders by the rulers, and supported by the peasants—a regression pretty much to the medieval model.

In fact, every man should be a warrior and/or a citizen soldier. You should be competent with firearms, and other weapons. This, along with martial arts training, is foundational.

PAINTBALL/AIRSOFT—Playing paintball is loads of fun, and an excellent supplement to your gun training. It will teach you loads of practical skills should you ever get into a real gunfight. One of the big pluses is that you'll find how easy it is to get hit. We're used to watching movies where the good guys rarely get hit, which can lead to a cavalier attitude. Figure that if it's easy to get hit with a relatively slow-moving paintball from an inaccurate weapon—and you almost certainly will get hit—that experience will disincline you from having anything to do with a real gun fight.

That said, your experience playing paintball will be very valuable if you're unfortunate enough to ever get into a real gunfight. Play a bunch of paintball games, they're a genuine high adrenaline experience. Do it either before or after taking proper gun training. But definitely do it.

ARCHERY—learning the basics of archery isn't hard; it's quite intuitive. You'll start out with a simple conventional bow, then move up to a recurve bow, and then a compound bow using pulleys. After basic instruction, practice makes perfect. Many expert bowmen go on to hunting. It's a worthwhile thing to learn, from the stalking to the butchering of the animal. I passed on the hunting, mostly for aesthetic reasons. Archery clubs and lessons are available everywhere.

SAILING—It's mostly—almost entirely— a recreational activity, but like most things on this list it's also a survival skill. 70% of the world is covered in water, and it's essentially the last free and unowned space on the planet. The day may come when you want to get out of Dodge, and a sailboat is the least noticeable way to do so.

SCUBA—It will take some pool sessions, some classroom time, then some open water dives to get your C-Card from one of several certifying organizations. I've dived most of my adult life, in a dozen countries. On wrecks in the cold open ocean, lots of reefs in tropical seas, with sharks, at night, and in caves. It's essential that you get the basics down and get experience whenever and wherever you can.

Like many activities in this part of The Preparation, it's a skill worth having, but typically for only occasional use. I went on a three-month long treasure hunting expedition (ill— starred, but a fine adventure), for which diving skills were a pre-requisite. It's better to have skills and not need them, then need skills and not have them.

SKYDIVING—A tandem jump, where you're buckled up with your instructor, is available to anyone with a day and $200 to spare. That's fine, but it's only an experience, similar to taking a bungee jump, or a hairy roller coaster ride. I learned by joining a parachute club, which instructed how to handle various emergencies, how to land properly (military canopies aren't like modern sport chutes—if you don't do a proper PLF (parachute landing fall) you can get hurt) and pack my own chute. I never liked that part, always fearing I wouldn't be neat enough, and cause a malfunction.

Learning to skydive isn't terribly useful or important, but I think it's worth doing simply because it's so exciting.

I have 59 jumps. The pros have many hundreds, or even thousands. On my first jump (you always jumped solo, with a military canopy then), I sat on the passenger side of the plane, seat removed, door off, back to the dashboard. My chute hooked up to a static line that would open it automatically. The jumpmaster guided the pilot over the DZ. He yelled (wind and engine noise are high) "Get out on the wing". The pilot cut the engine. I hoisted myself out, holding onto the Cessna 182's strut, feet on a specially added little pipe, and waited. The jumpmaster tapped me on the shoulder and yelled "Go!". I was afraid there was something wrong with my hookup and started crawling back in the plane. The Jump Master had been there before, and forcibly pushed me into the void. I assumed the "frog" position, the chute deployed, and all ended well. On my second jump, knowing what was coming, I was actually more afraid, but proceeded without aid. Three more static line jumps, and then it was off to pulling my own ripcord. I gradually got up to 30 second delays from about 7200 feet. After a while it became as natural as stepping out of a car in a parking lot. That said, it's probably a less dangerous (although much more spectacular) sport than scuba.

Is there anything you can gain from something like skydiving, which serves no useful purpose in the real world? It led me to a realization about life. As you leave the plane at altitude, it seems you can fall forever. But after about 15 seconds you realize things are accelerating. When it's time to pull the ripcord at around 2000 feet you feel "ground rush". Life is like that. When you're young it seems you have lots of time, you're trying to stave off boredom, looking for something to do. As you get older you don't have enough time to do all you'd like. The end is visibly approaching. It's the ground rush effect, and you're approaching the end at terminal velocity.

That perception underlines the importance of completing The Preparation while you're young. It will give you the tools to make wise choices before time starts moving too fast.

BUNGEE JUMPING—It's worthwhile mentioning bungee jumping in this context. It's not really a sport as much as a proof you have the nerve to do it. Which is how and why it originated. Natives on Pentecost Island in Vanuatu tied vines around their ankles and jumped off homemade towers about 60 or 70 feet high. Very low tech, and it takes real nerve.

Starting in 1979 Westerners have duplicated the experience with rubber bands. Some would call it "cultural appropriation", a fashionable meme favored by many leftists. They don't seem to realize the primitive cultures have done exactly that with all of the West's inventions—medicine, aviation, computers, and literally thousands of other technologies. But back to bungee jumping…

I did one in New Zealand; Kiwis are big on extreme sports, and they popularized the activity. It's probably scarier than your first parachute jump because everything is silent, and you're stationary—you're not distracted by the wind, engine noise, and the motion. Worse, your feet are bound together, as if you're about to be executed. The ground is close, maybe 200 feet away, as opposed to 2000, making everything seem imminent.

Should you do it? Of course. For the same reasons a native on Pentecost would. There are any number of things, which serve no economic or educational purpose, that you should consider doing. Not for bragging rights or to impress anyone else. But to conquer your own innate fears.

WEIGHTLIFTING—If you're not actively working to make your body stronger and more effective, you're making a mistake. Making a habit of weightlifting a few times a week really pays off. We're not saying you need to become a gym rat, if you lift heavy weight at lower reps, you can have an excellent workout in 30min or less–The key is consistency. The stronger your body is, the more effective you'll be at everything you do.

OTHER OUTDOOR ADVENTURE SKILLS

There are plenty of other outdoor activities worth exploring—things that get you outside, challenge you physically, and become a gateway to explore the world.

At the entry level, **HIKING** which is just walking along marked trails or paths. Many hikes are easy, but you can take it to extremes if you like. Colorado has 58 14ers – that's a mountain peak that exceeds 14,000ft in elevation. Some hikers make a sport of "peak bagging" as many as they can. We can promise you, even the easiest 14er hike is hard.

BACKPACKING builds upon hiking, combining it with camping as you carry all essential gear needed for multiple-day wilderness trips.

CANYONEERING offers an adventurous step up, involving traveling through canyons using techniques like hiking, rappelling, scrambling, and sometimes swimming. Canyoneering was a rite of passage for the kids of the Smith household.

Probably the highest level, **MOUNTAINEERING**, involves technical climbing and navigating challenging mountain terrain, often at high altitudes, requiring specialized gear and advanced skills.

Everyone uses GPS today, but **ORIENTEERING** is a valuable skill which helps you become comfortable in unfamiliar territory using just a map and compass.

PARAGLIDING frees you from the usual two-dimensional ways of exploring the world, giving you a completely new perspective on landscapes. Once you're comfortable with that, you can step it up to **paramotor**–which removes many of the limits of gliding. With a paramotor you can literally fly and explore – almost anywhere.

RAFTING and **KAYAKING** are great as well. From easy lake kayaking to intense river rapids. Finally, **FLY FISHING**, though quieter, can be deeply rewarding, demanding patience and skill as you closely connect with rivers and streams.

The common thread – all these activities get you outside and engaging with nature. The level of intensity is up to you.

SOCIAL SPORTS & GAMES

Everybody loves games and sports. There's a reason why sports stars are among the highest paid people on the planet.

It's a good idea to learn how to hit a baseball, throw a football, or kick a soccer ball. And play all aspects of the games built around their specialized balls. It can test your physical limits, and allow you to demonstrate leadership skills. Those are good things. But do you really need to be regimented and organized to play recreational sports?

Kid's team sports are largely dysfunctional once they're organized. Especially for kids who are only there because of peer or parental pressure. Learning team sports when you're a kid is good—if you like it, and you find you're good enough not to be among the last chosen when teams are picked. It's great to have learned that skill when you're a kid—if you enjoy the game.

Generally speaking, adults don't do team sports unless they either really like it, or plan to be professionals. And the odds of making pro in any sport are about (reasonable guess) one in 10,000. If you're natural, you'll play pick up games from time to time. But most sports are just for young people. You're young now, but you also want something that you can excel in after you're 30.

There are better "adult" games we suggest you learn will not only be enjoyable, but will pay off throughout life.

SKIING—Like scuba, this is a "must learn". You want to be able to do it when the occasion arises. Great social activity, great exercise, and great fun. But, all-in, it's become quite expensive. On the bright side, it's much easier to learn than ever before because of huge improvements in the boots, bindings, and the skis themselves. When I think of the old lace-up leather boots, beartrap bindings, and long skinny downhill skis we used to use, I'm surprised we bothered. Downhill skiing today is a piece of cake, the lifts, the equipment and clothing have improved so radically. It's no longer a cheap sport, like it was when I learned in Switzerland. At Aspen, the most expensive resort in the US, lift tickets are around $250 a day, and rental of boots and skis are about $80 more.

Lift tickets vary with the resort, but accommodations are expensive at any resort. Learn at a cheap resort. You'll want classes to speed your progress and insure that you don't pick up bad habits.

GOLF AND TENNIS—Maybe professionalism has ruined tennis and golf, not to mention polo. The money has become so big that, like Tiger Woods, families who are so inclined immerse prospects in these sports from just past the age when they can walk. You'll never compete with them, nor would you want to. Most serious athletes live in a bubble and have limited knowledge or abilities outside their specialty.

As with most things in this area, you just want to achieve basic competence. Real competence will come later, if the sport really grips you.

You may not want to run with the country club set (I certainly don't), but it helps to have what it takes to socialize with them when it makes sense. That's apart from the fact tennis and golf are fun. At least for most people. I took some (informal and inadequate) tennis lessons, and played very casually, never taking it seriously, or practicing enough to be any good. Don't make that mistake. I took golf lessons late in life, and played a couple of rounds, but could never get into the game. I'd say golf is a good way to ruin a nice walk through a meadow—except most people today use a cart. So you don't even get the benefit of a walk, just the frustration of playing.

You can get lessons in both sports with a pro at your local country club. Both are worth pursuing.

HORSE RIDING AND POLO—Polo is the top of the pecking order. I played for almost 20 years. You might be asking yourself why it's being listed here, since it's very costly, and therefore impractical for The Preparation. But it's aspirational, and something you should consider once you start earning serious money. Sports like this are one of the reasons you want to become wealthy.

PRO TIP

All these activities can lead to what I call the secondary game–a whole new world of connections and unexpected opportunities. This happened a lot to me, and hopefully it does to you too. Why? Because, it turns out, the side games are almost always where the most interesting things are found. This is a theme that comes up over and over again. You'll learn chess for enjoyment, to develop the ability to think several steps ahead, to learn direct and indirect consequences of your actions, and how to size up your opponent. That's the primary game. But there is a secondary game as well. It revolves around the relationships you can build and the doors it opens up for you. Most things have "secondary game" possibilities. Be on the lookout for them.

Polo was a hobby I picked up in my 40s. Incidentally, it probably isn't the best idea to start playing polo in your 40s. It's dangerous, and it's good to know how to ride a horse before you start. I thought I knew how to ride a horse because I could stay on when it went faster than a trot. It turns out, I picked up all kinds of bad riding habits, and they were hard to shake.

The primary game in polo is, of course, the sport itself involving hitting a ball on horseback. It's exhilarating. It can be the most fun you can have with your clothes on. If you have a polo handicap, you can visit any major city anywhere in the world. The chances are good there's a Polo Club.

My first actual tournament Polo was in Accra, Ghana. The Accra Polo Club invited the Stowe Vermont Polo Club, all expenses paid, including First Class on American Airlines. I went with the Stowe club because they could only round up three guys in a position to go. One of them, an old friend, called me to fill in. We had an all-expense paid trip to Ghana for 10 days. Things like that happen in the polo world.

The most interesting part is the secondary game. Polo players are among the wealthiest and most connected people, at the top of the social and economic pecking order. It's very international, with lots of exotic characters. Later I was a member of the New Zealand Ambassadors Polo Club.

I played in New Zealand for years. Basically, a bunch of tough farm boys that like to play horse hockey when they aren't playing rugby. It's a different class of Polo than in the US in general, and Aspen or Palm Beach in particular. But fun for that reason. I could have gone on a junket sponsored by the Tehran Polo Club, to play three tournaments in three Iranian cities.

It would have been most interesting to run with the top of society for a week in a country few people go to. But I didn't because I was recently injured. I could have faked it, but it would have been dishonest to make everyone count on an injured teammate. Missing that series of tournaments remains a great regret. But a man's got to know his limitations.

Regardless, I can still show up in any city in the world, go to the Polo Club, and get to know the guys. I recommend playing Polo for that reason alone. Winston Churchill said, "a polo handicap is better than a passport." And he was right.

It's a lifelong advantage to play all of these games at least competently, if not expertly. As a young man, without a lot of experience or financial resources, you'll have to utilize the resources you have in abundance: energy and drive.

As with golf and tennis, you're best off being born into a rich family that plays and has a bunch of horses. Unlike golf and tennis, polo is quite a dangerous game. It's a contact sport played at high speed with 800 LB animals, and hard balls that can come out of nowhere at 100 mph. You might call it horse hockey. But unlike ice hockey it's quite expensive. If you're going to play seriously you'll need at least 4 or 6 horses. They all need to be fed, groomed, exercised daily, and kitted out with saddles and bridles. They'll each need a new pair of shoes about every month which runs about $75 per hoof and occasional visits to the horse dentist and the veterinarian.

Even if you never get involved with polo, you'll want to spend some serious time learning to ride properly. When you're learning you may find muscles that you never knew existed will ache so badly that you can hardly turn over in bed. That's because you'll be overly tense. The good news is that familiarity with riding will mitigate that in the future. It's a major reason you want to learn the basics of as many sports as you can while you're under 30—to save yourself a lot of pain and possible embarrassment later.

Then you can either find a local Polo Club or get in touch with the USPA for a reference to a professional class. Most of those are either in Southern California or Florida. A usually better, and much cheaper alternative, is to do it in Argentina, the Mecca of polo. I spent a week with a top Argentine polo family at their estancia, riding so much that I could hardly move (obviously, I needed a lot more conditioning than I thought). FWIW, it was relatively inexpensive partly because Argentina was, and still is, a lot cheaper than the US. But also because your hosts are hoping to sell you a horse or two, though there's no obligation to buy anything.

BILLIARDS/POOL—It's easy to pick up a cue and use an intuitive knowledge of geometry and physics to make the balls go where you want—to a degree. But a limited amount of instruction (along with a lot of practice) will vastly improve your game and make it much more fun. Losing at pool is frustrating, and can be costly, since it's usually a betting game. The class of people you'll meet at pool halls (although they're mostly family friendly these days, often attached to bowling alleys) is typically a couple of standard deviations lower than golf or tennis. In-person instruction from an expert is worth the price. But reading a couple of How-To books will put you way above most everyone playing the game. You might try "Basic Pool", Cranfield, 232 pp. To gain an appreciation for the game, you can't go wrong watching these two classic movies about pool. FWIW, Cruise spent many hours learning the game, and did all but a few shots himself. If he can do it, so can you.

- ▶ "The Hustler" (1961) with Paul Newman and Jackie Gleason
- ▶ "The Color of Money" (1986). With Paul Newman and Tom Cruise.

SOCIAL GAMES

You'll want to know how to play the next four games. Learning them is very simple and won't take you more than 1/2 an hour or so each. Becoming competent in any of them can take years. What you want to do is learn the basics in all of them. Spend at least a day or two with each to see which ones you like and have an aptitude for. Be careful though, because all of them, not just poker, are played for money. That's the danger with just knowing the basic rules: A little knowledge is a dangerous thing.

CHESS, GO, POKER AND BRIDGE. Each teaches different ways of thinking and relating to your opponent. And all, for what it's worth, offer a potential income. Most people are untutored and poorly self-disciplined. If you make yourself an expert (to some degree— and there are many degrees in each), it can be both intellectually and psychologically gratifying. And enjoyable, because they are games. Everybody loves games because they mimic life itself, but on a bitesize scale. That they can be financially beneficial in addition is a huge extra benefit. Give yourself the opportunity to feel the thrill of victory in as many ways as possible.

Chess emphasizes strategy, forethought, thinking several moves ahead, and seeing not just the immediate and direct consequences of making a move or taking a piece, but the indirect and delayed consequences. It's helpful in economic thinking, and business planning. You might think the Soviets, who were notoriously strong chess players, might have understood economics, but they were effectively economic idiots.

Go is much more complex and strategic, offering many more possible outcomes.

Poker is a game of psychology and aggression.

Bridge is a game of memory and understanding your partner.

CHESS—I learned chess at about age 10. I don't remember from whom, but I certainly didn't have a tutor—which was a mistake. You want a tutor in most things that involve the concept "Do". It saves lots of time and you avoid picking up bad habits. Why try to reinvent the wheel? It makes more sense to take advantage of what others, who've spent years getting into details, have learned. It takes a normal person perhaps 30 minutes, one session, to learn how the pieces move. The basics of chess are simple.

In high school on Saturday afternoons, a bunch of us would play. None of us had formal instruction in chess. But if you do something enough, and you figure out what works. I found—partly from applying the principles of warfare taught in military class— that what worked was being aggressive (moving capital pieces out quickly), capturing the high ground (the middle of the board) and employing the principle of mass (concentrating firepower on the opposing king). Et cetera. Simple enough to remember.

I learned about the principles of warfare in my military high school. High school was much more valuable for me than college. We had both sergeants and officers that were, all of them, experienced veterans. They were very politically incorrect. SFC Shanahan liked to tell stories about the Korean War. "Well, we were experimenting, wondering, You know what? My .45 will go further than your .30 Carbine. So we'd line up some prisoners to find out. We'd experiment."

In those days, you could say things like that. It was a bona fide war crime. But the Korean War wasn't far in the past, and was in some ways a race war, as was WW2 in the Pacific against the Japanese.

Self-taught chess had some advantages. Chess books were of use, but a tutor is more helpful in climbing the ladder of knowledge. But all we had were chess books. Nobody had an uncle or an older cousin who was rated. No one could afford a tutor or even knew where to get one. But today there are excellent free tutorials on the internet. You can stand on the shoulders of giants, easily, and for free.

One key to an education is learning who the Giants are, and how you can get on their shoulders.

I got my real comeuppance in chess from a Soviet. I was living in DC, just out of college, selling disability insurance by cold calling on the phone. I'd explain that I had a policy which would pay if he were sick or injured, then close for an in-person meeting. I solicited Yuri Barsukov, who was the head of Izvestia's Washington bureau. Why not? I'd already called the guys from AP, UPI, and Reuters.

Barsukov undoubtedly thought that I was speaking spook code to him. "We can pay you if you're sick or injured. I'd like to get together and talk about it." I'm sure that what was going through his mind was "What is this guy trying to tell me?" I met him at the Russian embassy, which certainly earned me another file with some US agency; it's not like he wouldn't have been watched at the time. Pretending to be a reporter is a standard cover for spooks. We met for dinner a couple of times, and he took me to his chess club once. He was a very, very good player. He sized up my amateur level play quickly, and then the game really picked up speed. It was Muhammed Ali against Dylan Mulvaney.

I'd never played with somebody that was really good before. It was devastating, shocking, and humbling. Not that he was ever a good prospect, but I didn't even try to sell him insurance. It was bad salesmanship on my part, I should have put the pen in his hand and asked him to "sign on the line which is dotted." Simply to get his reaction. I was chasing a rabbit down a different hole at the time, and I forgot why I was really there. I got interested in the side game as opposed to the reason I'd called Yuri to start with.

Chess is in essence a military game. You and your opponent have exactly equal forces on the proverbial level playing field. I went to a four-year military boarding high school. A bunch of us would get together and play every Saturday afternoon, trying to apply the principles of warfare to the game. I'll list them here, because they're simple and valuable in many areas of life. You might want to memorize them.

1. **Objective**—Always keep in mind the objective isn't taking enemy pieces (although that is helpful). The objective is to checkmate the enemy king.

2. **Offensive**—You want to be the aggressor—fortune favors the bold. When you're on the defensive, you're the effect of your opponent's cause, forced to respond, unable to be proactive.

3. **Mass**—Try to overwhelm the enemy with concentrated power. In warfare, it's ideal to out-power the enemy by 3–1 when on the attack. Same here, several pieces should control the crucial squares.

4. **Economy of Force**— The obverse of #3. Keep the minimum necessary in places that won't win the game.

5. Security— Guard the home front, your plans, and the King.

6. **Maneuver**— Don't box yourself in so your own pawns are blocking your major pieces, or jam your pieces too close together. You may wind up like the Romans against Hannibal at Cannae.

7. **Unity of command**— Maybe not very applicable to chess, but in the real world you have to know who's running the show, and that orders are followed.

8. **Surprise**— Amateur players get tunnel vision, watching their game, not the enemy's. What might he be planning to spring on you? How can you take him off guard?

9. **Simplicity**— Plans are important. Complex plans, however, are usually only good in theory. As Clausewitz said, "No plan survives first contact with the enemy". Or as Mike Tyson put it "Everybody's got a plan, until they get punched in the face".

10. **Initiative**— It's best to be white, the side that moves first has the advantage. Like the Germans against the Soviets in June 1941, or the Japanese against the Americans in December 1941.

11. **Morale**—You might think this one irrelevant to chess, since you're moving objects, not soldiers. But Bobby Fisher was a master at intimidating and discombobulating opponents to throw them off their games.

Gaining expertise in chess trains you to think a few moves ahead, something most people don't do. Most people live in the world of "It seemed like a good idea at the time".

Gaining expertise is easier today than ever before, by taking advantage of the Internet for both instruction and practice.

If you get good it's possible to hustle chess, just like poker, pool, and most other games.

Chess has principles that can be applied on its 64 squares, where the battle is straight forward, with principles Clausewitz would approve of.

GO— Go (the Japanese name for this Chinese game) is also a military game. It feels as if Sun Tzu would be at home playing.

It's played on a 19x19 board (sometimes a smaller board, to accommodate beginners, or for a quick game) but with identical pieces. Not on the squares, but on the junctions between them. The object is to surround the opponent on its board of 361 squares. Unlike chess, once a piece is played, it stays there. The game is, paradoxically, although simpler than chess, much more complex and strategic, offering many more possible outcomes. That's indicated by the fact a computer, IBM's Deep Blue, was able to beat Gary Kasparov, the world champion in 1997, 3&1/2–2&1/2, but it wasn't until 2015 that Google's Deep Mind Alpha Go beat Fan Hui, the European Go champion, 5–0.

It's said that Go has more possible moves and outcomes than there are atoms in the universe. I find that hard to believe, or at least unfathomable, considering there are supposedly 2 trillion galaxies, each with, on average perhaps 200 million suns. Our sun has about $1.2 \times 10-57th$ atoms. The universe may have, therefore $10-81th$, or so, atoms. Go is intuitive, and about patterns, more than logical rules in Western chess.

Ancient Chinese aristocrats were expected to be competent at least four skills. The **qin** (a stringed instrument), **qi** (the game of Go), **shu** (Chinese calligraphy) and **hua** (Chinese painting). The four are called **qínqíshūhuà**. Not so different from the medieval Western quadrivium. When living in Hong Kong I pursued qi and shu, but regrettably remain at the beginner level. I suggest you give them all a try, but especially Go. And substitute the guitar for the qin.

There are an order of magnitude more chess players. Most Go aficionados are in East Asia. but you can, and should, learn Go online.

The eleven rules of warfare still apply, but in different ways. Go is paradoxical.

As always, the Internet is your friend. The Wikipedia article, Go, is an excellent introduction. You-tube offers lots of tutorials.

POKER—There was a worldwide poker boom back in the 2000s. It seemed like everybody was playing. Some people consider poker to be gambling but it's not. There's a large element of chance, of course. You never know what cards you're going to be dealt. But the key with poker is taking advantage of the fact that nobody else knows what you've been dealt. It's a game of bluffing and figuring out the other players' psychology. There have been hundreds of books written on poker. Reading them won't do you much good until you have a certain amount of experience playing. You might have an uncle or a cousin who can teach you the basics and give you a few tips. Learning the basic hands is simple. The problem is finding a friendly local game with low stakes, or your education can become very expensive.

A man I once knew wrote a poker book (there are hundreds) called "Poker: A Guaranteed Income for Life". It was built around a couple of simple valid concepts (mainly, only betting if the "pot odds"—potential return on your bet—significantly exceeds the actual odds of getting a winning hand. I'm unconvinced he was able to put the theory into practice, but he definitely made a lot selling a book with a great title.

One key with poker is the fact most people believe it's a game of chance. And that's true in one way; over the long run everybody gets the same cards. But as the Kenny Rogers song observed, "every card's a winner, and every card's a loser". That's true; it's a question of how they're played, which is all about betting.

Poker is a game of psychology and aggression. Remember the military motto: "Fortune favors the bold".

One possibility is to play online poker, where it's possible to enter a large game for only $0.25 or $1.00. After doing that for a few hours reading a book on poker strategy will have some practical value.

> **PRO TIP**
>
> It's one thing to play on a Monday night for low stakes with some friends. If you pay attention, you'll improve your game, and probably win some money, since the others likely won't treat the game seriously. I also recommend it because you'll learn a lot about your associates in an informal, mildly stressful environment where money, judgment, and bluffing are all involved.

That's very different from playing for high stakes. The two movies below are warnings: Most poker players, like almost all gamblers, aren't made of the right stuff.

MOVIES—There are two classics centering on poker. The Cinncinnati Kid (1965) with Steve McQueen, and The Rounders (1998) with Matt Damon. They're both good dives into the sleazy world of card sharps.

BRIDGE— You need to know how to play if you wish to move in certain social circles. Bridge players have a very different demographic from poker players. They're generally older, better educated, and more polite. Unlike poker, which is a game of aggression and psychology, bridge is a game of memory and strategy. Unlike poker, there are lots of bridge clubs. The government can't overtly accuse them of gambling, as they do with poker. That's not to say bridge isn't about gambling. All four of these games are played for money, and they're all full of hustlers. I don't suggest you wager more than pocket change until you reach the level of a hustler yourself.

Learning bridge with a book is slow. Youtube offers many entertaining courses; it's your huckleberry.

ARTS & CRAFTSMANSHIP

DRAWING—Some people are naturals, most aren't. But learning the basics is important for things like architecture and mechanical engineering. The best, sometimes the only, way to learn some things (like dancing) is with an instructor. But you can get drawing by following the instructions of a book. Get a copy of "How to Draw and Think like a Real Artist: A 30-Day Drawing Guide from the Fundamentals to Step-by-Step Instructions with Detailed Illustrations and Comprehensive Explanations". That's quite a promise, but it's worth an hour or so for 30 days to pick up the basics, and see if you want to go further.

This is a skill that, at least in my opinion, won't require any in-person instruction. So you, your pencil, drawing pad, and guide book, can pursue it any time, anywhere.

It's a valuable skill. Some people are naturals, most aren't. But learning the basics is important for professions like architecture and mechanical engineering.

PAINTING— On first glance, you might think this is like drawing. But not really. Drawing is essentially the precise creation of images on paper, using pencil. Painting can be like that, but there are many different media (oil, tempura, gouache), techniques (brush, pallet, pointillist), and styles (realist, abstract, surreal).

I collect art. My main criteria are technical skill (how perfect is the execution) and ideational value (how well is the artist presenting an aspect of life or thought that I'm interested in). As a cultured man, you need the ability to judge quality. You'll have vastly more appreciation of an artist's skill if you try to do it yourself. The work of art is, according to Alberti, so constructed that it is impossible to take anything away from it or to add anything to it, without impairing the beauty of the whole.

Unless you're extremely talented, or later become famous, there's no money in being a painter. Large, competent canvases go for $10 or $100 at auction all the time— a fraction of the hard costs of materials alone.

There are plenty of painters who are skilled enough to teach a class even though they can't make a living doing paintings. It's a rare town where one of them isn't running a school.

Going to a painting class once a week, where they'll provide all the materials you need as well as guidance in using them, is an excellent use of that time.

PRO TIP

I've found an understanding of painting and sculpture to be quite valuable in traveling. When visiting a foreign city, I'm not interested in just being another tourist. So I always made a practice of reaching out to at least three groups: lawyers, real estate brokers, and art gallery owners. Why? Because they all run in the top levels of the local society, dealing with others who are rich and connected. Better, they're all willing to talk to an outsider— he might turn into an excellent client. Of course you have to call or email for an appointment with lawyers, and possibly with the brokers. With galleries you only need to walk in. The key is to have something relevant and worthwhile to talk to them about—business in the case of the lawyers and brokers.

After a day of interesting interviews, as often as not I found myself invited to a party, or referred to someone else, or invited home for dinner with the family. The more knowledge and experiences you have, the more likely "good luck" will materialize. Don't, therefore, view a knowledge of art as irrelevant to life, off by itself in a dusty corner.

As with music, art has two aspects: creation, and appreciation. You're probably not interested in becoming an art historian, but rather in gaining a broad understanding.

MUSIC— You'll recall the Trivium and Quadrivium, the foundations of an education in ancient Greece and Rome. Music is one of the quadrivium. In those days it meant learning the theory and practice of the lute or lyre. Today I'd say it includes two things: a familiarity with the great music that's been composed since around the time of JS Bach (1685–1750), and the ability to play at least one instrument.

It seems few young men—or most anyone—knows much about classical music. The radio plays current favorites, of which many have no rhythm, no melody, and actively degrading lyrics. Even if you find a classical station, you can't always rely on the taste of the moderator. There's a surprising amount of pseudoclassic junk that's played for political reasons.

You can't possibly become more than superficially familiar with more than just the highlights of the great masters in the time we have available—but you must.

The good news is that the pieces we've listed are not only among the most famous, but I'd argue the best. They're as enjoyable as anything ever done. That's why they're classics, and why they're still popular today, centuries later. It will take days of listening, even though we're just skimming the surface. But you're in for a treat.

As for instruments, take your choice. But, certainly to start, some are much better choices than others. The bass fiddle, trombone, and tuba are somewhat impractical. The most useful choices are the guitar and the piano. Everybody likes them, they're available everywhere, and there's a lot of music written for them.

It's one of my regrets that I didn't at least get the basics in either. It takes years of practice to become competent. But if you get the basics down, it's largely a matter of practice— which you can fit in when you have spare time, or a break.

As a bonus, a degree of competence means you may be able to join an amateur group doing gigs at clubs or parties. It's a great way to pick up extra income while being paid to practice. Charles Knight, the hero of my novels, uses his ability to play the piano to great advantage.

It's best to get an instructor to make sure you get the basics down. Then, once you do, there are loads of free courses on the Internet.

IMPROV/COMEDY—I think this is a self-taught skill. There are courses on offer, but I think they're an unnecessary expense. It's unlikely anyone can be taught a sense of humor, or irony.

You'll want to go to a local comedy club— not to be entertained, but to take notes. Watch what the performers are doing, how they're succeeding or failing. Put together your own act and give it a try. It's not hard to talk the management into an audition— they're looking for free talent. FWIW, you'll find most aspiring comedians are quite intelligent—which is great—but often psychologically troubled. Which means you should be more discriminating than usual with your choice of friends. This is true across the board in the artsy world.

Comedy may be an intuitive gift. But there are tricks to every gig. At a minimum, you'll learn to read a crowd.

PUBLIC SPEAKING—Good public speakers share many skills with actors and comedians. It's said that most people would rather face a firing squad than speak in public. I doubt that's true. But, apart from the fact most don't have anything valuable to say, we're herd animals, and there's a degree of safety in not standing out. Unlike being an actor, or even a comic, a speaker isn't just exposing a character or pretending. He's putting himself forward. And trying to accomplish a specific objective. I was lucky, and chosen for my High School debate team. But there really aren't many places to learn and (especially) practice speaking in public.

Our old friend Youtube has dozens of excellent short courses that are full of excellent tips. It will take only two hours to watch them all. Make some notes. Practice a few as if you're shadow boxing, or practicing karate katas. Repeat the process a week later, and see how many of their tips you can remember and apply.

The real key to speaking is genuine expertise in the subject you're talking about. You'll find speaking gets easier and easier the more you know about any given subject—that's the basis of the confidence you need to give a proper speech. The key is practice. If you have an idea you want to communicate, contact local clubs like the Lions and Rotary. They're always looking for luncheon and dinner speakers. They're composed of businessmen who are always on the lookout for talented young men. It's a great way to broaden your horizons while you're perfecting a new skill. When I had a company selling gold and silver it was a great way to get leads, get to know successful people, practice speaking, and fielding questions. And, FWIW, get a free lunch, which serves as a fee.

If you're in an area that has a Toastmasters club, participate.

ACTING—It's odd how some actors have become among the richest, most famous, and therefore influential, people in the world. It's odd because acting has historically been among the world's least honored—actually despised— professions. Since at least the days of ancient Rome actors have been viewed as "poseurs", pretending to be something they're not. A variety of professional liars, someone who's skilled at displaying false emotions, and saying things he doesn't believe. Actresses were at least amateur, and often professional, prostitutes. But despite being despised, they were popular because they entertained. And in today's world, which is rich enough to be an entertainment (as opposed to an agricultural, industrial, or information) economy, the profession has been upgraded. The huge face and name recognition actors get, not to mention their skills in deception, qualify them for politics. Acting is no longer considered to be a dishonorable occupation.

That's on the bright side. In the real world, acting is an ultra-hard way to make a living. The competition is brutal. That's why most actors have to pay the rent with low-skill part— time "real" jobs— like waiting tables.

That said, taking acting classes, and then getting unpaid parts in plays, is valuable experience and a skill worth learning. You'll learn to control and project your emotions, and present the most advantageous social veneer.

A downside is that most aspiring actors are short on cash, and some are desperate; you want to avoid those types wherever you find them; it's usually evidence of a character flaw. The trade is full of homosexuals (it's true, they're arty) and sexually promiscuous. Some say it's a genetic condition. Maybe. But it's also a red flag. The casting couch, recently made notorious by Jeffrey Epstein, is real, and an effective way to open doors.

PHOTOGRAPHY—Because everyone today has a camera in their pocket, true skill in videography and photography is massively underrated. Too many people are constantly looking at their phones and snapping pictures -yet when you pick up a camera with intention, you become an active participant in life, not just a spectator.

It's more than capturing moments; it's about noticing stories others overlook, offering a unique perspective, and, if you're skilled enough, shaping the way others see the world. At the very least, you're creating something enduring—documenting adventures, preserving memories, and producing a meaningful visual legacy.

METALWORK/WELDING/BLACKSMITHING— Since the end of the Stone Age, about 5000 years ago, the world has been built on metal. It's primal to know how to use oxyacetylene and arc—welding torches to cut things apart or repair them. Melting metals and shaping them into almost anything. Learning to work with metals doesn't have to be very costly. All you need are a proper hammer, tongs, a forge, and a bit of common-sense safety gear. With some instruction you'll soon be able to craft your own handmade knives and hatchets.

MAGIC—Illusions are underrated as a skill, seen as the province of nerdy teenagers and guys who put on low budget performances at kids' birthday parties. There's probably no point in trying to become Houdini or David Blaine. But Blaine noted that "magic" is math, logic, science, psychology, performance, public speaking, statistics, and estimation. It makes a lot of sense to practice the basics of tricks with coins, string, and cards. I'm not talking about imitating the spectacular and extremely dangerous stunts they're famous for—things like being placed in a straight jacket, chained, and locked in a box before being thrown into any icy river. But simply gaining the ability to manipulate reality, or perceptions of reality, on a superficial level. The tricks are especially fun when you use them unexpectedly, in the mode of a "cool uncle" not a wannabe magician. Lots are available on Youtube. The encyclopedia of tricks is probably Tarbells' seven volume encyclopedia. It's expensive, at $250. But unnecessary. You really only need a good guide that offer a few dozen tricks. The key, as in martial arts moves, is to practice them enough that they become automatic.

COOKING—This is an essential skill. It's really just applied chemistry. All the ingredients are just compounds of the elements on the Periodic Table. There are two approaches to cooking.

One is to master the basics of common dishes—perfectly. You'll have a limited repertoire, but quality always trumps quantity. And, as with martial arts, it's much better to repeat something many times until it's right than to have only a glancing familiarity with many poorly done things.

There are certain dishes that are reliable favorites but usually poorly executed. You should learn an elegant and perfect way to deal with eggs—scrambled, omelet's, and poached. Hamburger and steak. Fish, particularly salmon. And salads—particularly Caesar. And one outstanding dessert; I'd choose a tiramisu. If you can deliver on those (and most people can't) you'll be loved, respected, needed, and wanted wherever food is served. You'll be able to hire out as a short order cook (if you can add speed to the mix) if you need cash.

When I was on a three month long treasure hunting expedition on a converted WW2 minesweeper (like Jacque Cousteau's Calypso, except ours looked more like a target drone), I wound up as the ship's Cook. It was a plus for me because cooking is creative, unlike doing scut work. And it was a plus for the crew, since I took the job seriously.

There are some courses that can guide you, and you should take at least one.

The second approach is to train as a professional. But it may be a wasted block of knowledge if you don't plan on being a pro and don't keep in practice.

PRO TIP

Top quality ingredients are critical. This is where you don't cut corners. Buying the best ingredients will make up for lots of errors (within reason) in preparation.

MIXOLOGY—The bartenders art, mixing drinks from vodka, gin, whiskey and other hard liquors. It might be worthwhile taking a class. But all you really need is a Mr.Boston manual or a video course. Then reach out to find a bar or a nightclub in need of talent, and improve your skills while being paid.

BEER BREWING—There are thousands of craft beers now. It's worthwhile to learn how to brew pilseners, porters, stouts, ales.

Chapter 15

UNLOCKING NEW POSSIBILITIES BY HOLDING YOURSELF ACCOUNTABLE

BY MAXIM SMITH

Something that became clear to us after just a couple months of my time in The Preparation was that I needed a way to hold myself accountable. My father was deeply interested in knowing about everything I was doing, so I was held accountable through him but, as family, he is more likely to let moments of laziness slide from time to time.

The solution then came down to publishing a summary of everything I did in the past week on Substack where my action (or lack of it) would face the judgment of at least a few people. Now, that audience has grown to a total of around 5,000 people.

I started publishing my What I Did This Week posts on Substack when I was 18 weeks into The Preparation. As I write this, I am about to publish my 74th week and publish my weekly "What I did this week."

As the audience has grown, I've felt an ever-increasing pressure to produce consistent positive results.

It's a heavy burden to carry at times since it requires my sincere effort to not only learn new skills, garner knowledge, and have unique experiences—I also have to make sure I understand everything I learn so that I can explain everything in a way which can be understood to people who don't know me or what I'm learning.

Yet, it's been great for me to hold myself accountable in this way. I've had the opportunity to meet a few of my readers and they all were seeking to help me in some way—giving me books to read, advice, potential opportunities, and unique experiences.

For a time, I was focusing on improving my horsemanship. I'd ride my horse, Comanche, at least once a week to build both of our skills. One of my readers reached out to me to offer that I go to his ranch in Colorado and learn horse/mule packing. It's a niche skill, and few people possess it. So, when I left Uruguay and went back to Colorado, I took him up on his offer, drove to his ranch, and spent a few days learning foundational packing techniques.

Not only did I get to learn a skill, but I had the opportunity to meet someone rare. This reader was a professional meat cutter by 16, started multiple businesses, and shifted gears to become a hunting guide in Africa–just to name a few things. He had the life experience of 15 men and, for that alone, it was good to meet him.

Another man had heard about my work in The Preparation from my father and decided on his own accord to check out my Substack page. Later on, he reached out to me with an offer. He said that I could head down to Puerto Rico to learn acupuncture from him and potentially sail the Caribbean.

After completing EMT school an entrepreneur/paramedic ended up offering me a job which involved working on wildfires. Eagerly, I pursued that path and spent 41 total days on fires in 2024.

Most recently, while making my way through flight school, I was told about a completely unique opportunity that was available to me...If I wanted to, I could travel to Nevada and work on a geophysics crew for a few weeks. Along with that, I'd essentially be apprenticed to a man who had been in that line of work for nearly 40 years. It didn't turn out exactly how I thought it would, but I was grateful to have met some of the people there, learned a few things, and absolutely thankful to have been given that opportunity.

From those three examples I was able to: Become a Type 2 firefighter, take a rope rescue course, earn money working on fires, learn navigation skills, improve my social skills, improve my horsemanship, learn foundational mule/horse packing skills, earn money on a geophysics crew, learn some of the basics of IP geophysics (and mining in general), learn a little more about geology, collect rock samples with a crew of geologists, and come in close contact with highly impressive men.

Those are the sort of experiences that you can have when you say, "Here I am, and here's what I'm doing." If it's impressive then people will be more than happy to help you along your path. You may not learn packing in the Colorado mountains, but other wild and unexpected things will be offered to you...things you never could have imagined.

When you publish your accomplishments they act as your resume, they are proof that you are continuously improving and putting your all-out effort into gaining skills, knowledge, friends, and experiences. Those 3 major opportunities from the men mentioned above came either directly through them noticing my proof of work on my Substack page, or their desire to aid me was (or could have been) slightly increased from the evidence that my weekly letter provides.

HOW TO HOLD YOURSELF ACCOUNTABLE

To hold yourself accountable you will be using either beehiiv or Substack to publish a weekly summary of everything you did/learned. Create an account on either publishing platform and title your publication: Your name's Preparation

From there, send us an email (FirstStep@ThePreparation.com) so that we can follow along with all that you're doing and help hold you accountable. You can do as I did and title each one of your weekly summaries: What I Learned This Week (Add the week number that you're on). Or, call it anything you want. The point is to publish some detailed account of your progress, lessons learned, and activities each and every week.

At first it will feel like you're publishing into the void. You won't have many people following your posts, but that doesn't matter because it'll still be an opportunity to improve your writing and put your thoughts and weekly accomplishments in writing.

If, however, you are making serious progress over several months there is no doubt that more and more people will flock to your page to read about what you're doing. From there, keep making progress, keep improving your writing, and use the weekly updates to reflect on your progress.

Readers will have recommendations for you–books, courses, activities–and they will help you think about things you can add, subtract, or improve in your preparation.

The Substack/beehiiv method is by far the most effective as it puts you in a position to receive scrutiny from others if you fail to show good work. Yet, we recommend that you also hold yourself accountable by creating a To-Do list every day. It's something that will drastically improve your productivity and, as you will see, when you fail to check all of the daily boxes you'll be disappointed with yourself when you realize that you likely had time to do it all.

You should also be tracking your accomplishments each month as a method of self— motivation. Write down every achievement–large or small. In the months where the list is much shorter than it could have been, or the content isn't impressive you'll be able to recognize that and course correct.

Chapter 16

MANAGING YOUR MIND

BY MAXIM SMITH

OVERCOMING SOCIAL ANXIETY

When I originally wrote this section for the book I was 9 months into The Preparation. Now, I'm two years into it, but at that time I had completed EMT school, become an EMT, increased my Brazilian Jiu Jitsu skills, worked two menial jobs, started writing on my substack page, learned skills on our ranch in Uruguay, and then went back to the states.

I was back in the states to prepare for a wildland firefighting job I was offered. I was staying in Denver until I would eventually get the call to head out to a fire in Oregon. Until then I stacked my schedule with many different things to pursue. I continued taking BJJ classes, rock climbed for the first time, took woodworking classes, a motorcycle driving course, and met a man that taught me horse and mule packing in the Colorado mountains.

Around that time I also spent 5 days learning basic rope rescue skills in South Dakota and went back to Colorado to complete the required S-130 training to become a certified wildland firefighter.

I was doing new things (and lots of them) which caused me to directly confront a fear I had: Social anxiety. Though, because of the effort I put in throughout the first 7 months of the program, the fear was easier to overcome. Being more than a year into The Preparation now, I can tell you that I rarely ever experience that fear.

The fact is, there are always challenges to be faced and most of them are internal challenges...the most difficult of those challenges to overcome being fear.

Fear will never disappear, but it can be mastered slowly but surely over time. No doubt, you will experience different forms of fear throughout your preparation. Social anxiety may be one of the fears that you, like myself, will have to directly confront. If it is, this may be of help to you...

Before The Preparation (and through at least 7 months of it) I had terrible social anxiety. I would get nervous anytime I met someone new or entered into an unfamiliar situation. Well, everyone might get a bit nervous in a new situation, but what I suffered was complete fear. I did anything I could do to avoid interacting with people or doing something

I should do. And I always had an excuse to justify that decision.

A few months into the program I decided to take Brazilian Jiu Jitsu (BJJ) classes. My father's encouragement pushed me to actually do it. I immediately concocted a few alibis to convince myself not to go. Yet upon examining my excuses, I saw they held no weight (the same thing happened before I started EMT school).

Pushing past the first layer of fear, I took the first free class the BJJ gym offered. Nervous, I walked through the doors. At the front desk I was greeted by a kind woman who told me to go to a secluded room to meet my instructor. A small setting with one instructor and one other student? Unpleasant, but not terrible for my social anxiety.

My first official class with the gym was much more stressful. I arrived 15 minutes early and sat in my car. My heart was beating hard enough that you could hear it if you were in the passenger seat next to me. Before I even started the hour's worth of grappling, I started to sweat. My hands and feet turned cold, my vision went blurry, and my coordination was off. I had to put my full focus into grabbing the door handle, pulling the door open, and walking into the place. I was that anxious.

I did learn good skills in the class. But I let anxiety stop me from learning more and trying as hard as I could. Many of my thoughts focused on the imaginary criticism I might receive from looking like a fool.

I'd dealt with social anxiety for years. But now, because I wanted to truly improve myself, I faced it head-on.

Most of my social anxiety is gone now. It took many months to get over it, but I can tell you one thing with certainty: The effort to rid myself of anxiety literally changed my life. I've learned a lot from it too. Any young man who goes through The Preparation will face many difficulties, just as I have. Social anxiety may imprison you the way it once imprisoned me.

Well, I've thought of a few methods that, if used together, can free you from persistent anxiety...

EAGLE'S EYE VIEW

You've probably seen an old video of San Francisco or New York in the early 20th century. Cars, trolleys, horses, and people–hundreds of them–all passing one another in the street.

All the emotions of the people and problems of the time are not taken into account. The scene is pleasant as you watch people go about their business so long ago.

I play these historical videos in my mind whenever I sense anxiety poking its ugly head around the corner. They're a clear reminder of the passage of time, that all that is will soon be gone. And that every emotion, potent or airy, shall soon disappear.

This is not meant to be a nihilistic view of the world, but a practical one. It's simply the truth. The nihilist will adopt this mental tool to indulge in self-pity. The man who seeks greatness will use it to free himself from the thoughts of others and, more importantly, from his own negative emotions.

The eagle's eye view helps you step back from the world and measure it with reason. Instead of getting caught up in emotions, you begin to observe them, toss out the negative ones (fear, jealousy, hatred, anger...), and replace them with positive sentiments (love, faith, compassion, courage...).

The economic idea of low time preference applies here. The objective is, in certain moments, to view the bigger picture. Once we do, we can act in ways that serve others, and ourselves.

So, when you feel anxiety creep in, take a step back. Play the old-timey videos of 1920s New York in your mind. Understand the passage of time and how emotions come and go like the wind. Step outside yourself. Feel the pleasantness of the moment.

But there's another component to this method that I must mention...

HARMONY

Marcus Aurelius said that humans are all made for one another. I rejected this idea for a brief period of time. Not wanting to view myself as the same as other people, or obligated to them in any way, I ignored those parts of Meditations. Yet, I've come to realize it is true.

I specifically remember in one translation of Meditations Marcus Aurelius calling other people his "brothers and sisters". I began to do the same. As I'd walk down the street, I'd see a man and in my mind, I'd say, "he is my brother". As I passed a woman on the sidewalk I'd say, "she's my sister". Suddenly, with that simple comment, all my anxiety fell away. Along with that, any criticism I had of the person turned to dust. What is there to be anxious about when I walk among my brothers and sisters? And why would I want to criticize them?

Most of the greatest ways to reduce social anxiety involve stepping outside yourself. What most people fail to properly describe regarding the removal of social anxiety is consideration of other people's thoughts and potential criticisms.

Many of the influential figures of our time, especially those who act as motivational speakers, will say things like, "Screw what other people think. It doesn't matter." Is this true? Yes, but this way of thinking about it puts you in opposition to other people. It assumes their thoughts, especially those about you, are negative.

The last thing you want to do when killing off anxiety is to assume the thoughts of others. We tend to think other people are critical of us. The "screw them" mentality assumes as much, providing justification for your anxiety, leading you further into it, and away from good, free, and useful action.

Marcus Aurelius spoke of this as well: Never assume the thoughts of others. Whenever you are in public or engaged in a specific activity that causes you to think someone may be critical of you, always remind yourself, "I will not assume their thoughts".

The fact is, it doesn't matter what people think. But never assume the worst from them. Don't degrade yourself by placing false criticism in the mind of another, because that also degrades them in your own mind.

Don't view other people as your opponent or enemy. Never assume the worst from others. It makes it impossible to destroy social anxiety and advance toward action. Instead, take the eagle's eye view, separate yourself from negative emotions, and seek harmony with yourself and others.

LEAN INTO IT

The previous methods are meant for use in the open world (when you're not directly engaged with anything). This one is for engaging in direct action with a person or event. It includes several components.

Anxiety encourages inaction. It wants you to sit still, to hide from everything that draws it out. It steals our opportunities by making us feel small, unworthy, insignificant. It throws us in our cell but always slides the key under the door. We can get out, but we will come face-to-face with the thing.

It's only through action that we recognize anxiety as a misty, harmless figure that often reveals the right path to take.

It's taken months of hard work to get where I am. Now, could I make a presentation in front of a crowd of people? No. At least not without running out of breath, stumbling over my words, and sweating like crazy. Getting comfortable with something like that will come with time.

My social anxiety is largely gone because I've been leaning into uncomfortable situations. EMT school, BJJ classes, and being apprenticed to a Uruguayan gaucho to name a few. You must first step into discomfort and then force yourself to stay there. Soon it won't seem so bad, but that's when you need to take the next step by doing it again.

NOTE: Since originally writing this section, I've worked on wildfires in Oregon, sailed around the Falkland Islands and through the Strait of Magellan, started flight school, and worked on a geophysics crew for a couple weeks in Nevada to name a few more things... The social anxiety I once had is now gone. The more you do, the more confidence you gain, the more relaxed you'll feel in any situation. Don't avoid. Push through.

When you enroll in a course to learn a new skill, you must force yourself to speak to the instructors and other students in the class. In fact, anytime you have the opportunity to talk to someone... take it. In the elevator, at a restaurant, on the street. Ask people how they're doing or just say "hi". Make conversation. I can tell you from personal experience that this reduces anxiety. Anytime I even consider speaking to someone, I force myself to do so right away.

I was walking down the street the other day when I saw a nurse walking home from a hospital near my house. I was about to take a ride along with an ambulance service, and I had a question I thought he might be able to answer. We crossed the street at the same time, and I took the opportunity to ask him. He didn't have the answer to my question, but I took immediate action, overcame anxiety, and grabbed an opportunity to be kind to a stranger.

It's self-induced exposure therapy. Yet it is much more effective. Let me explain...

As you go through your version of The Preparation, you (in order to gain skills) will put yourself in places to learn valuable lessons. Yes, you'll force yourself to look social anxiety dead in the eye. But more importantly, you'll gain competency...one of the greatest antidotes to anxiety.

Competency = Confidence

Build skills to confront discomfort. The war on anxiety is fought on multiple fronts. With persistence, you'll win.

When learning a skill or interacting with someone, your mind should be completely present and engaged. This is when you shift your perspective from the "eagle's eye" view to that of a person whose full attention is on whatever they are engaged in.

What has worked best for me is trying to never let my mind wander. Practice this when learning a skill and you'll quickly advance. Do so with people, and anxiety will fade as relationships grow.

I'll always remember the words tattooed on my father's arm, "Lean into it". Let those words echo in your mind whenever you're doing something to benefit yourself or another person.

In some cases, you want to step outside yourself to see the bigger picture. In others you want to be fully engaged with whatever is at hand. The proper timing of these shifts in perspective can only be learned through continuous effort. Build skills to become competent. Rid yourself of the fear of looking like a fool by looking like a fool over and over again. Seek harmony with others and yourself. Never assume the worst of other people. That is the method to overcome anxiety.

MANAGING YOUR OWN PSYCHOLOGY

In college your peers are all with you going through the same process. In the military you and your buddies are all suffering together. At a dead-end job you and your coworkers are all punching the clock together.

The shared experience provides a sense of comfort. Any suffering that comes with it is easier to endure because that, too, is shared. When large groups of people follow the same path, it instills belief in a common goal or outcome. The primary motivation comes from the collective, not the individual. Competition and conformity are the primary drivers of action in most groups. Small portions of the group compete among each other, but everyone is pressured to conform.

In The Preparation you go at it alone. No peer group to follow, society doesn't cheer you on, and many of the social norms agreed upon are opposed to you. There is no clear-cut path to follow. You're in the dark, and all you've got is your ambition and willpower to succeed. Every act is a self-made decision, every pain is yours to bear, every achievement is brought about through your ability to imagine what the man you'd like to be would do, and to act upon it.

You stand alone, building yourself brick by brick.

It won't be easy for you. Trust me, there was a time when I questioned if any of this mattered. I didn't know if what I was doing would make any difference. When you are on your own path you have no guarantee of anything. No diploma, no Dress Blues, no salary.

But – you are free.

Your success is self-driven and self-determined. There will be many times where you are going to be brought down by the uncertainty of your situation...Be ready for it.

I want to give you some solutions to the difficulties that I have faced, and that you will face as well.

WHO COULD YOU BE?

"Know thyself" is an ancient Greek maxim that was inscribed on the Temple of Apollo. It takes time to know thyself. You must start on your own path to figure out who you are. To do that, you must first know who you want to be. The ultimate version of yourself...Who is he? What is he capable of? How does he live his life? Burn these questions into your mind until you find the answer.

For myself, I want to emulate Maximus from Gladiator and Edmond Dantes from The Count of Monte Cristo. I know their stories, I know who they are. They are men of courage, compassion, strength, virtue, influence, capability, confidence, and sheer will. They learn, they persist, they overcome.

The thought of being like them uplifts me. Becoming that type of man is my path. When I live in accordance with that idea I am reassured by the sense of fulfillment I receive.

With a precise vision of who you could be, of who you want to be, you can pull yourself out of any rut and get back on your path.

YOUR COUNCIL

Speaking of Maximus and Dantes, these men are on my "council". A personal council is a concept Napoleon Hill came up with in his book Think and Grow Rich. Each night before bed, Hill would assemble his council of men he admired in his mind. He imagined himself sitting at the head of a table with his council of admirable men sitting around the table before him.

He did this to get insights from each of these men. He wanted to know what they would do if they were in his shoes. One by one, he'd go around the table, soliciting perspectives from Emerson, Paine, Edison, Darwin, Ford, Napoleon Bonaparte, Lincoln, Burbank, and Andrew Carnegie.

Oftentimes, the hardest part of anything is figuring out what to do. When your mind assembles a personal council of people you wish to emulate (real or fictional), they can help you determine how you want to walk, talk, and act. It becomes easier to make the decisions you need to make.

WIN YOUR OWN FAVOR

Most of your peers who find a job, join the military, or go to college will do the bare minimum to coast through. It's the natural impulse for most humans.

But ambition is coded into certain individuals. You may be one of them. Ambition has to be backed by grit, which must be trained and developed. Our progress can stall when circumstances bring us down. The challenge lies in getting back up and re-gaining momentum as quickly as possible.

The most difficult times for me have come not from external, unchangeable circumstances, but from deteriorating understanding of what I'm doing and why I'm doing it. Several times I have lost the "big picture", and I'm sure you will too. It sucks because you lose faith in yourself, making it easy to reduce effort in whatever you're doing, leading to a downward spiral where you lose conviction in your "why".

When we are young, we don't have many achievements in life to enhance our confidence. We don't yet know exactly who we are. Our "why" is both our Fortress of Solitude and our driver of action. It is our shield and our sword. Only with a "why" can we become who we want to be.

When you forget your "why" and drop your weapons, you open yourself up to outside attack. You become vulnerable to the blows of negative thoughts from yourself and others.

You must first realize you've lost sight of your cause. It takes true determination to do so because you must keep watch over your thoughts and actions.

It's essential to notice when you become:

- ▶ Lazy
- ▶ Complacent
- ▶ Fearful
- ▶ Anxious
- ▶ Jealous
- ▶ Angry

These are all indicators that you've lost your path.

Second, you must gather your "council", which I mentioned earlier. Address each member and ask, "What would you do from here?" The answer will come to you right away.

Third, you need to take direct and immediate action. If you've already planned your day, ensure you do all you committed to do. If you haven't planned your day, you need to do so right away and follow through with everything. Place yourself in the present. Focus on today and accomplish what you say you will.

Fourth—and this is if you need an extra push—do something uncomfortable. It could be as simple as going to the gym. But you need to do something challenging, something that the person you want to be would do if they were in the same situation you're in. This will bring you back into alignment with your "why".

I've had days where I've completely lost sight of my "why". After realizing that this happened, I went to the gym, stayed longer than I wanted to, and left the gym with the clear image of my "why" back in my mind.

Put simply: the key is to act.

Do things that win the favor of your ultimate self. With time, the blessing of the lack of peer support will shine through. By starting your version of The Preparation, you are creating your fate, not letting it fall to the hands of the crowd.

REST

Making significant improvements in yourself and aiming toward your "why" is no small task. It's a grind requiring continuous daily effort, which is good. But it's easy to burn out.

I neglected rest for a long time. I wanted to keep going, to keep moving forward even when it was clear mental and physical fatigue were keeping me from producing my best results. I'm glad I learned the lesson the hard way, and I encourage you to burn out a few times in the beginning stages of The Preparation. You've got to pick up the pace as quickly as possible, to see how much you can get done with the time you have each day.

Once I began to incorporate short periods of rest, I was able to enhance my focus and effort when I was aiming to get things done. Burn out a few times, find your limit, and then rest for a day every once in a while. Chances are you'll find that you can continue without rest for much longer than you may believe.

But what do I mean by rest?

You need time away from everything, time to clear your head. Find a place where you can sit down, take a drive, or go for a walk. Don't use electronics, don't read books, don't do anything that requires substantial focus. Let your mind rest. Some of your best ideas will come when you have nothing to do and you let your mind wander. You'll think of a place you should go, a thing you should do, a better way to learn a skill, or a new way to orient your day for increased productivity.

Use rest to recoup. It energizes your mind and body while giving you time to step back and analyze where you're at.

DO FUN SHIT

I've viewed pretty much everything I do for The Preparation as work—the games, activities, occupations, studies I treat it all as if I have employed myself to do it (at least most of the time). Why? Well, you can't daydream about the future all the time, about who you could be, if you did you wouldn't actually get anything done. When I view it as work, I have an obligation to show up and get things done every day.

But I've also come to think that you really can't be all work and no play, at least that's my experience so far. I've burnt out, noticed it, and rested—but I still felt like I needed something more. I was missing something. Well, I didn't want to admit it for a long time, but you need to do fun things sometimes.

Having fun is a form of rest (that should be had in moderation) and it enriches the spirit. Take a drive, go white water rafting, hike a mountain—anything to get the dopamine flowing for a bit.

THE GREATEST MOTIVATION

All these personal anecdotes and ideas are meant to assist you in managing your own psychology when dealing with hardship on your own path. I'm sure that as you and I progress through The Preparation we will find other more specific ways of combating discouragement and rising above difficulty.

The idea that gave me the greatest motivation, especially in the beginning, was that I was going at this alone. I've always loved the idea of the hero's journey, the outline is nearly always the same, but the challenges and triumphs change from story to story. The hero does it alone. He either dies in the process or comes out on the other side as a man among men.

Our peers live in a silo, one that they will likely never escape. Some may view their place among their mass of peers as a blessing, but really, it's a curse. You can be free, but you must bear the burden of your freedom and make the decisions of your life for yourself. It's daunting, but nothing compares to it.

Maybe this thought brings you the same strength and motivation it brings me.

THE
CYCLES

PART

3

CYCLE #1: MEDIC

ANCHOR COURSE

Find an EMT school in your area. Depending on what the school in your area offers, you could complete the course in as little as two months. You'll average 14–16 hours a week for 2 months. The cost is $1,500–$3,000.

There is no single list of EMT schools in the US, but there are many. Google EMT classes or schools in your Local Area.

Anchor................168 hours

ACADEMICS

Core Classes:

A1: Biology and Human Behavior
A2: Medical School for Everyone: Emergency Medicine
A3: Medical School for Everyone: Grand Rounds

Electives; choose in OPT (Optional) Classes

▶ ....

▶ ....

▶ ....

▶ ....

Academics................120 hours

Core................36/120

12
12
12

Add 84 hours

................Total hours

Reading:

B1: Discovering the German New Medicine
B2: Caveman Chemistry

Choose Books in OPT to complete 12 hours

▶ ....

▶ ....

Reading................72 hours

10
50

................Total hours

Do Fun Shit: At least 5 hours a week

EMT classes are often offered just 2–3 days a week. That leaves plenty of time to be filled in exploring novel experiences or continuing your progress with martial arts, a musical instrument, or something like chess.

► ....

► ....

► ....

DFS: .... 60 Hours Minimum

.... Total hours

Reflection/Accountability: 5 hours a week

Write and publish an explanation of what you learned/did in the past week to Substack. Find time to reflect on how you're doing and how you can improve.

Reflection: .... 60 hours

Anchor: .... ~$1500–3000

Academics: .... $37.5 (~$12.50/month subscription to Great Courses Plus)

Reading: .... $40 ($20/Book x 2)

Total = ... **$1577.5–3077.5**

+ OPT Courses/Reading $_____

DFS Hobbies + ... $_____

COSTS TOTAL = ... $_____

480/minimum hours in a cycle

CYCLE #2: PILOT

ANCHOR COURSE

Private Pilot course in Alaska. This course will take around 150 hours of study, ground school, and active flight time total to complete over the course of as little as 2 months. You'll average 19 hours a week including ground school (which can be done online). Total cost is a minimum of $11,350.

(There are, of course, additional pilot schools all over America)

Pilot

Anchor................300 hours

ACADEMICS

Core classes:

A4: The Science of Flight
A5: The Science of Extreme Weather

Reading:

B3: Stick and Rudder
B4: Mental Math for Pilots

Choose Books in OPT to read if you have time

▶ ....

▶ ....

▶ ....

Academics

Core...................27 hours

15
12

Reading................17 hours

12
5

.... Total hours

Do Fun Shit: 6.5 hours a week.

With the unique opportunity of being in Alaska we want you to take advantage of your time there. You can go to the **Alaska Department of Fish and Game website** (or go to one of their locations in person) to purchase a non-resident (if you're not from there) fishing license and sport fish for several hours a week.

▶ ....

▶ ....

▶ ....

DFS: .... 76 hours

.... Total hours

Reflection/Accountability: 5 hours a week

Write and publish an explanation of what you learned/did in the past week to Substack. Find time to reflect on how you're doing and how you can improve.

Reflection: .... 60 hours

Anchor: $11,350

Academics: .... $37.5 (Great Courses Plus)

Reading: .... $40 ($20/Book x 2)

Total = ... **$11, 407.50**

+ OPT Courses/Reading $_____

DFS Hobbies + ... $_____

COSTS TOTAL = ... $_____

480/minimum hours in a cycle

CYCLE #3: COWBOY

ANCHOR COURSE

For this quarter you'll be heading to Texas to complete the **Beginner Ranch work and Horsemanship** from the American Cowboy Academy for ~$1,500. (1 week to complete course, ~40 hours)

After that week-long course you're going to Idaho for 3 weeks to learn how to **pack horses and mules into the backcountry** from Middle Fork Outfitters. The cost of the course is $4,400. (~120 hours to complete)

Cowboy

Guide Packer

Anchor................160 hours

ACADEMICS

Core classes:

A6: A History of the United States 2nd Ed
A7: The America West: History, Myth and Legacy
A8: Trials West: How Freedom Settled The West
A9: Skeptics Guide to American History

Academics................120 hours

Core................81/120

42
12
15
12

Elective classes; Now choose classes in OPT

▶ ....

▶ ....

▶ ....

Add 39 Elective hours

................Total hours

Reading:

B5: Blood and Thunder
B6: Education of a Wandering Man
B7: Empire of the Summer Moon
B8: The Sackett Series

Choose Books in OPT you like

▶ ....

▶ ....

Reading................80 hours

15
5
16
44

................Total hours

Do Fun Shit: For this cycle, nearly a month is tied up with Anchor courses. For the other two months, be sure to make plenty of time for exploring novel experiences or continuing your progress with martial arts, a musical instrument, or something like chess. Choose your Activities:

▶ ....

▶ ....

DFS:............ 60 Hours Minimum

.... **Total hours**

Reflection/Accountability: 5 hours a week

Write and publish an explanation of what you learned/did in the past week to Substack. Find time to reflect on how you're doing and how you can improve.

Reflection.................... 60 hours

Anchor: $6,015

Academics: .... $42.5 (GCP) + Liberty Classroom

Reading: .... $80 ($20/Book x 4)

Total = ... **$6,137.50**

+ OPT Courses/Reading $_____

DFS Hobbies + ... $_____

COSTS TOTAL = ... $_____

480/minimum hours in a cycle

CYCLE #4: BUILDER

ANCHOR COURSE

Taking the **2-Week Design Build Course** from the Shelter Institute for $5,000.

Builder

Anchor	112 hours

ACADEMICS

Academics	120 hours
Core	50/120

Core Classes:

A10: The Big History of Civilizations — 13
A11: Understanding The Worlds Greatest Structures — 13
A12: Understanding Greek and Roman Technology — 12
A13: The Rise of The Novel: Exploring History's Greatest Early Works — 12

Elective classes; Now choose classes in OPT

Add 70 Hours

▶ ....

▶ ....

▶ ....

▶ ....

.... Total hours

Reading:

Reading 72 hours

B9: Virtue of Selfishness — 4
B10: Modern Man in Search of a Soul — 9
B11: The Iliad — 9
B12: Only Yesterday — 10
B13: The Law — 2

Choose Books in OPT to complete 38 hours

▶ ....

▶ ....

.... Total hours

Do Fun Shit: You'll be totally absorbed during your visit to the shelter institute, but classes are only 2–3 weeks long. You'll have more than two months to fill with Academic & reading work, but don't forget to make time for novel experiences and continued practice of the core hobbies like chess, martial arts, becoming competent with a musical instrument, etc.

▶ ....

▶ ....

DFS: .... 60 hours

.... Total hours

Reflection/Accountability: 5 hours a week

Write and publish an explanation of what you learned/did in the past week to Substack. Find time to reflect on how you're doing and how you can improve.

Reflection: .... 60 hours

Anchor: $5,000

Academics: .... $37.5 (GCP)

Reading: .... $100 ($20/Book x 5)

Total = ... **$5,137.5**

+ OPT Courses/Reading $_____

DFS Hobbies + ... $_____

COSTS TOTAL = ... $_____

480/minimum hours in a cycle is the goal

CYCLE #5: CHEF

ANCHOR COURSE

You're going across the world in this next course to Florence, Italy to take the **1-month Professional Italian Cuisine cooking program** from Florence Culinary Arts School for around 5,500 euros.($6,500) (~240 hours to complete)

Chef

Anchor	240 hours

ACADEMICS

Core Classes:

	Academics	120 hours
	Core	77/120 hours
A14: The Rise and Fall of the Roman Republic	7	
A15: The Italian Renaissance	18	
A16: How To Look At And Understand Great Art	13	
A17: European Paintings: From Leonardo to Rembrandt to Goya	14	
A18: A History of European Art	25	

Electives; choose in OPT (Optional) Classes

Add Elective 43 hours

▶ ....

▶ ....

▶ ....

▶ ....

Total hours

Reading:

	Reading	40–72 hours
B14: Greek Art	7	
B15: Roman Art	6	
B16: The Republic	3	
B17: Gorgias	2	
B18: Trial and Death of Socrates	3	
B19: Way of the Superior Man	5	

Choose Books in OPT to complete 14 hours

▶ ....

▶ ....

▶ .... Total hours

Do Fun Shit: Look, you'll be in Florence Italy. It's easy to get all over much of Europe from there. You should travel to new places. Go hiking (or skiing) in the Alps. See Art. Study Architecture. Take an art class. Choose your adventure:

DFS: .... 40–60 hours
(at a minimum!)

▶ ....

▶ .... Total hours

Reflection/Accountability: 3 hours a week
Write and publish an explanation of what you learned/did in the past week to Substack. Find time to reflect on how you're doing and how you can improve.

Reflection .... 40–60 hours

Anchor: .... $6,120 (Course + Twin Room)

Travel: .... $400–$1,300 for a round-trip flight to Florence from the US

Academics: .... $37.5 (GCP) + Edx (Free to Audit no certificate)

Reading: .... $120 ($20/Book x 6)

Total = ... $5,117.5

+ OPT Courses/Reading $_____

DFS Hobbies + ... $_____

COSTS TOTAL = ... $_____

480/minimum hours in a cycle is the goal

CYCLE #6: HEAVY EQUIPMENT OPERATOR

ANCHOR COURSE

Now, it's time that you make your way down to Green Cove Springs, Florida where you will be taking the Heavy Now course from the Earth Movers School. This course will teach you how to operate heavy machinery over the course of 4 weeks and will cost you $15,000.

Heavy Equip

Anchor	160 hours

ACADEMICS

Core Classes:

	Academics	120 hours
	Core	90/120

A19: Geology Series — 30
A20: Planet Earth... and You! — 41
A21: Practical Geology — 12
A22: Law School for everyone: Contracts — 7

Elective classes; Now choose classes in OPT

Add 30 hours

► ....

► ....

► ....

► ....

Total hours

Reading:

Reading 72 hours

B20: The Count of Monte Cristo — 30
B21: Adventures of Huckleberry Finn — 9
B22: Underland: A Deep Time Journey — 14

Choose Books in OPT to complete 19 hours

► ....

► ....

Total hours

Do Fun Shit: Turn to the Activities page of the book and find something that looks interesting to you. All things are hard at first, but novel action is the way forward. Find something do-able and take action:

▶ ....

▶ ....

▶ ....

DFS: 50–60 hours

.... Total hours

Reflection/Accountability: 4 hours a week

Write and publish an explanation of what you learned/did in the past week to Substack. Find time to reflect on how you're doing and how you can improve.

Reflection: 50–60 hours

Anchor: $15,000

Academics: .... $37.5 (GCP) + Edx (Free to Audit no certificate)

Reading: .... $40 ($20/Book x 2)

+ OPT Courses/Reading $_____

DFS Hobbies + ... $_____

COSTS TOTAL = ... $_____

480/minimum hours in a cycle is the goal

CYCLE #7: WORK CYCLE

ANCHOR COURSE

Opportunities will come your way in the form of work. Sometimes it makes sense to take a job for a cycle to earn money and learn on the job.

Two Examples: Maxim leveraged his EMT to work on wildfires earning $600/day. He was also offered a paid internship writing advertising copy – which he passed on. Examples like this will come your way.

Anchor:	160 hours minimum

ACADEMICS

Core Classes:

Academics	100 hours
Core	70/100

A23: Argumentation: The Study of Effective Reasoning — 12
A24: Successful Negotiation: Essential Strategies and Skills — 17
A25: Malcom Gladwell Teaches Writing — 4
A26: History of the English Language 2nd Edition — 13
A27: Foundations of Western Civilization — 24

Elective classes; Now choose classes in OPT

Add 30 Hours

▶ ....

▶ ....

▶ ....

▶ ....

Total hours

Reading:

Reading 72 hours

B23: Poke the Box — 2
B24: Atlas Shrugged — 36
B25: On Writing, A Memoir of the Craft — 6
B26: The Creature from Jekyll Island — 10
B27: Consider This — 8
B28: The Elements of Style — 2
B29: Thank You for Arguing — 6

Choose Books in OPT to complete 9 hours

- ▶ ....
- ▶ .... **Total hours**

Do Fun Shit: With developing your novel hobbies, flexibility is key. If, like Maxim, working on wildfires, You might focus on chess, poker, or improving your guitar playing skills. You'll be sitting around much of the time with other guys looking for entertainment too. That's an opportunity.

If you're working in a regular office-type gig, take the opportunity to get started or double down on your Brazilian Jujitsu. Join a local gym and go as often as possible. It's your choice, but make it count.

DFS:.................... **80 hours**

- ▶ ....
- ▶ ....
- ▶ .... **Total hours**

Reflection/Accountability: 4 hours a week

Reflection:.... **50–60 hours**

Write and publish an explanation of what you learned/did in the past week to Substack. Find time to reflect on how you're doing and how you can improve.

Anchor:.................... $Make Money

Academics:.................... $50 (Great Courses Plus
                  + Masterclass)

Reading:.................... $100 ($20/Book x 5)

Total =.................... $137.5

+ OPT Courses/Reading $_____

DFS Hobbies + ... $_____

COSTS TOTAL = ... $_____

480/minimum hours in a cycle is the goal

CYCLE #8: WELDER

ANCHOR COURSE

For your last course of the year you will be going to Canada to take a course from General Welding School where you will be learning the basics of welding from highly trained professionals over a total of 160 hours. The cost of the course will be $3,750.

Welder

Anchor: .... 160 hours

ACADEMICS

Academics .... 114 hours

Core Classes:

Core 114

A28: The Science of Energy: Resources and Power Explained   14
A29: Pre-U Calc, physics, chemistry ($135)   100

Reading:

Reading .... 72 hours

B30: Zen and the Art of Motorcycle Maintenance   12
B31: True Believer   4
B32: Gulliver's Travels   6
B33: The Prize   23

Choose Books in OPT to complete 27 hours

▶ ....

▶ ....

▶ ....

.... Total hours

Do Fun Shit: As always, what you do here is dependent on location. When you'll be in a fixed position for a period of time, this presents a good opportunity to dive deeper into a particular activity. No matter what, there's always plenty to do.

Close to the welding school are two boxing gyms, it's a chance to expand your martial arts capability. Or you could devote your energies to becoming competent at one of the local rock climbing gyms. The choice is yours, but don't waste it.

► ....

► ....

► ....

DFS: .... 68 hours

.... **Total hours**

Reflection/Accountability: 5 hours a week

Write and publish an explanation of what you learned/did in the past week to Substack. Find time to reflect on how you're doing and how you can improve.

Reflection: .... 60 hours

480 hours in a cycle

Anchor: $3,750

Academics: .... $37.5 (GCP) + Coursera (Free to Audit no certificate)

Reading: .... $80 ($20/Book x 4)

+ OPT Courses/Reading $_____

DFS Hobbies + ... $_____

COSTS TOTAL = ... $_____

CYCLE #9: FIGHTER

ANCHOR COURSE

For this cycle you'll head to Thailand to train Muay Thai for 3 months at one of the most recognized Muay Thai gyms in the world.

Two hour classes X 4–6 days a week

Fighter

Anchor	192 hours

ACADEMICS

Academics	100 hours

Core Classes

Core	97/100

A30: Understanding the human body/ Anatomy & Physiology — 24

A31: Masters of War: History's Greatest Strategic Thinkers — 12

A32: Foundations of Eastern Civilization — 24

A33: History of the Ancient World: A Global Perspective — 24

A34: Life Lessons From the Great Books — 13

Choose any Elective courses you want to add.

Add 3 hours

▶ ....

.... Total hours

Reading

Reading	61 hours

B34: Meditations — 6

B35: The Art of War — 1

B36: Bobby Fischer Teaches Chess — 3

B37: A War Like No Other — 9

B38: Beowulf — 4

B39: Book of Five Rings — 2

B40: The Guns of August — 13

B41: The Moon is a Harsh Mistress — 10

Choose Books in OPT to complete 13 hours

▶ ....

▶ ....

▶ ....

.... Total hours

Do Fun Shit: The school has two locations. One in the Mountains, one near the ocean. Depending on which you choose, the activities will follow. If you're on the beach this is the perfect time to get your Scuba certification. Learn archery or practice firearms skills at Phuket Shooting Range. Take a Thai cooking class.

If in the mountains, get 1–1 training in archery at Archery Chiang Mai, Spend a day doing jungle-based canyon trekking, water rafting, or jungle kayaking. Or do some motorbike Adventure riding. Your Choice.

▶ ....

▶ ....

▶ ....

▶ ....

DFS: .... 67 hours minimum

.... Total hours

Reflection/Accountability: 5 hours a week

Write and publish an explanation of what you learned/did in the past week to Substack. Find time to reflect on how you're doing and how you can improve.

Reflection: .... 60 hours

Anchor: .... $3,845 (3 Months All Inclusive Muay Thai classes, training gear, prepaid meal card, and standard accommodations)

Travel: .... $600-$1,100 for airfare from US to Thailand

Academics: .... $37.5 (GCP)

Reading: .... $160 ($20/Book x 8)

Total = ... **$4,642.50**

+ OPT Courses/Reading $_____

DFS Hobbies + $_____

COSTS TOTAL = $_____

480 hours in a cycle

CYCLE #10: SAILOR

ANCHOR COURSE

Your objective for this cycle is to complete the 16-day voyage near the Cape Horn of Chile and become a competent crew member aboard a sailing boat with Pelagic Expeditions. The trip itself will cost $12,000.

Sailor

Anchor	120 hours

ACADEMICS:

Core Classes:

	Academics	100 hours
	Core	56/100

A35: Our Night Sky	6
A36: The Natural Navigator	6
A37: Introduction to Celestial Navigation for Mariners	2
A38: Everyday Engineering: Understanding the Marvels of Daily Life	18
A39: The Evidence of Modern Physics: How We Know What We Know	12
A40: Heros and Legends: The Most Influential Characters of Literature	12

Elective classes; choose courses in OPT   Add 44 hours

▶ ....

▶ ....

▶ ....

Total hours

Reading:

	Reading	60 hours

B42: Endurance	7
B43: Brave New World	7
B44: The Odyssey	6
B45: The Travels of Marco Polo	7
B46: 1493	11
B47: The Last Place on Earth: Scott and Amund	12.5
B48: Cosmos	6.5

Choose Books in OPT to complete 3 hours

▶ ....

▶ ....

Total hours

Do Fun Shit: Location matters. You'll be in the Southern Cone of South America anyway. What else can you do while you're there? Hiking and mountaineering in Patagonia. Fly fishing or rafting? Study the architecture of Buenos Aires, learn to paraglide in Punta del Este, Uruguay. If you've been practicing Brazilian JuJitsu, you could drop in on a class in one of the famous schools in Brazil. There are so many possibilities. Again, the key is novel action or using the time to improve your competency in a particular craft.

▶ ....

▶ ....

▶ ....

DFS: .... 100 hours

.... Total hours

Reflection/Accountability: 5 hours a week

Write and publish an explanation of what you learned/did in the past week to Substack. Find time to reflect on how you're doing and how you can improve.

Reflection: .... 60 hours

Costs: .... ~$12,000 ($1,000–$1,500 for airfare costs from US to Puerto Williams, Chile)

~$12.50/month for Great Courses Subscription

Anchor: $3,750

Academics: .... $37.5 (GCP) + Coursera (Free to Audit no certificate)

Reading: .... $100 ($20/Book x 5)

Total = ... **$4,025**

+ OPT Courses/Reading $_____

DFS Hobbies + ... $_____

COSTS TOTAL = ... $_____

480 hours in a cycle

CYCLE #11: SURVIVALIST

ANCHOR COURSE

Utah is going to be your home base for a short time as you take the 14-day Primitive Living Intensive course from Boulder Outdoor Survival School.

Survivor

Anchor	160 hours

ACADEMICS

Core classes:

	Academics	120
	Core	116/120

A41: Foraging Wild Mushrooms — 20
A42: Music Theory Comprehensive Complete Part 1, 2, &3 — 12
A43: How to Listen to and Understand Great Music 3rd Edition — 36
A44: Music As A Mirror of History — 12
A45: Classical Music Guide by Doug Casey — 36

Elective classes; Now choose at least 4 hours

Add 4 hours

▶ ....

▶ ....

	Total hours

Reading:

	Reading	80 hours

B49: The Revenant — 8
B50: Undaunted Courage — 11.5
B51: One Man's Wilderness — 8
B52: Man's Search for Meaning — 4
B53: Touching the Void — 6
B54: 1984 — 8
B55: Animal Farm — 3
B56: 1177 B.C. — 7

Choose Books in OPT to complete 24 hours of Reading

▶ ....

▶ ....

▶ ....

	Total hours

Do Fun Shit: After a couple of weekends roughing it in the wilderness, you'll have a new appreciation for the finer things in life. Use the clean-slate energy to do something new, fun, and challenging.

DFS: .... 60 hours

▶ ....

▶ ....

▶ ....

▶ .... Total hours

Reflection/Accountability: 5 hours a week

Reflection: .... 60 hours

Write and publish an explanation of what you learned/did in the past week to Substack. Find time to reflect on how you're doing and how you can improve.

Anchor: $3,980

480 hours in a cycle

Academics: .... $57.5 (GCP)
+ $20 Foraging Course

Reading: .... $160 ($20/Book x 8)

Total = ... $4,197.50

+ OPT Courses/Reading $_____

DFS Hobbies + ... $_____

COSTS TOTAL = ... $_____

CYCLE #12: FARMER

ANCHOR COURSE

There's no guarantee that you'll be accepted to learn and work at Polyface Farms for a summer; Joel only accepts people that he thinks can hack it. There's no cost for as an intern to learn the fundamentals of regenerative farming; your tuition is paid in the form of your labor.
(May 1st–September 30th).

In our book, Joel Salatin is the gold standard, but there are plenty of other internship opportunities available on regenerative farms all over the world.

Farmer

Anchor................................320 hours

ACADEMICS

No core academic required

Elective classes; Now choose any courses of interest to you.

Electives

▶ ....

▶ ....

....Total hours

Reading

B57: Man, Cattle and Veld
B58: The Ascent of Money
B59: How to Draw Like A Real Artist
B60: Logic: A Very Short Introduction
B61: The Art of Thinking Clearly

Reading................................80 hours

14
10
30
2.5
7

Choose Books in OPT to complete 19 hours

▶ ....

▶ ....

....Total hours

Do Fun Shit: When you're working on a farm for three months (or more) you've got to focus on accessible hobbies. Fitness, Music, Poker, Chess, guitar etc. It's also a great time to pick up or practice your drawing.

DFS: .... 60 hours

▶ ....

▶ ....

▶ ....

.... Total hours

Reflection/Accountability: 5 hours a week

Reflection: .... 60 hours

Write and publish an explanation of what you learned/did in the past week to Substack. Find time to reflect on how you're doing and how you can improve.

Anchor: .... $80 for Travel

Academics: $0

Reading: .... $60 ($20/Book x 3)

Total = ... **$140**

+ OPT Courses/Reading $_____

DFS Hobbies + ... $_____

COSTS TOTAL = ... $_____

480 hours in a cycle

CYCLE #13: ENTREPRENEUR

ANCHOR COURSE

Hopefully, you've already been thinking about a business you could create or service you could offer. If that's you, this is your time for a test run.

Don't make it complicated. If it involves manufacturing, forget it. You don't have enough time. What you're looking for is a product you can create (a course or newsletter) or a service you can sell.

Selling is the key word here, because much of Entrepreneurship is figuring out who your potential clients are and how to sell it to them.

Our goal here is to get someone to willingly and happily fork over their hard-earned money for a solution you offer.

If you really have no product or service idea, you'll likely come up with one as you follow the course material.

Anchor................255 hours

Do Fun Shit: During this cycle, routine will do you a lot of good. Starting a business is novel enough. Focus your hobby time on activities that give your life structure and your mind a release. Fitness, chess, music, etc. Save your creative energies for figuring out how to make the business work.

DFS:................60 hours

▶ ....

▶ ....

▶ ....

................Total hours

ACADEMICS

A46: Modern Marketing with Seth Godin
A47: Sales Training: Practical Sale Techniques
A48: Social Media Marketing Masterclass
on 10+ platforms

Reading

B62: The Reluctant Entrepreneur
B63: The Lean Startup
B64: The Million-Dollar, One-Person Business
B65: Ready, Fire, Aim
B66: The 1-Page Marketing Plan
B67: The Boron Letters
B68: Influence
B69: Think and Grow Rich
B70: Great Leads
B71: How to Win Friends and Influence People
B72: PreSuasion
B73: Never Split the Difference
B74: Good Strategy/Bad Strategy

Academics	20 hours
	6
	3
	11
Reading	81 hours
	5
	6
	5
	7
	4
	4
	8
	6
	4
	7
	10
	9
	6

Reflection/Accountability: 5 hours a week

As a lifelong entrepreneur, I can say without doubt:
This is the time to keep your day organized, planned,
and structured. Start your day with a plan. Remove all
unnecessary decisions and use your reflection time to think
through each obstacle as you come to it.

Reflection: 60 hours

Anchor: $0

Academics: $230 Udemy courses

Reading: $260 ($20/Book x 13)

Total = $4,025

+ OPT Courses/Reading $_____

DFS Hobbies + $_____

COSTS TOTAL = $_____

480 hours in a cycle

CYCLE #14: INVESTOR

ANCHOR COURSE

You'll be making investments in the public stock market. First, we'll use a trading simulator as you learn. You'll start with $100,000 and learn to make it grow.

You'll build the foundation necessary to invest OR speculate in the markets. The Courses and books are wide ranging and designed to give you both practical tools as well as the context to make intelligent decisions.

Before you get started on the curriculum, create a simulator brokerage account at Investopedia (QR code to the right). You'll be given a fake $100,000 to invest. Along the way you'll learn how to determine what's a good investment by looking at it in two ways:

1. Securities analysis, which involves evaluating the fundamentals and financials of an individual company.

2. Macro analysis, which looks at broader economic trends, interest rates, sector cycles, and geopolitical factors that affect entire markets or industries.

And since history rhymes, you'll get a lot of exposure to financial and economic history.

Anchor	100 hours

Do Fun Shit: 5 hours a week

DFS:	60 hours

▶ ....

▶ ....

▶ ....

	Total hours

ACADEMICS

A49: Stock Market Investing for Beginners	10
A50: Investing In Stocks The Complete Course!	18
A51: The Art of Investing: Lessons from Histories Great Traders	12
A52: The Complete Financial Analyst Course 2025	22

Academics................75 hours

Reading

B75: Economics in One Lesson	6
B76: The Intelligent Investor	13
B77: The Most Important Thing	6
B78: Market Wizards	9
B79: When Money Dies	8
B80: Lords of Finance	14
B81: When Genius Failed	8
B82: Manias, Panics & Crashes	12
B83: Common Stocks & Uncommon Profits	8
B84: The World for Sale	9
B85: A Random Walk Down Wall Street	13
B86: Against the Gods	9
B87: You Can Be a Stock Market Genius	7
B88: Reminiscences of a Stock Operator	9
B89: Berkshire Letters to Shareholders	16
B90: The Great Crash 1929	6
B91: The Lords of Easy Money	10
B92: This Time Is Different	13
B93: Devil Take the Hindmost	12
B94: The Dao of Capital	7

Reading................195 hours

Reflection/Accountability: 4 hours a week

Write and publish an explanation of what you learned/did in the past week to Substack. Find time to reflect on how you're doing and how you can improve.

Reflection:................50 hours

Anchor:................	$0
Academics:................	$77 Udemy courses + Great Courses Subscription
Reading:................	$400 ($20/Book x 20)
Total =................	$477
+ OPT Courses/Reading..	$_____
DFS Hobbies +............	$_____
COSTS TOTAL =............	$_____

480 hours in a cycle

CYCLE #15: HACKER

ANCHOR COURSE

AI is the future. This cycle is about leveraging it in productive ways. You'll learn to use AI and other tools to build real products, apps and websites. You don't need to be a techie to make things happen.

By the end of the cycle you will build and launch a product for fun or profit.

Hacker

300 hours

ACADEMICS

Academics .... 57 hours

Core:

A53: Prototyping with AI Bootcamp — 22
A54: Python for Beginners — 15
A55: AI Builders Bootcamp — 20

Elective classes; Now choose any courses of interest to you.

▶ ....

▶ ....

Reading:

Reading .... 60–72 hours

B95: Antifragile — 12
B96: Don't Make Me Think — 3.5
B97: The Three Body Problem — 10
B98: Foundation Trilogy — 17

Choose Books in OPT to complete 17.5 hours of Reading

▶ ....

▶ ....

▶ ....

Total hours

Do Fun Shit: 5 hours a week

▶ ....

▶ ....

▶ ....

DFS: .... 60 hours

.... Total hours

Reflection/Accountability: 5 hours a week

Write and publish an explanation of what you learned/did in the past week to Substack. Find time to reflect on how you're doing and how you can improve.

Reflection: .... 60 hours

Anchor: $2149

Academics: $0

Reading: .... $80 ($20/Book x 4)

Total = ... $2229

+ OPT Courses/Reading $_____

DFS Hobbies + ... $_____

COSTS TOTAL = ... $_____

480 hours in a cycle

CYCLE #16: MAKER

ANCHOR COURSE

Maker—throws you into a FabLab stocked with nine powerhouse machines and challenges you to turn raw ideas into a finished product, fusing all the skills you've gathered in The Preparation; whether you mill a flat-pack chair, 3-D-print a drone frame, or CNC-carve an acoustic guitar, you'll prototype fast, master every tool, document the journey, and exit as a self-directed creator who can bend imagination into reality at minimal cost in publicly accessible labs across the country.

FabLabs

200 hours

ACADEMICS

A56: Autodesk Fusion 360 (Year 2025)–Complete Beginners Guide
A57: Introduction to CAD, CAM, and Practical CNC Machining for Milling
A58: Introduction to CAD and CAM for Milling and Turning
A59: 3D Modeling for 3D Printing and Laser Cutting on Fusion 360

Reading

B99:   The War of Art
B100: Nicomachean Ethics
B101: Scientific Revolution (VSI)
B102: The Diamond Age
B103: The Martian

Choose Books in OPT to complete 3 hours of Reading

▶ ....

Academics	31 hours
11	
15	
11	
4	
Reading	80hrs
6	
4	
13	
10	
40	
	Total hours

Do Fun Shit: 5 hours a week

> ▶ ....

> ▶ ....

> ▶ ....

DFS:................................ 60 hours

.... Total hours

Reflection/Accountability: 5 hours a week

Write and publish an explanation of what you learned/did in the past week to Substack. Find time to reflect on how you're doing and how you can improve. (Minimum of 5 credit hours must be hit)

Reflection:................................ 60 hours

Anchor:................................ $0

Academics:................................ $547 Udemy OR MITX + Great Courses Subscription

Reading:................................ $120 ($20/Book x 6)

+ OPT Courses/Reading $_____

DFS Hobbies + ... $_____

COSTS TOTAL = ... $_____

480 hours in a cycle

Chapter 18

HOW TO BUILD YOUR OWN CYCLE

BY MAXIM SMITH

We gave you 16 packaged cycles, but, naturally, there are thousands more possibilities. For those wanting more, in this section we'll show you how to build your own cycle.

Planning out exactly what to do is hard without a template to follow. We spent months coming up with a winning structure. So–don't reinvent the wheel.

A cycle is 12 weeks (plus or minus depending on circumstances) where you want to commit at least 40 productive hours a week to the program. Each cycle has 5 components: An Anchor Course, Academics, Reading, Activities for doing fun shit, and Reflection/Accountability.

The Anchor Course is the most important aspect of the cycle and will set the tone for everything else–including where you'll physically be. So, choose an Anchor that gets you fired up to get started.

Building out a cycle requires lots of pre-planning, so get started early and gather all the facts–who, what, where, when, and how much.

During your research you'll find options–cheaper Anchor course options that offer less or teach virtually, don't disregard the real thing just because it costs much more.

Sometimes the expensive courses cost more because they're worth it. Planning and hard work can overcome most problems you might encounter including a temporary shortage of cash. Remember–choose physical experience over virtual education 9 times out of 10.

Once the Anchor course is settled in your plan, fill in the Academics, Books you plan to read along with activities. If there are things on our resource list of courses and books that you haven't completed yet, we encourage you to start there.

You want to carefully document the hours and costs involved with each. If you're attending a two-week in-person anchor course, calculate your hours by multiplying 14/days by 8–10 hours/day to get 112 total hours for the Anchor activity. And get clear on all the costs involved.

If it's an online course on Coursera, EDX, MIT Online, or another online learning platform, that requires 3 hours a week for 12 weeks that'd be 36 academic hours. Most books you can google how long on average it takes to read. Basically, most books are read at one page per minute (on average).

> **PRO TIP:**
>
> Once you've got a few cycles under your belt, a good rule of thumb is to let passion and curiosity be your guide–but do so with rigor. By rigor we mean, make sure you've got a smart plan in place before the cycle begins.

We generally try to match the Academic and Reading content to be in theme or related to the anchor course. It isn't always easy or even possible. But, give it your best shot. Intentional or not, a cycle always has a theme, try to structure your "electives" within the context of that theme.

One last note, avoid the tendency to fall back on subjects you're comfortable with. I like history and if I'm not careful, I'll limit myself to topics like Hannibal's invasion of Rome. It's okay to make time for that, but the juice of life comes from novel action. Make sure that's a big part of your plan.

USING THE TEMPLATES BELOW

In the template below, we recommend how many hours you might spend on each of the key areas. 160 for Anchor courses, 120 for Academic, 72 for reading, 60 for fun shit, and another 60 for reflection & writing.

There are no fixed rules, however. So, if you've done at least a cycle or two–feel free to be flexible. Just be sure you hit your 40 productive hours each week. A total of 480 for the cycle. But, what's the big deal with 40 hours/week?

The truth is, most humans average between 15–20 total productive hours a week (including those with full-time jobs!). The Preparation is about shattering these pathetic benchmarks by choosing intentional activities that drive our lives forward in interesting and profitable ways. Don't let the inertia of the lost, the slackers, and the ne'er do wells keep you from realizing your potential.

BACK TO THE TEMPLATES

On the left column you write the name of the courses and books you've selected. On the right column you fill out how many hours it takes to complete, then total them up. Revise as needed.

Finally, list all the costs for the Anchor activity, courses, books, and everything else to the bottom row of the table. Usually the largest costs are the anchor courses.

Based on my experience, sometimes you'll end up with way more hours than 480, by choice. If you have free time you can always fill it in with something productive. Hit the gym or try out one of the novel activities we listed earlier.

Oh, and if you discover and take an incredible anchor course, I'd love to hear about it.

Reach out to me at **www.MaximSmith.com**. I might want to try it as well!

CYCLE THEME:

ANCHOR COURSE

Anchor .... 160 hours

ACADEMICS

Academics .... 120 hours

....

....

....

....

....

....

.... Total hours

Reading

Reading .... 72 hours

....

....

....

....

....

.... Total hour

Do Fun Shit: At least 5 hours a week

....

....

....

....

DFS:............. **60 Hours Minimum**

.... **Total hours**

Reflection/Accountability: 5 hours a week

Write and publish an explanation of what you learned/did in the past week to Substack. Find time to reflect on how you're doing and how you can improve.

Reflection:.................. **60 hours**

Anchor:.................... ~$ _____

Academics:.............. $ _____

Reading:................... $ ($20/Book x)

DFS Hobbies:........... $ _____

Costs Total=.............. $ _____

480/minimum hours in a cycle

CYCLE THEME:

ANCHOR COURSE

Anchor .... 160 hours

ACADEMICS

Academics .... 120 hours

....

....

....

....

....

....

.... Total hours

Reading .... 72 hours

Reading

....

....

....

....

....

.... Total hour

Do Fun Shit: At least 5 hours a week

DFS: .... 60 Hours Minimum

....

....

....

....

.... Total hours

Reflection/Accountability: 5 hours a week

Reflection: .... 60 hours

Write and publish an explanation of what you learned/did in the past week to Substack. Find time to reflect on how you're doing and how you can improve.

Anchor: .... ~$ _____

Academics: .... $ _____

Reading: .... $ ($20/Book x)

DFS Hobbies: .... $ _____

Costs Total= .... $ _____

480/minimum hours in a cycle

CYCLE THEME:

ANCHOR COURSE

Anchor .... 160 hours

ACADEMICS

Academics .... 120 hours

....

....

....

....

.... Total hours

....

Reading .... 72 hours

Reading

....

....

....

....

.... Total hour

Do Fun Shit: At least 5 hours a week

....

....

....

....

.... **Total hours**

Reflection/Accountability: 5 hours a week

Write and publish an explanation of what you learned/did in the past week to Substack. Find time to reflect on how you're doing and how you can improve.

Reflection:.................... 60 hours

Anchor:............................ ~$ _____

Academics:....................... $ _____

Reading:.......................... $ ($20/Book x)

DFS Hobbies:.................... $ _____

Costs Total=..................... $ _____

480/minimum hours in a cycle

Chapter 19

RESOURCES

ACADEMICS, BOOKS, CLASSICAL MUSIC GUIDE, MOVIES WORTH WATCHING

RESOURCES

- ▶ Academics List (CORE A1 – A59 OPT A60- A153)
- ▶ Book List (Core B1 – B103 OPT B104 – B184)
- ▶ Classical Music Guide & List
- ▶ Movies Worth Watching

Disclaimer: Links to websites may change if a QR code does not work email us at **Help@thepreparation.com**

CORE

	Title	Genre	Source	Hours	QR Code	Completed
A1	Biology and human Behavior	Biology	Great Courses	12		☐
A2	Medical School for Everyone: Emergency medicine	Biology	Great Courses	12		☐
A3	Medical School for Everyone: Grand Rounds Cases	Biology	Great Courses	12		☐
A4	The Science of Flight	Physics	Great Courses	15		☐
A5	The science of Extreme weather	Meterology	Great Courses	12		☐
A6	A History of the United States 2nd Ed	American History	Great Courses	42		☐

	Title	Genre	Source	Hours	QR Code	Completed
A7	The America West: History, Myth and Legacy	American History	Great Courses	12		☐
A8	Trials West: How Freedom Settled The West	American History	Liberty Classroom	15		☐
A9	Skeptics Guide to American History	American History	Great Courses	12		☐
A10	The Big History of Civilizations	World History	Great Courses	13		☐
A11	Understanding The Worlds Greatest Structures	World History	Great Courses	13		☐
A12	Understanding Greek and Roman Technology	World History	Great Courses	12		☐
A13	The Rise of the Novel: Exploring History's Greatest Early Works	Literature	Great Courses	12		☐
A14	The Rise and Fall of the Roman Republic	World History	Hillsdale College	7		☐
A15	The Italian Renaissance	World History	Great Courses	18		☐

Title		Genre	Source	Hours	QR Code	Completed
A16	How To Look At And Understand Great Art	Art	Great Courses	13		☐
A17	European Paintings: From Leonardo to Rembrandt to Goya	Art	Edx	14		☐
A18	A History of European Art	Art	Great Courses	25		☐
A19	Geology Series by Nick Zentner	Geology	Youtube/ CWU	30		☐
A20	Planet Earth... and You! Stephen Marshak	Geology	Coursera	41		☐
A21	Practical Geology	Geology	Great Courses	12		☐
A22	Law School for everyone: Contracts	Law	Great Courses	7		☐
A23	Argumentation: The Study of Effective Reasoning	Law	Great Courses	12		☐
A24	Successful Negotiation: Essential Strategies and Skills	Law	Coursera - Umich	17		☐

Title	Genre	Source	Hours	QR Code	Completed
A25 Malcom Gladwell Teaches Writing	Literature	Masterclass	4		☐
A26 History of the English Language 2nd Edition	Literature	Great Courses	13		☐
A27 Foundations of Western Civilization	World History	Great Courses	24		☐
A28 The Science of Energy: Resources and Power Explained	Physics	Great Courses	14		☐
A29 Pre-U Calc, physics, chemistry	Chemistry/ Physics	EDX ($135)	100		☐
A30 Understanding the human body/ Anatomy & Physiology	Biology	Great Courses	24		☐
A31 Masters of War: History's Greatest Strategic Thinkers	World History	Great Courses	12		☐
A32 Foundations of Eastern Civilization	World History	Great Courses	24		☐
A33 History of the Ancient World: A Global Perspective	World History	Great Courses	24		☐

	Title	Genre	Source	Hours	QR Code	Completed
A34	Life Lessons From the Great Books	Literature	Great Courses	13		☐
A35	Our Night Sky	Astronomy	Great Courses	6		☐
A36	The Natural Navigator	Astronomy	60 dollars	6		☐
A37	Introduction to Celestial Navigation for Mariners	Astronomy	Udemy (free)	2		☐
A38	Everyday Engineering: Understanding the Marvels of Daily Life	Chemistry/ Physics	Great Courses	18		☐
A39	The Evidence of Modern Physics : How We Know What We Know	Physics	Great Courses	12		☐
A40	Heroes and Legends: The Most Influencial Characters of Literature	Literature	Great Courses	12		☐
A41	Foraging Wild Mushrooms	Biology Lab	learnyour land ($375)	20		☐
A42	Music Theory Comprehensive Complete Part 1, 2, &3 by Jason Allen	Music Theory	Udemy	12		☐

	Title	Genre	Source	Hours	QR Code	Completed
A43	How to Listen to and Understand Great Music 3rd Edition	Music Theory	Great Courses	36		☐
A44	Music as a Mirror of History	Music Theory	Great Courses	12		☐
A45	Classical Music Guide	Music Theory	Dougs list	36		☐
A46	Modern Marketing with Seth Godin	Marketing	Udemy ($200)	6		☐
A47	Sales Training: Practical Sale Techniques	Sales	Udemy ($14)3			☐
A48	Social Media Marketing Masterclass on 10+ platforms	Marketing	Udemy ($14)11			☐
A49	Stock Market Investing for Beginners	Investing	Udemy (&150/yr)	10		☐
A50	Investing In Stocks The Complete Course!	Investing	Udemy ($159)	18		☐
A51	The Art of Investing: Lessons from Histories Great Traders	Investing	Great Courses	12		☐

	Title	Genre	Source	Hours	QR Code	Completed
A52	The complete Financial Analyst Course 2025	Accounting		22		☐
A53	Prototyping with AI Bootcamp	Tinker	Maven ($799)	22		☐
A54	Python for Beginners	Tinker	Maven ($999)	15		☐
A55	AI Builders Bootcamp	Tinker	Maven ($995)	20		☐
A56	Autodesk Fusion 360 (Year 2025) - Complete Beginners Guide		Udemy	11		☐
A57	Introduction to CAD, CAM, and Practical CNC Machining for Milling	Tinker	AutoDesk (Free)	15		☐
A58	Introduction to CAD and CAM for Milling and Turning	Tinker	AutoDesk	11		☐
A59	3D Modeling for 3D Printing and Laser Cutting on Fusion 360		Udemy	4		☐

OPTIONAL

Name	Source	Hours	Cycle	Qr code	Completed
BS CHEMISTRY OPT					
A60 Chemistry 2nd	Great Courses	18	Welder		☐
A61 The Nature of Matter: Understanding the physical world	Great Courses	12	ALL		☐
A62 Chemistry and Our Universe	Great Courses	28	Welder		☐
A63 Foundations of Organic Chemistry	Great Courses	18	Welder		☐
A64 Science and Cooking	Harvard ($672)	104	Chef		☐
BS PHYSICS OPT					
A65 How things work: An Intro to Physics	Coursera / UVA	14	Pilot		☐
A66 Physics and Our Universe: How it all Works	Great Courses	30	Pilot		☐
A67 Introduction to Engineering Mechanics	Georgia Tech	14	Pilot		☐

	Name	Source	Hours	Cycle	Qr code	Completed
A68	Fundamentals In Flight Mechanics	Coursera Georgia Tech	10	Pilot		☐
A69	Introduction to Aeronautical Engineering	EDX	50	Pilot		☐
A70	Introduction to Aerodynamics	EDX	150	Pilot		☐
A71	The Joy of Science	Great Courses	30	ALL		☐
A72	Great Ideas of Classical Physics	Great Courses	12	ALL		☐
A73	Impossible: Physics Beyond the Edge,	Great Courses	12	ALL		☐
A74	Principles of Welding	ASME (395)	5	Welder		☐
A75	Practical Welding Technology	ASME (1595)	10	Welder		☐
A76	Elements of Metallurgy	ASME (2050)	16	Welder		☐

	Name	Source	Hours	Cycle	Qr code	Completed
A77	Beginner MIG Welding	Udemy ($20)	1	Welder		☐
A78	CWI Pre Seminar	AWS Certified $1000	80	Welder		☐
A79	Welding Math	Weblink	5	Welder		☐
A80	MIT Calculus 1A	MIT	13	Welder		☐
A81	Classic Mechanics MIT	MIT	5	Welder		☐
A82	Do It Yourself Engineering	Great Courses	12	Maker		☐
A83	Circuits and Electronics	MITX ($510)	100	Builder / Maker		☐
A84	DIY Geiger Counters	MIT DIY LAB + Textbook PDF	10	Maker		☐
A85	FAB LAB	YOUTUBE/ MIT	40	Maker		☐

	Name	Source	Hours	Cycle	Qr code	Completed
A86	3D Printing Course	Udemy ($14)	4	Maker		☐
A87	Crash course Electronics and PCB Design by Andre La Mothe	Udemy ($14)	112	Maker		☐
A88	Learn to Repair & Troubleshooting	Udemy ($10)	6	Maker		☐
A89	Physics In Your Life	Great Courses	18	Builder		☐
A90	Classical Mechanics by Walter Lewin	MIT - Youtube	100	Heavy Equipment		☐
BS Geology/ Astronomy						
A91	How the Earth Works	Great Courses	24	Heavy Equipment		☐
A92	New History Of Life	Great Courses	15	Heavy Equipment		☐
A93	Big History	Great Courses	24	Heavy Equipment		☐
A94	Understanding the Universe: Intro to Astronomy	Great Courses	48	Sailor		☐

Name	Source	Hours	Cycle	Qr code	Completed
A95 The Inexplicable Universe: Unsolved Mysteries	Great Courses	3	Sailor		☐
A96 Introduction to Palentology	Great Courses	12	ALL		☐
A97 Cosmology	DVD GC		ALL		☐

BS Biology OPT

Name	Source	Hours	Cycle	Qr code	Completed
A98 The Science of Life	Great Courses	36	Medic		☐
A99 Biochemistry and Moleular Biology	Great Courses	18	Medic		☐
A100 Infectious Diseases	Great Courses	12	Medic		☐
A101 Physiology and Fitness	Great Courses	13	Fighter		☐
A102 Eat for Your Health	Great Courses	6	Farmer		☐
A103 Human Behavior by Robert Sapolsky	Youtube - Stanford	30	Hacker		☐

Name	Source	Hours	Cycle	Qr code	Completed
A104 Trees in All Seasons	leanyourland ($375)	25	Survivor		☐
A105 The science of Gardening	Great Courses	12	Farmer		☐
A106 Pioneering Skills for everyone	Great Courses	12	Cowboy		☐
A107 Food A Cultural History	Great Courses	12	Chef		☐
A108 The Everyday Gourmet Rediscovering the Lost Art of Cooking	Great Courses	12	Chef		☐
A109 Introduction to Jungian Psychology	Jung Plat 167	7	Builder		☐
A110 Personality and its Transformations by Jordan Peterson	Youtube	72	Builder		☐

BA World History OPT

Name	Source	Hours	Cycle	Qr code	Completed
A111 Greece and Rome: An Integrated History	Great Courses	1	Chef		☐
A112 How the Medici Shaped the Renaissance	Great Courses	6	Chef		☐

	Name	Source	Hours	Cycle	Qr code	Completed
A113	Western civilization II	Great Courses	24	Cowboy		☐
A114	Hannibal: The Military Genius Who Almost Conquered Rome	Great Courses	7	Fighter		☐
A115	The Decisive Battles of World History	Great Courses	13	Fighter		☐
A116	Alexander the Great and the Macedonian Empire	Great Courses	13	Fighter		☐
A117	Turning Points in Modern History	Great Courses	12	Fighter		☐
A118	The Real History of Pirates	Great Courses	12	Sailor		☐
A119	History's Greatest Voyages of Exploration	Great Courses	12	Sailor		☐
BA American History						
A120	What American Founders Learned from Antiquity	Great Courses	13	Cowboy		☐
A121	The Civil War and reconstruction 18450 1877	Yale Open Course	22	Cowboy		☐

Name	Source	Hours	Cycle	Qr code	Completed
BA Literature					
A122 The Western Literary Canon in Context	(only DVD/ internet archive)	19	Cowboy		☐
A123 36 Books that Changed the World	(only Dvd)	18	Sailor		☐
A124 Dantes Divine Comedy	Great Courses	12	ALL		☐
BA Economics					
A125 Speeches by Milton Friedman	Free to Choose	15	Hacker		☐
A126 1980 TV Series by Milton Friedman	PBS/ Free to Choose	10	Hacker		☐
A127 Economics 101 by Rothbard	Mises Institute	11	Hacker		☐
A128 Austrian Economics step by Step by Jeff Herbener	Liberty Classroom	15	Hacker		☐
BA Music Theory / Art					
A129 The 30 Greatest Orchestral Works	Great Courses	26	Survivor		☐

	Name	Source	Hours	Cycle	Qr code	Completed
A130	Great Masters Tchaikovsky - His Life and Music	Great Courses	6	Survivor		☐
A131	Real World Music Production	Studio ($450)	14	Maker		☐
A132	The Worlds Greatest Paintings	Great Courses	12	Chef		☐

BA Law

	Name	Source	Hours	Cycle	Qr code	Completed
A133	Contract Law: From Trust to Promise to Contract	EDX - Harvard	20	Builder/ Heavy Equipment		☐
A134	Art of Conflict Management	Great Courses	12	Fighter		☐
A135	Art of Critical Decision Making	Great Courses	12	Hacker		☐
A136	Law School for everyone: Criminal + Civil	Great Courses	24	Hacker		☐
A137	Law School for Everyone: Corporate Law	Great Courses	6	ALL		☐
A138	Law School for Everyone	Great Courses	24	ALL		☐

Name	Source	Hours	Cycle	Qr code	Completed
MBA Investing					
A139 Financial Markets	Coursera Yale	33			☐
A140 Stock Market for Beginners	Udemy ($14)	9	Investor		☐
A141 Blockchain and Money	MIT	25	Investor		☐
A142 How Does the Stock Market Work	Great Courses	9	Investor		☐
A143 Financial Markets	Great Courses	12	Investor		☐
A144 How to Invest - Understanding Investment Markets	Great Courses	12	Investor		☐
A145 Wall Street Survivor	Simulator		Investor		☐
A146 How the Market Works	Simulator		Investor		☐
A147 Investopedia	simulator		Investor		☐

Name	Source	Hours	Cycle	Qr code	Completed
MBA Accounting OPT					
A148 Intuit Academy Bookkeeping Professional Certificate	Coursera	65	Farmer		☐
A149 Bookkeeping Certification		30	Farmer		☐
A150 Accounting & Financial Statement Analysis	Udemy ($14)	4	Farmer		☐
A151 Mastering Quickbooks online 2025	Udemy ($14)	180	Hacker		☐
MBA Sales OPT					
A152 Mastering Sales by Craig Wortmann	Northwestern (2K)	40	Entrepreneur		☐
A153 Seven Figure Copywriting	AWAI		Worker		☐
MBA Marketing OPT					
A154 Intro to Marketing	Coursera Upenn	10	Hacker		☐
A155 Presenting to Persuade by Seth godin	Udemy (30)	1	Fighter		☐

Name	Source	Hours	Cycle	Qr code	Completed
A156 Google Digital Marketing	Coursera	10	Hacker		☐

MBA OPT

A157 A guide to Making a Career on Upwork	Udemy ($14)	8	Entrepreneur		☐
A158 Freelancers Course	Udemy ($200)	5	Entrepreneur		☐
A159 How to Turn Your Passion into Profit	Great Courses	11	Maker		☐
A160 Critical Business Skills for Success	Great Courses	30	Farmer		☐

BOOK LIST CORE & OPTIONAL

CORE

	Title	Author	Hours	Why	Completed
Medic					
B1	Discovering the German New Medicine	Caroline Markolin	10	Challenges conventional medical thinking by exploring the mind-body connection in illness	☐
B2	Caveman Chemistry	Kevin M. Dunn	50	Hands On Projects in Chemistry	☐
Pilot					
B3	Stick and Rudder	Wolfgang Langewiesche	15	One thorough reading of it is the equivalent of many hours of practice.	☐
B4	Mental Math for Pilots	Ronald D. McElroy	5	Sharpens your cockpit calculation skills with quick, practical shortcuts every pilot needs in-flight.	☐
Cowboy					
B5	Blood and Thunder	Hampton Sides	15	Frontier expansion & leadership under fire	☐
B6	Education of a Wandering Man	Louis L'Amour	5	Lifelong autodidact's field notes	☐
B7	Empire of the Summer Moon	S. C. Gwynne	14	Adaptation and resistance on the plains	☐
B8	The Sackett Series	Louis L'Amour	44	Frontier virtue saga	☐
Builder					
B9	Virtue of Selfishness	Ayn Rand	4	Rational selfinterest argument	☐
B10	Modern Man in Search of a Soul	Carl G. Jung	9	Intro to depthpsychology tools	☐
B11	The Iliad	Homer	9	Western archetype of honor & courage	☐
B12	Only Yesterday	Frederick Lewis Allen	10	Roaring '20s as cautionary mirror	☐
B13	The Law	Frédéric Bastiat	2	how economic liberty thrives and warns against government overreach.	☐
Chef					
B14	Greek Art	John Boardman	7	Visual language of classical power	☐
B15	Roman Art	Paul Zanker	6	Propaganda & identity in empire	☐

	Title	Author	Hours	Why	Completed
B16	The Republic	Plato	3	Blueprint of justice & civic order	☐
B17	Gorgias	Plato	2	Dissects rhetoric & moral responsibility	☐
B18	Trial and Death of Socrates	Plato	3	Moral integrity under pressure	☐
B19	Way of the Superior Man	David Deida	5	Purposedriven relationships	☐
Heavy Equipment					
B20	The Count of Monte Cristo	Alexandre Dumas	30	Strategic patience and just vengeance	☐
B21	Adventures of Huckleberry Finn	Mark Twain	9	Individual conscience vs. social norms	☐
B22	Underland: A Deep Time Journey	Robert Macfarlane	14	reveals hidden worlds beneath our feet—and our place in deep time.	☐
Work					
B23	Poke The Box	Seth Godin	2	Bold call to stop waiting and start initiating—because the world needs your action, not just your ideas	☐
B24	Atlas Shrugged	Ayn Rand	29	Production vs. predation dramatized	☐
B25	On Writing, A Memoir of the Craft	Stephen King	6	How to become a better writer	☐
B26	The Creature from Jekyll Island	G. Edward Griffin	10	Controversial origin story of the Fed	☐
B27	Consider This	Chuck Palahniuk	8	Excellent book on writing	☐
B28	The Elements of Style	Strunk & White	2	Write clearly or die vaguely	☐
B29	Thank You for Arguing	Jay Heinrichs	6	Persuasion from Aristotle to memes	☐
Welder					
B30	Zen and the Art of Motorcycle Maintenance	Robert Pirsig	12	Inquiry into quality & selfmaintenance	☐
B31	The True Believer	Eric Hoffer	4	Psychology of mass movements	☐
B32	Gulliver's Travels	Jonathan Swift	6	Satire exposing the follies of power	☐
B33	The Prize	Daniel Yergin	23	Energy's grip on geopolitics & growth	☐
Fighter					
B34	Meditations	Marcus Aurelius	6	Stoic operating system	☐
B35	The Art of War	Sun Tzu	1	Timeless asymmetric strategy	☐
B36	Bobby Fischer Teaches Chess	Bobby Fischer	3	Structured problemsolving pattern	☐

	Title	Author	Hours	Why	Completed
B37	A War Like No Other	Victor D. Hanson	9	Logistics & cost of a grinding conflict	☐
B38	Beowulf	Douglas Wilson (tr.)	4	Protoentrepreneurial monsterslaying ethic	☐
B39	Book of Five Rings	Miyamoto Musashi	2	Duelling insights †' competitive edge	☐
B40	The Guns of August	Barbara Tuchman	13	Missignals that triggered WW I	☐
B41	The Moon is a Harsh Mistress	Robert Heinlein	10	Libertarian revolt & systems hacking	☐

Sailor

	Title	Author	Hours	Why	Completed
B42	Endurance	Alfred Lansing	7	Crisis leadership in extreme conditions	☐
B43	Brave New World	Aldous Huxley	7	Soft tyranny via pleasure	☐
B44	The Odyssey	Homer	6	Model of grit, ingenuity and homebuilding	☐
B45	The Travels of Marco Polo	Marco Polo	7	Early global view of trade & culture	☐
B46	1493	Charles Mann	11	Columbian Exchange's secondorder effects	☐
B47	The Last Place on Earth: Scott and Amundsen's Race to the South Pole	Roland Huntford	12.5	Redefines the legendary race to the South Pole	☐
B48	Cosmos	Carl Sagan	6.5	Voyage through the universe, blending science, history, and humanity to show how the cosmos came to know itself	☐

Survivalist

	Title	Author	Hours	Why	Completed
B49	The Revenant	Michael Punke	8	Grit & wilderness craft	☐
B50	Undaunted Courage	Stephen Ambrose	11.5	Decisionmaking on an uncharted frontier	☐
B51	One Man's Wilderness	Richard Proenneke	8	Blueprint for radical selfreliance	☐
B52	Man's Search for Meaning	Viktor Frankl	4	Purpose amid suffering	☐
B53	Touching the Void	Joe Simpson	6	Decisions at the edge of death	☐
B54	1984	George Orwell	8	Total surveillance & language control	☐
B55	Animal Farm	George Orwell	3	Satire on revolutionary rot	☐
B56	1177 B.C.	Eric Cline	7	Complexity collapse across an entire era	☐

Title	Author	Hours	Why	Completed
Farmer				
B57 Man, Cattle and Veld	Johann Zietsman	10	How traditional African pastoralism shaped societies, landscapes, and survival in Southern Africa	☐
B58 The Ascent of Money	Niall Ferguson	11	Panoramic history of money & capital flows	☐
B59 How to Draw and Think like a Real Artist: A 30-Day Drawing Guide from the Fundamentals to Step-by-Step Instructions with Detailed Illustrations and Comprehensive Explanations	Fabrizio Secolo	30	A practical guide to drawing	☐
B60 Logic: A Very Short Introduction	Graham Priest.	2.5	Distills the foundations of reasoning into a concise guide to how arguments work—and how to spot bad ones	☐
B61 The Art of Thinking Clearly	Rolf Dobelli	7	Reveals the most common cognitive biases that cloud your judgment—and how to avoid them	☐
Entrepreneur				
B62 The Reluctant Entrepreneur	Mark Ford	5	guide for people who want to start a business but aren't natural risk-takers.	☐
B63 The Lean Startup	Eric Ries	6	Still the best intro to rapid experimentation and building something people actually want, before you waste money.	☐
B64 The Million-Dollar, One-Person Business	Elaine Pofeldt	5	Real-world examples of solo entrepreneurs making real money without investors, employees, or BS.	☐
B65 Ready, Fire, Aim	Michael Masterson	7	How to grow from zero to $100M in practical stages. If you liked Reluctant Entrepreneur, this is its aggressive big brother.	☐
B66 The 1-Page Marketing Plan	Allan Dib	4	Simple, practical, and high-impact. Gets you from scattered ideas to a coherent marketing strategy fast.	☐
B67 The Boron Letters	Gary Halbert	4	A raw, direct education in marketing, copywriting, and life. One of the best places to start learning to sell.	☐
B68 Influence	Robert Cialdini	8	Six universal persuasion levers	☐

	Title	Author	Hours	Why	Completed
B69	Think and Grow Rich	Napoleon Hill	6	Goaldirected mindset classic	☐
B70	Great Leads	Micheal Masterson & John Forde	4	The underrated blueprint for writing marketing that actually converts	☐
B71	How to Win Friends and Influence People	Dale Carnegie	7	Timeless influence toolkit	☐
B72	PreSuasion	Robert Cialdini	10	Position the audience before you ask	☐
B73	Never Split the Difference	Chris Voss with Tahl Raz	9	Sales & Negotiation Tips From FBI Negotiator	☐
B74	Good Strategy/Bad Strategy	Richard Rumelt	6	Spot & craft true strategic leverage	☐
Investor					
B75	Economics in One Lesson	Henry Hazlitt	6	Fast, clear mental model of markets	☐
B76	The Intelligent Investor	Benjamin Graham	13	Classic on value & margin of safety	☐
B77	The Most Important Thing	Howard Marks	6	Secondlevel risk thinking	☐
B78	Market Wizards	Jack Schwager	9	Playbooks of elite traders	☐
B79	When Money Dies	Adam Fergusson	8	Hyperinflation case study & fiat collapse lessons	☐
B80	Lords of Finance	Liaquat Ahamed	14	Centralbank missteps & Great Depression origins	☐
B81	When Genius Failed	Roger Lowenstein	8	LTCM & the dangers of leverage	☐
B82	Manias, Panics & Crashes	Charles Kindleberger & Robert Aliber	12	Contagion model of financial crises	☐
B83	Common Stocks & Uncommon Profits	Philip Fisher	8	Qualitative scuttlebutt investing method	☐
B84	The World for Sale	Javier Blas & Jack Farchy	9	Modern commodity trading house exposÃ©	☐
B85	A Random Walk Down Wall Street	Burton Malkiel	13	Indexing & market efficiency primer	☐
B86	Against the Gods	Peter Bernstein	9	How humans learned to price risk	☐
B87	You Can Be a Stock Market Genius	Joel Greenblatt	7	Specialsituations edge	☐
B88	Reminiscences of a Stock Operator	Edwin LefÃ¨vre	9	Trading psychology canon	☐
B89	Berkshire Letters to Shareholders	Warren Buffett	16	Compounding & culture in practice	☐

Title	Author	Hours	Why	Completed
B90	The Great Crash 1929	John Kenneth Galbraith	6	Definitive narrative of the 1929 bubble burst	☐
B91	The Lords of Easy Money	Christopher Leonard	10	Inside story of post2008 QE regime	☐
B92	This Time Is Different	Carmen Reinhart & Kenneth Rogoff	13	Eight centuries of sovereign default data	☐
B93	Devil Take the Hindmost	Edward Chancellor	12	500 years of bubble patternspotting	☐
B94	The Dao of Capital	Mark Spitznagel	7	Austrian patience +' convex payoff	☐

Hacker

B95	Antifragile	Nassim Taleb	12	Systems that gain from volatility	☐
B96	Don't Make Me Think	Steve Krug	3.5	Firstprinciple UX instinct	☐
B97	The Three Body Problem	Cixin Liu	10	Systems thinking at cosmic scale	☐
B98	Foundation Trilogy	Isaac Asimov	17	Macrostrategy & decay cycles	☐

Maker

B99	The War of Art	Steven Pressfield	4	Beat resistance, ship work	☐
B100	Nicomachean Ethics	Aristotle	6	Virtue as habit framework	☐
B101	Scientific Revolution (VSI)	Lawrence Principe	4	How experiment dethroned authority	☐
B102	The Diamond Age	Neal Stephenson	13	Nanotech & education thoughtexperiment	☐
B103	The Martian	Andy Weir	10	Engineering mindset under duress	☐

OPTIONAL - OPT

	Title	Author	Hours	Why	Completed
Genre: Classics & Storytelling					
B104	The Divine Comedy	Dante	9	Journey from error to enlightenment	☐
B105	Blood Meridian	Cormac McCarthy	13	Consequences of nihilistic violence	☐
B106	The Lord of the Rings	J. R. R. Tolkien	40	Epic teamwork & moral clarity at scale	☐
B107	Stranger in a Strange Land	Robert Heinlein	13	Outsider's lens on culture & faith	☐
B108	The Jungle	Upton Sinclair	13	Industrial excess †' reform catalyst	☐
B109	The Old Man and the Sea	Ernest Hemingway	2	Stoic perseverance distilled	☐
B110	The Fountainhead	Ayn Rand	28	Creative integrity vs. conformity	☐
B111	Decline & Fall of the Roman Empire Volume 1	Edward Gibbon	17	Longform case study in institutional decay	☐
B112	The Canterbury Tales	Geoffrey Chaucer	9	Medieval mosaic of classes & motives	☐
B113	War and Peace	Leo Tolstoy	48	Human dimension of grandscale war	☐
B114	Don Quixote	Miguel de Cervantes	33	Comic anatomy of heroic idealism	☐
B115	Glory Road	Robert Heinlein	8	Hero's quest with libertarian edge	☐
B116	Novum Organum	Francis Bacon	3	Birth of the modern scientific method	☐
B117	The Time Machine	H. G. Wells	3	Evolutionary warning in novella form	☐
B118	Hitchhiker's Guide to the Galaxy	Douglas Adams	4	Absurdist creativity & curiosity	☐
B119	Dragon's Egg	Robert Forward	8	Extremeenvironment life & rapid evolution	☐
B120	MobyDick	Herman Melville	18	Obsession, leadership & risk at sea	☐

	Title	Author	Hours	Why	Completed
B121	Slaughterhouse Five	Kurt Vonnegut		Nonlinear meditation on war trauma	☐
B122	One Second After	William Forstchen	9	EMP scenario & local resilience	☐
B123	Lonesome Dove	Larry McMurtry	24	Widely considered one of the greatest American novels, especially in the Western genre.	☐
B124	In the Heart of the Sea	Nathaniel Philbrick	8	True story of the whaleship Essex—a tale of survival that inspired Moby-Dick	☐
B125	For Whom The Bell Tolls	Ernest Hemingway	11	Sacrifice and courage when every decision counts.	☐
Genre: Power, State & Strategy					
B126	The Portable Greek Historians	M. I. Finley	9	Primary sources on war & politics	☐
B127	The Enlightenment	Billy Wellman	4	Ideas that powered the modern project	☐
B128	Confessions	St Augustine	8	Birth of the introspective conscience	☐
B129	Before France & Germany	Patrick Geary	8	How medieval Europe first cohered	☐
B130	The Carolingians	Pierre Riché	8	Dynastybuilding playbook	☐
B131	Magna Carta	Dan Jones	7	First contractual brake on monarchy	☐
B132	Heart of Europe	Peter Wilson	17	1 000year overview of HRE complexity	☐
B133	The Fall of Rome	Bryan WardPerkins	6	Material evidence of true collapse	☐
B134	The Holy Roman Empire	Peter Wilson	15	Deepdive into a multistate organism	☐
B135	Collapse: How Societies Choose to Fail or Succeed	Jared Diamond	18	Why some societies fall while others survive, revealing how environmental choices and leadership shape the fate of civilizations	☐
B136	What Has Government Done to Our Money	Murray Rothbard	12.7	Powerful, concise argument for sound money and a critique of inflationary monetary policy	☐

	Title	Author	Hours	Why	Completed
B137	The Silk Roads: A New History of the World	Peter Frankopan	20	Reframes world history through the vibrant trade routes that connected East and West, placing Asia—not Europe—at the center of civilization	☐
B138	The Russian Revolution	Sheila Fitzpatrick	7	Anatomy of ideological upheaval	☐
B139	The Gulag Archipelago	Aleksandr Solzhenitsyn	46	Lived indictment of totalitarian systems	☐
B140	Hagakure	Yamamoto Tsunetomo	4	Samurai code in aphorisms	☐
B141	Bhagavad Gita	Vyasa	4	Duty, detachment & right action	☐
B142	A History of the United States in Five Crashes	Scott Nations	8	Pattern recognition across U.S. panics	☐
B143	A Demon of Our Own Design	Richard Bookstaber	7	Why complexity breeds fragility	☐
B144	Once in Golconda	John Brooks	7	Wall Street drama 192038	☐
B145	Skeletons on the Zahara: A True Story of Survival	Dean King	7.5	True survival story of shipwrecked sailors enduring slavery and starvation in the unforgiving Sahara Desert	☐
B146	The Prince	Niccolò Machiavelli	3	Realpolitik for builders & CEOs	☐
Genre: Personal Mastery & Psychology					
B147	Outwitting the Devil	Napoleon Hill	7	Facing fear & internal saboteurs	☐
B148	Put Your Ass Where Your Heart Wants to Be	Steven Pressfield	3	Commit physically to your calling	☐
B149	Memories, Dreams, Reflections	Carl G. Jung	10	Map of an examined inner life	☐
B150	12 Rules for Life	Jordan Peterson	10	Order & responsibility playbook	☐
B151	About Face	David Hackworth	19	Gritty, frontline leadership lessons	☐
B152	With the Old Breed	E. B. Sledge	8	Unfiltered grunt's view of Pacific war	☐

	Title	Author	Hours	Why	Completed
B153	Napoleon: A Life	Andrew Roberts	25	Strategic genius & ambition case study	☐
B154	Stilwell and the American Experience in China	Barbara Tuchman	16	Alliance management in real time	☐
Genre: Enterprise & Innovation					
B155	The Fourth Turning	William Strauss & Neil Howe	8	Cyclical model of historical risk	☐
B156	Dumbing Us Down	John T. Gatto	2	Why factoryschooling breeds mediocrity	☐
B157	The Singularity is Near	Ray Kurzweil	10	Exponential tech & its societal shocks	☐
Genre: Money & Markets					
B158	The Machinery of Freedom	David Friedman	8	Radical market fixes for social problems	☐
B159	The Bitcoin Standard	Saifedean Ammous	7	Why sound money may be digital	☐
B160	The Wealth of Nations	Adam Smith	31	Bedrock text of voluntary exchange	☐
B161	Wealth, War & Wisdom	Barton Biggs	10	Markets as earlywarning system	☐
B162	Beating the Street	Peter Lynch	9	Scuttlebutt investing in practice	☐
B163	The Little Book That Still Beats the Market	Joel Greenblatt	5	Simple formula, big results	☐
B164	What Works on Wall Street	James O'Shaughnessy	12	Factor evidence over 90 years	☐
B165	Adaptive Markets	Andrew Lo	13	Evolutionary finance bridges EMH & behavior	☐
B166	The Alchemy of Finance	George Soros	14	Reflexivity and macro trading philosophy	☐
B167	House of Morgan	Ron Chernow	22	Institutional history of modern banking power	☐
B168	The Panic of 1907	Robert Bruner & Sean Carr	7	Liquidity freeze that birthed the Fed	☐
B169	Misbehavior of Markets	Benoit Mandelbrot	7	Fractal mathematics & wild price swings	☐

	Title	Author	Hours	Why	Completed
B170	Financial Statement Analysis & Security Valuation	Stephen Penman	20	Accounting detective work for valuation	☐
B171	The Psychology of Money	Morgan Housel	5	Storydriven lessons on money behavior	☐
B172	The Price of Time	Edward Chancellor	9	Interest rates as moral compass of capital	☐
B173	The Fruits of Graft: Great Depressions Then & Now	Wayne Jett	14	Contrarian take on the economic system	☐
B174	Only Yesterday	Frederick Lewis Allen	10	Roaring '20s as cautionary mirror	☐
Genre: Skills & Craft					
B175	The Hard Thing About Hard Things	Ben Horowitz	9	Brutally honest lessons on building and leading a startup through the toughest challenges no one warns you about	☐
B176	Confessions of the Pricing Man	Hermann Man	6	Insider strategies and real-world lessons on how to set prices that maximize profit and customer value	☐
B177	Zig Ziglar's Secrets of Closing the Sale	Zig Ziglar	6	Timeless, practical techniques to master the art of persuasion and confidently close deals.	☐
B178	The Resilient Farm and Homestead	Ben Falk	12	Practical strategies to build a sustainable, self-reliant farm that thrives through changing seasons and challenges	☐
B179	Holistic Management Handbook	Allan Savory; Jody Butterfield; Sam Bingham	12	Guides you to make smarter land-use decisions by balancing ecological, economic, and social factors for sustainable farming	☐
B180	Breakthrough Copywriting: How to Generate Quick Cash with the Written Word	David Garfinkel	5	Proven techniques to craft persuasive sales copy that drives fast, measurable results	☐
B181	Scientific Advertising	Claude Hopkins	3	Reveals how data-driven principles make advertising more effective and profitable	☐

	Title	Author	Hours	Why	Completed
B182	Making Them Believe	Dan Kennedy	7	Psychology and storytelling secrets behind crafting messages that truly persuade and inspire action	☐
B183	The 10 Commandments of A-List Copywriters	John Bejakovic	3	Essential principles that top copywriters live by to create irresistible, high-converting copy	☐
B184	The No-Code Revolution	Nolan Gray	6	How no-code tools are democratizing software creation, empowering anyone to build apps without programming skills	☐

Classical Music Starter Guide

DOUG CASEY

Music as a Mirror of History—24 lectures of 45 minutes. The prof who teaches this course is one of the best. I believe that (as with literature) the best way to appreciate it is by listening to the works, rather than being told about them. But this course is exceptional.

Course

You already have more familiarity with classical music than you know. Listen to these four compilations. They'll act as an overture to what will follow. You could spend years becoming familiar with great music, but we don't have years right now. And you're not majoring in music. These four shorts are practically a cheat sheet for someone looking to recognize pieces for a test, but they're really appetizers to the main courses.

32 REALLY FAMOUS CLASSICAL PIECES YOU'VE HEARD AND DON'T KNOW THE NAME!

PART II - 16 REALLY FAMOUS CLASSICAL PIECES YOU'VE HEARD AND DON'T KNOW THE NAME!

PART III - 24 FAMOUS CLASSICAL PIECES YOU'VE HEARD AND DON'T KNOW THE NAME!

21 FAMOUS PIANO PIECES YOU'VE HEARD BUT DON'T KNOW THE NAME!

7 EPIC SYMPHONY ENDINGS

Armed with that introduction, you can simply find the music from composers you like and listen to it. Dave Hurwitz gives a superb explanation of classical music, in particular symphonies—he's almost as good as listening to the music he discusses

These are what he calls

"10 ESSENTIAL SYMPHONIES FOR BEGINNERS".

I've put together the most important composers and a selection of their work. You'll find, after listening for a few hours each, that they all have musical signatures and distinct styles—as distinct and easily identifiable as the Beach Boys are from the Rolling Stones, for those of you familiar with Rock, the modern era's answer to Classical. At the end of this segment of The Preparation you will be able to pick out one from the other, and determine which you prefer.

SCAN HERE TO LISTEN TO OUR MUSIC LIST ON YOUTUBE

 **SCAN HERE TO LISTEN TO OUR MUSIC LIST ON SPOTIFY**

Rec #	Length	Name / Description	Completed
Johann Sebastian Bach			
M1	1 hr 40 min	**Brandenburg 6 Concertos** Six instrumental works showcasing a variety of styles and instruments.	☐
M2	45 - 80 min	**Goldberg Variations, BWV 988** First listen to this very amusing explanation. Then the variations themselves.	☐
M3	4 hrs	**The Well-Tempered Clavier, Books I and II, BWV 846-893**	☐
M4	2 hours	**Mass in B minor, BWV 232**	☐
M5	15 min	**St. Matthew Passion, BWV 244 Intro**	☐
M6	2 hrs 40 min		☐
M7	8 - 10 min	**Toccata and Fugue in D minor, BWV 565**	☐
M8	5 min	**Air on the G String**	☐
M9	35 min	**Violin Concertos, BWV 1041 and BWV 1042** Celebrated for their lyrical melodies and intricate interplay between the violin and orchestra.	☐
M10	2 hr 15 min	**Cello Suites, BWV 1007-1012** A collection of six suites that are foundational to cello repertoire, known for their melodic beauty and technical challenges.	☐

Rec #	Length	Name / Description	Completed
Georg Frederic Handel			
M11	2 hr 30 min	**Messiah** famed for its "Hallelujah" chorus.	☐
M12	50 min	**Water Music** A collection of orchestral suites composed for a royal boat outing on the River Thames.	☐
M13	20 min	**Music for the Royal Fireworks** A celebration for a fireworks display, featuring grand orchestral writing.	☐
M14	3 hr 30 min	**Giulio Cesare** An opera full of dramatic arias and notable for its rich character development.	☐
M15	3 hr	**Rinaldo** Another opera, well-known for the aria "Lascia ch'io pianga."	☐
M16	6 min	**Zadok the Priest** A choral work often performed at royal coronations.	☐
M17	3 hr 15 min	**Alcina** An opera that features lush melodies and poignant arias.	☐
Johannes Brahms			
M18	40 min	**Symphony No 3**	☐
M19	45 min	**Symphony No. 1 in C minor, Op. 68** Often referred to as "Beethoven's Tenth,"	☐
M20	45 min	**Symphony No. 4 in E minor, Op. 98** A powerful work that concludes with a moving passacaglia based on a theme by Bach.	☐
M21	40 min	**Violin Concerto in D major, Op. 77**	☐
M22	50 min	**Piano Concerto No. 1 in D minor, Op. 15**	☐
M23	75 min	**A German Requiem, Op. 45**	☐
M24	50 min	**Hungarian Dances (21 Dances)**	☐
Pyotr Ilyich Tchaikovsky			
M25	16min	**1812 Overture** commemorating Russia's defense against Napoleon.	☐
M26	2hr 30 min	**Swan Lake**	☐
M27	1 hr 30 min	**The Nutcracker**	☐
M28	50 min	**Symphony No. 6 in B minor, Op. 74 (Pathétique)** His final symphony	☐
M29	20 min	**Romeo and Juliet (Fantasy Overture)**	☐

Rec #	Length	Name / Description	Completed
M30	40 min	**Piano Concerto No. 1 in B-flat minor, Op. 23**	☐
M31	35 min	**Violin Concerto in D major, Op. 35** A staple of the violin repertoire known for its lyrical beauty and virtuosic passages.	☐

Felix Mendelssohn

Rec #	Length	Name / Description	Completed
M32	60 min	**A Midsummer Night's Dream** the "Overture" (13 min) and the "Wedding March," (5 min) often played at weddings.	☐
M33	30 min	**Violin Concerto in E Minor, Op. 64**	☐
M34	30 min	**Symphony No. 4 in A Major, Op. 90 (Italian Symphony)**	☐
M35	35 min	**Symphony No. 5 in D Major, Op. 107 (Reformation Symphony)**	☐
M36	22 min	**Piano Concerto No. 1 in G Minor, Op. 25**	☐
M37	2 hrs	**Songs Without Words**	☐
M38	2 hrs 15 min	**Elijah, Op. 70**	☐
M39	12 min	**The Hebrides Fingal's Cave**	☐

Wolfgang Amadeus Mozart

Rec #	Length	Name / Description	Completed
M40	27 min	**Symphony No. 40 in G minor, K. 550**	☐
M41	2 hrs 40 min	**The Magic Flute (Die Zauberflöte)**	☐
M42 M43	30 min 6 - 7 min	**Piano Concerto No. 21 in C major, K. 467** second movement, often referred to as "Elvira Madigan."	☐
M44	20 min	**Eine kleine Nachtmusik, K. 525**	☐
M45	55 min	**Requiem in D minor, K. 626** Mozart's unfinished masterpiece	☐
M46	20 min	**Piano Sonata No. 11 in A major, K. 331** Includes the famous Rondo Alla Turca	☐
M47	2 hr 45 min	**Don Giovanni** A dramatic opera based on the legends of Don Juan.	☐
M48	36 min	**Symphony No. 41 in C major, K. 551 (Jupiter Symphony)**	☐

Claude Debussy

Rec #	Length	Name / Description	Completed
M49	5 min	**Clair de Lune**	☐
M50	11 min	**Prelude to the Afternoon of a Faun (Prélude à l'après-midi d'un faune)**	☐

Rec #	Length	Name / Description	Completed
M51	25 min	**La Mer** – one of his masterworks.	☐
M52	10 min	**Arabesque No. 1 and No. 2**	☐
M53	10 min	**Gymnopédies**	☐
M54	7 min	**L'isle Joyeuse**	☐
M55	17 min	**Children's Corner** – includes the famous piece "Golliwogg's Cakewalk.	☐
Richard Wagner			
M56	5 - 6 min	**The Ride of the Valkyries**	☐
M57	15 hours	**The Ring Cycle (Der Ring des Nibelungen)** I've watched the entire cycle twice, once at the NY Met and once at the National Opera in DC. These are just a few more recognizable snippets	☐
M58	2 hr 30 min	**Das Rheingold**	☐
M59	4 hrs	**Die Walküre**	☐
M60	4 hrs	**Siegfried**	☐
M61	4 hrs 30 min	**Götterdämmerung**	☐
M62	4 hrs	**Tristan und Isolde**	☐
M63	2 hrs 30 min	**The Flying Dutchman (Der fliegende Holländer)**	☐
M64	3 hr 30 min	**Tannhäuser**	☐
M65	3 hr 30 min	**Lohengrin** – Known for the wedding march, "Here Comes the Bride,".	☐
George Gershwin			
M66	18 min	**Rhapsody in Blue (1924)**	☐
M67	3 hrs	**Porgy and Bess (1935)**	☐
M68	20 min	**An American in Paris (1928)**	☐
M69	35 min	**Concerto in F**	☐
Frederic Chopin			
M70	5 min	**Nocturne in E-flat Major, Op. 9 No. 2**	☐
M71	10 min	**Ballade No. 1 in G minor, Op. 23**	☐

Rec #	Length	Name / Description	Completed
M72	6 min	**Prelude in D-flat Major, Op. 28 No. 15 ("Raindrop Prelude")**	☐
M73	10 min	**Scherzo No. 1 in B minor, Op. 20**	☐
M74	7 min	**Polonaise in A-flat Major, Op. 53 ("Heroic")**	☐
M75	4 min	**Waltz in C-sharp Minor, Op. 64 No. 2**	☐
Antonín Dvořák			
M76	45 min	**Symphony No. 9 in E minor, Op. 95 ("From the New World")**	☐
M77	40 min	**Slavonic Dances, Op. 46**	☐
M78	40 min	**Cello Concerto in B minor, Op. 104** This concerto is highly regarded for its emotional depth and lyrical beauty, making it a staple in the cello repertoire.	☐
M79	30 min	**String Quartet No. 12 in F major, Op. 96 ("American")** Composed during his time in the United States, this quartet reflects his adaptation of American folk elements.	☐
M80	40 min	**Symphony No. 8 in G major, Op. 88** Known for its optimism and pastoral character, this symphony is a favorite among orchestras	☐
Edvard Grieg			
M81	30 min	**Piano Concerto in A minor, Op. 16**	☐
M82	30 min	**Peer Gynt Suites** Composed for Henrik Ibsen's play "Peer Gynt," features well-known pieces like "Morning Mood" and "In the Hall of the Mountain King."	☐
M83	2 hr 30 minI	**Lyric Pieces** A collection of 66 short piano pieces, with some of the most famous ones being "Nocturne," "Butterfly," and "Wedding Day at Troldhaugen."	☐
M84	40 min	**String Quartet in G minor, Op. 27**	☐
Johann Strauss II			
M85	10 min	**The Blue Danube (An der schönen blauen Donau)**	☐
M86	15 min	**Tales from the Vienna Woods (Geschichten aus dem Wienerwald)**	☐
M87	12 min	**Emperor Waltz (Kaiser-Walzer)**	☐
M88	2 hr 30 min	**Die Fledermaus (The Bat)** The overture of his most famous operetta. memorable arias.	☐

Rec #	Length	Name / Description Honorable Mentions	Composer	Completed
M89	17 min	**Boléro**	Maurice Ravel	☐
M90	2 hr 15 min	**La Traviata**	Giuseppe Verdi	☐
M91	2 hr 30 min	**Aida**	Verdi	☐
M92	2 hr 15 min	**Rigoletto**	Verdi	☐
M93	2 hr 15 min	**Il Trovatore**	Verdi	☐
M94	1 hr 50 min	**La Bohème**	Giacomo Puccini	☐
M95	2 hr 30 min	**Madama Butterfly**	Puccini	☐
M96	8 min	**Le Dance macabre**	Camille Saint Saens	☐
M97	45 min	**Scheherazade**	Nikolai Rimsky-Korsakov	☐
M98	10 min	**Orpheus in the Underworld**	Offenbach	☐
M99	35 min	**thus Spake Zarathustra**	Richard Strauss	☐
M100	60 min	**Carmina Burana**	Carl Orff	☐
M101	10 min	**Hungarian Rhapsody no. 2**	Franz Liszt	☐
Ludwig van Beethoven				
M102	35 min	**Symphony No. 5 in C minor, Op. 67**	Beethoven	☐
M103	75 min	**Symphony No. 9 in D minor, Op. 125**	Beethoven	☐
M104	40 min	**Symphony N. 7**	Beethoven	☐
M105	45 min	**Symphony No. 6 in F major, Op. 68**	Beethoven	☐
M106	15 min	**Piano Sonata No. 14 in C-sharp minor, Op. 27, No. 2**	Beethoven	☐
M107	40 min	**Piano Concerto No. 5 in E-flat major, Op. 73**	Beethoven	☐
M108	20 min	**Piano Sonata No. 8 in C minor, Op. 13**	Beethoven	☐
	122 HOURS			

MOVIES WORTH WATCHING

The American West is about myths that are almost as important as those of the ancient Greeks, Romans, and Norse. A civilization's myths tell people what's right and what's wrong, what's noble and what's base. What to strive for and what to avoid. They offer moral guidance that's more practical and useful than what you're likely to hear from any preacher.

A good part of this mythos has been enshrined in movies—Westerns. They've fallen out of favor over the last few generations because the values that they promote—which is their essence— are no longer held in high regard. What values might those be? The big ones are Courage, Honesty, Truthfulness and Independence. They're almost antithetical to everything Woke.

One of the great things about this Cycle is that it will not only be fun in the outdoors, but an excuse to watch a lot of truly great movies that most of your cohort won't have seen. Here's the list. There have been thousands of Westerns made over the years. We're missing some good ones, but these are among the best of the best. You don't want to waste your time on second-rate junk—in this like anything else. Watch them carefully. They're an education in myth, morality, history, and the art of making films—which itself could be an anchor course.

Western stories are moral laboratories. Enter each asking, "What kind of man will I be when the dust settles?"

As you can see, we love the morality tales of the old West. But much can be learned from modern movies too... while being entertaining. These are some of our favorites:

Films We Like

SCAN HERE TO SEE OUR MOVIE DATABASE

The Preparation is a new way of life... One of adventure, hard work, and eventual self-mastery. Both my dad and Doug had their own kind of "preparation"; but, let me tell you, they are both jealous that they didn't have this when they were 18 years old.

I hear them say it all the time...

So, you and I are getting something very special. We are being given the framework to view the world in a new light, not as a system of dull and formulaic paths to "success", but to view the world as unique ground to gain skills, live in virtue, and reap the unimaginable fruits of our own good labor.

But, beyond all of that, I truly believe in my heart that this is when a spark can be lit inside you that'll lead you to the person you can be This is a monumental moment, perhaps the most important moment of your life, just as it was for me back in August of 2023.

Doug came up with the idea of the program and my father developed it to where it is now. The tools are before you. I pray that you use this to embark on your own path.

It may be the best decision of your life.
Maxim Benjamin Smith

ABOUT DOUG CASEY

Best-selling author, world-renowned speculator, and libertarian philosopher Doug Casey has garnered a well-earned reputation for his controversial insights into politics, economics, and investment markets. He isn't your conventional financial guru—Doug is a globe-trotting maverick whose bold analyses and contrarian insights have shaken up markets and minds for decades. With boots-on-the-ground experience in over 100 countries, his investment strategies and no-nonsense perspectives have made him a uniquely compelling figure.

Doug literally wrote the book on profiting from periods of economic turmoil. His breakout best-seller, "Crisis Investing," spent weeks as #1 on the New York Times bestseller list and became the best-selling financial book of 1980. Following that debut, Doug penned books like "Strategic Investing," "Crisis Investing for the Rest of the '90s," and "The International Man." Venturing into fiction, he teamed up with John Hunt to create a gripping series of novels including "Speculator," "Drug Lord," and "Assassin," each weaving his ideas about wealth, freedom, and human nature into thrilling narratives.

He has been a featured guest on hundreds of radio and TV shows, including David Letterman, Merv Griffin, Charlie Rose, Phil Donahue, Regis Philbin, Maury Povich, NBC News, and CNN, and has been profiled in periodicals such as Time, Forbes, People, and the Washington Post. A regular keynote speaker, Doug continues to challenge mainstream thinking, inspiring readers worldwide to question, explore, and claim their own paths to freedom and prosperity. You can find him on YouTube at Doug Casey's Take, co-hosted with Matt Smith, and read his articles at International-Man.com and CrisisInvesting.com, where he shares his extensive body of work and insightful commentary on wealth, liberty, and individual sovereignty.

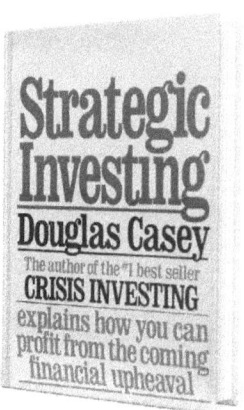

www.ingramcontent.com/pod-product-compliance
Lightning Source LLC
Chambersburg PA
CBHW041533120626
46551CB00019B/2680